CW00495406

INTERPRETING
ARCHAEOLOGY

INTERPRETING
ARCHAEOLOGY

What archaeological discoveries reveal about the past

NEIL FAULKNER

ARCTURUS

ARCTURUS

This edition published in 2022 by Arcturus Publishing Limited
26/27 Bickels Yard, 151–153 Bermondsey Street,
London SE1 3HA

Copyright © Arcturus Holdings Limited

All rights reserved. No part of this publication may be reproduced,
stored in a retrieval system, or transmitted, in any form or by any means,
electronic, mechanical, photocopying, recording or otherwise, without
prior written permission in accordance with the provisions of the
Copyright Act 1956 (as amended). Any person or persons who do any
unauthorised act in relation to this publication may be liable to criminal
prosecution and civil claims for damages.

ISBN: 978-1-83940-874-8
AD007997UK

Printed in China

Contents

Introduction 8

Timeline 12

Chapter 1: Dawn of the Hominins 16
The Evolutionary Tree – The First Hominins – The Australopithecines – The Earliest Tools – *Paranthropus* – Out of Africa – Fossil Hunting – The Neanderthals

Chapter 2: The First Modern Humans 32
The Upper Palaeolithic Revolution – What Makes Us Human? – The Upper Palaeolithic Crisis

Chapter 3: The Agricultural Revolution 42
An Early Neolithic Village – A New Way of Life – Bloody Stone Age – Australia – Primitive Matriarchy – From Mother-Right to Patriarchy

Chapter 4: Bronze Age Civilizations 56
The First Social Classes – The Bronzeworkers – The Land of Shinar – A Global Transformation – Basket-mavkers and Olmecs: the First Civilizations of the Americas – The Chavín – Akrotiri, Troy, Knossos and Mycaenae – A Late Bronze Age Arms Race – Bronze Age System Failure – The Collapse of Indus Civilization – The Shang Dynasty and its Overthrow

Chapter 5: Iron Age Worlds 90
The First Industrial Revolution – African Ironworking – Bantu Expansion – Sacred Metal – New Civilizations – Mesopotamia: the Assyrian Empire – Persia: the Achaemenid Empire – India: Warlords and Hindus – India: Merchants and Buddhists – Culture-History – China: the First Emperor – Classical Greece – The Macedonian Empire and the Hellenistic World – The Scythians – The Celts – Animal Power

Chapter 6: The Roman Empire 144
Archaeology and Myth – The First City of Rome – Roman Expansion – Caesar's Army – Roman Colonies – Roman Forts – Roman Towns – A Note on Roman Coins – Roman Villas – Roman Pottery

Chapter 7: The Post-Roman World 174
The Fall of the Roman Empire – The Byzantine Empire – The Germanic World – Carolingian Europe – Islamic Civilization – The Vikings – Maya and Moche

Chapter 8: The Medieval World 200
European Feudalism: Villages – Monasteries – European Feudalism: Castles – Novgorod – Mound-builders and Pueblo Farmers – Toltecs, Aztecs, Chimú and Incas – Wind Power – Angkor Wat – Ming China – Samurai Japan – Pacific Societies

Chapter 9: The Archaeology of Modernity 232
Settlers, Slaves and Ships – Tudor London – Victorian York – Conflict Landscapes – The Archaeology of the Contemporary Past

Conclusion 246

Recommended Further Reading 248

Index 251

Picture Credits 256

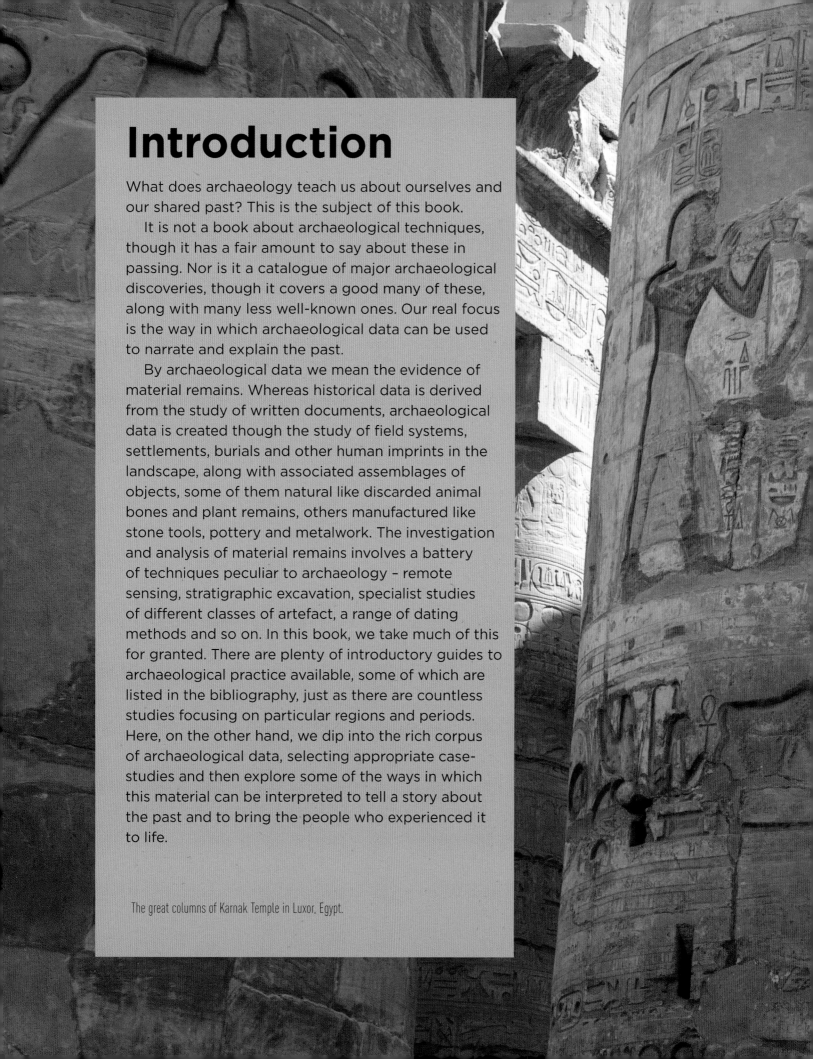

Introduction

What does archaeology teach us about ourselves and our shared past? This is the subject of this book.

It is not a book about archaeological techniques, though it has a fair amount to say about these in passing. Nor is it a catalogue of major archaeological discoveries, though it covers a good many of these, along with many less well-known ones. Our real focus is the way in which archaeological data can be used to narrate and explain the past.

By archaeological data we mean the evidence of material remains. Whereas historical data is derived from the study of written documents, archaeological data is created though the study of field systems, settlements, burials and other human imprints in the landscape, along with associated assemblages of objects, some of them natural like discarded animal bones and plant remains, others manufactured like stone tools, pottery and metalwork. The investigation and analysis of material remains involves a battery of techniques peculiar to archaeology – remote sensing, stratigraphic excavation, specialist studies of different classes of artefact, a range of dating methods and so on. In this book, we take much of this for granted. There are plenty of introductory guides to archaeological practice available, some of which are listed in the bibliography, just as there are countless studies focusing on particular regions and periods. Here, on the other hand, we dip into the rich corpus of archaeological data, selecting appropriate case-studies and then explore some of the ways in which this material can be interpreted to tell a story about the past and to bring the people who experienced it to life.

The great columns of Karnak Temple in Luxor, Egypt.

ABOVE: Excavation in action. An archaeologist carefully uncovers ancient pottery with a hand trowel.

In the popular mind, archaeology means excavating for buried remains. This is a misconception. It arises from the fact that much archaeology is indeed buried and has to be dug up. There are a number of reasons for this. Some remains were deliberately buried at the time, as with the burial of the dead or ritual deposits in sanctuaries. In other cases, old buildings get knocked down, the rubble is levelled and new ones are constructed on top; this is particularly the case in cities, where the earliest remains can often end up several metres below the modern ground-level as a result of continual redevelopment over hundreds or even thousands of years. On rural sites, on the other hand, a more common pattern is for the site to be abandoned, tumble into ruins and become overgrown; then, as material breaks down, humus forms and earthworms get to work, layers of soil accumulate

RIGHT: A still from *Indiana Jones and the Kingdom of the Crystal Skull*. Like Indiana Jones, the best archaeologists do their work in the field, rather than in the library.

and bury the remains. So many archaeologists are necessarily excavators: they have to dig for their evidence. But this does not define the discipline.

Many of those remains are still in existence as standing buildings or portable artefacts and these are as much objects of archaeological enquiry as the foundations, postholes, ditches and pits found in excavation. In this book, as we move forwards in time, an increasing proportion of our evidence will take the form of extant buildings and artefacts.

This study cannot be done in the confines of the library and the seminar room. Some people describe themselves as 'theoretical archaeologists' and take the view that fieldwork is optional. I beg to differ. Material remains are the foundation of archaeology as an academic discipline and I do not think I could have written this book if I had not spent more than

30 years working in the field, during which time I have explored sites of many different periods in many different places.

There is a scene in *Indiana Jones and the Kingdom of the Crystal Skull* (2008) in which the heroic professor crashes a motorbike into an Ivy League university library and is asked by a student for advice on reading. 'Forget Hargreaves,' Jones tells him. 'Read Vere Gordon Childe on diffusionism. He spent most of his life in the field. If you wanna be an archaeologist, you gotta get out of the library.' It is a scene beloved of informed archaeologists. Childe was probably the discipline's most brilliant scholar – an archaeological Darwin or Einstein. And without question, his combination of indefatigable fieldwork and artefact studies with exhaustive reading and thinking was the essential basis of his seminal contribution. Let him be our model.

Timeline

	3.5 MILLION YEARS AGO	300,000 YEARS AGO	50,000 YEARS AGO
GLOBAL	3.3 million–300,000 years ago **Lower Palaeolithic**	300,000–40,000 years ago **Middle Palaeolithic**	c. 40,000–20,000 years ago **Upper Palaeolithic**

	4500 BCE	3000 BCE	2000 BCE	1500 BCE

c. 10,000–4,500 BCE
Neolithic

c. 3300–1200 BCE
Bronze Age

ASIA

3300–1300 BCE
Indus Valley Civilization

1523–1027 BCE
Shang Dynasty China

EUROPE

2000–1600 BCE
Minoan Crete

1750–1050 BCE
Mycenae

2200–1500 BCE
El Argar Culture

MIDDLE EAST AND AFRICA

3000–6th century BCE
Troy

c. 4500–1900 BCE
Sumer

1650–1178 BCE
Hittite Empire

2700–2250 BCE
Egyptian Old Kingdom

2055–1650 BCE
Egyptian Middle Kingdom

1550–1077 BCE
Egyptian New Kingdom

AMERICAS

20,000 YEARS AGO | 10,000 BCE

c. 20,000 years ago–10,000 BCE
Mesolithic

c. 10,000–4,500 BCE
Neolithic

1000 BCE | 500 BCE | 0 CE

c. 1200 BCE–550 BCE
Iron Age

1300–300 BCE
Painted Grey Ware culture

321–184 BCE
Mauryan Empire

700–200 BCE
Northern Black Polished Ware culture

1027–221 BCE
Zhou Dynasty China

221–206 BCE
Qin Dynasty China

206 BCE–220 CE
Han Dynasty China

594–338 BCE
Classical Athens

359–323 BCE
Macedonian Empire

323 BCE–31 BCE
Hellenistic Civilization

c. 753–509 BCE
Roman Kingdom

509–30 BCE
Roman Republic

30 BCE–476 CE
Roman Empire

1200–500 BCE
Hallstatt culture

400–200 BCE
Celtic migrations

880 BCE–612 BCE
Assyrian Empire

550–330 BCE
Achaemenid Persia

1500 BCE–200 CE
Nok culture, Nigeria

1500 BCE–750 CE
Basketmaker culture

1000–300 BCE
Adena Culture

100 BCE–500 CE
Hopewell Culture

1200–300 BCE
Olmecs

750 BCE–250 CE
Preclassical Maya

1200–200 BCE
Chavín

	0 CE	500 CE	600	700	800	900	1000	1100	1200

ASIA

206 BCE–220 CE
Han Dynasty China

618–907
Tang dynasty China

960–1126
Song dynasty China

1185–1333
Kamakura period Japan

802–1431
Khmer Empire

EUROPE

c. 300–800
Migration Period

793–1066
Viking Age

9th–15th centuries
European feudalism

410–1066
Anglo-Saxon England

30 BCE–476 CE
Roman Empire

751–888
Carolingian Empire

395–1453
Byzantine Empire

1136–1478
Novgorod Republic

MIDDLE EAST AND AFRICA

622–711
Muslim Conquests

661–750
Umayyad Caliphate

800–909
Aghlabid Caliphate

1500 BCE–200 CE
Nok culture, Nigeria

11th century–15th century
Great Zimbabwe

AMERICAS

1500 BCE–750 CE
Basketmaker culture

700–1700
Mississippian Culture

100 BCE–500 CE
Hopewell Culture

1000–1600
Pueblo Culture

1st–7th centuries CE
Teotihuacán

950–1170
Toltecs

750 BCE–250 CE
Preclassical Maya

250–950 CE
Classical Maya

950–1550
Post-Classical Maya

1st century CE–750 CE
Moche civilization

900–1470
Chimu Empire

AUSTRALASIA/ POLYNESIA

700–850
Early period Easter Island culture

1050–1680
Middle period Easter Island culture

1300 1400 1500 1600 1700 1800 1900 2000

1279–1368
Yuan dynasty China

1368–1644
Ming dynasty China

1644–1912
Qing dynasty China

1467–1603
Sengoku Japan

1603–1868
Tokugawa Shogunate

1485–1603
Tudor England

1837–1901
Victorian Britain

1607–1776
Colonial America

1776–present
United States of America

1345–1519
Aztec Empire

1438–1533
Inca Empire

1350–1800
Classic Maori

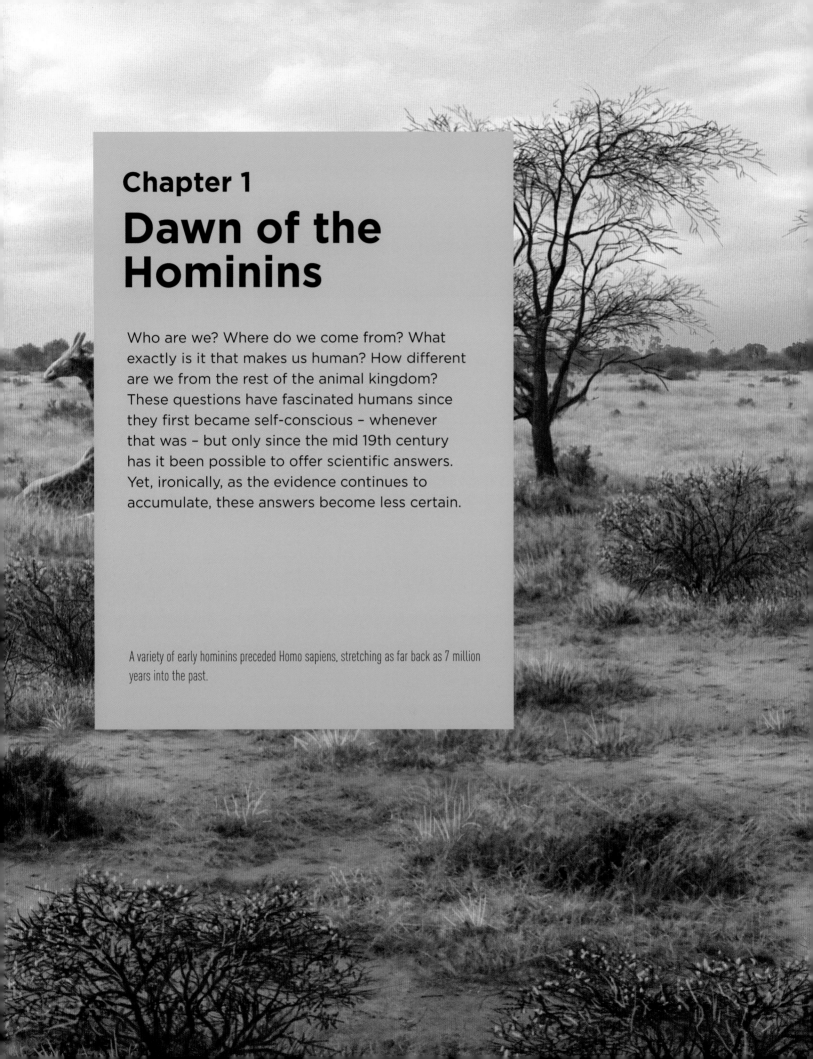

Chapter 1
Dawn of the Hominins

Who are we? Where do we come from? What exactly is it that makes us human? How different are we from the rest of the animal kingdom? These questions have fascinated humans since they first became self-conscious – whenever that was – but only since the mid 19th century has it been possible to offer scientific answers. Yet, ironically, as the evidence continues to accumulate, these answers become less certain.

A variety of early hominins preceded Homo sapiens, stretching as far back as 7 million years into the past.

The Evolutionary Tree

In this chapter we explore the current state of knowledge about human origins. We find ourselves at the intersection of two related disciplines: palaeo-anthropology – essentially the study of human evolution from fossil remains – and archaeology – essentially the study of the human past from material culture.

A generation ago it all seemed very simple. Palaeo-anthropologists imagined a more or less linear evolutionary process involving only about half a dozen hominin species. Now more than 20 species of hominin are known in the 7 million years since the evolutionary tree leading to modern humans separated from that of the chimpanzees. Not only that, but until as recently as 40,000 years ago there seem to have been several different species of hominin around at any one time. And instead of a simple linear progression, we now have multiple branches and 'failed' lines. This means more uncertainty than ever. It is as if we were doing a 1,000-piece jigsaw puzzle, but we only have a handful of pieces. And whereas we once had five pieces and imagined we could see a simple pattern, we now we have 50 and everything looks much messier.

For the entire hominin evolutionary tree there are three main types of evidence: the fossils themselves, the associated stone tools and a battery of scientific dating techniques. Since 2010, headway has also been made into the genetic relationships between Homo sapiens and our related cousins, notably the Neanderthals. Let us review what we think we know in the current state of research.

BELOW: A technician extracts DNA from a Neanderthal bone. Genetic evidence has rewritten our understanding of human evolution, revealing complex connections between the different hominid species.

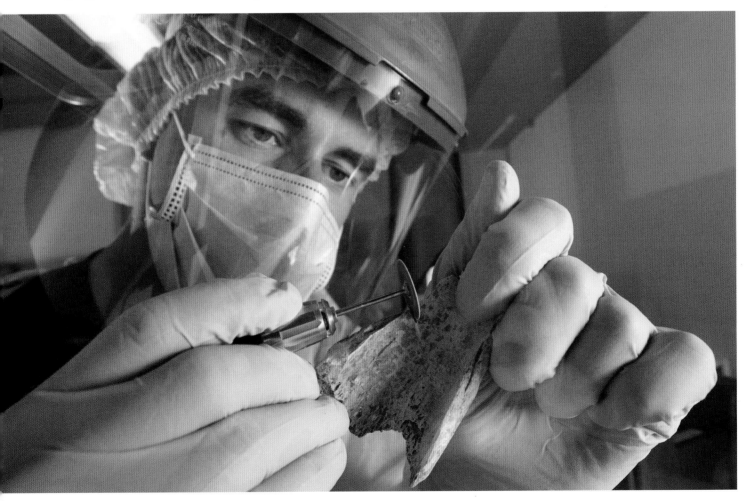

The Human Evolutionary Tree

HOMO GROUP

Homo sapiens

300,000 years ago–present

Homo neanderthalensis

400,000 years ago–40,000 years ago

Homo heidelbergensis

700,000–200,000 years ago

Homo floriensis

100,000–50,000 years ago

500,000 years ago

Homo erectus

1.9 million years ago–110,000 years ago

Homo habilis

2.4 million years ago–1.4 million years ago

Homo rudolfensis

1.9–1.8 million years ago

Homo antecessor

1.2–0.8 million years ago

1 million years ago

PARANTHROPUS GROUP

Paranthropus aethiopicus

2.7–2.3 million years ago

Paranthropus robustus

1.8–1.2 million years ago

Paranthropus boisei

2.3–1.2 million years ago

2 million years ago

AUSTRALOPITHECUS GROUP

Australopithecus africanus

3.3–2.1 million years ago

Australopithecus afarensis

3.85–2.95 million years ago

Australopithecus garhi

2.5 million years ago

3 million years ago

ARDIPITHECUS GROUP

Sahelanthropus tchadensis

7–6 million years ago

Ardipithecus ramidus

4.4 million years ago

7 million years ago

LEFT: A skull of the oldest hominin discovered, the *Sahelanthropus tchadensis*, which roamed Africa 7 million years ago.

The First Hominins

The animal kingdom is divided into families, genera (plural of genus) and species. In theory at least, species are defined by the fact that all members of one species can interbreed, whereas a genus is a group of closely related species and a family is broader still.

In 2003 palaeo-anthropologists working in Chad's remote Djurab Desert caused a sensation by discovering a new genus and species of early hominin dating from around 7 million years ago. They excavated parts of six individuals, including one largely complete though distorted cranium, of *Sahelanthropus tchadensis*, to give the new hominins their scientific name. The first part of the name refers to the genus, the second to the species and what justified this classification was the clear evidence that 'Saharan Hominin from Chad' walked upright. How do we know? Because *Sahelanthropus tchadensis*'s foramen magnum, the hole at the base of the skull where the spinal cord enters, was centrally placed – whereas in chimpanzees, our nearest relatives, who are four-limb ground walkers, it is placed towards the back.

Upright walking is an adaption to more open savannah landscapes, in contrast to the closed forest environments inhabited by the great apes. But it is an adaption with huge evolutionary potential, for once arms and hands are freed from their locomotive function, they are freed up for other tasks – like tool-making. And once that happens, we can be pretty certain that natural selection will tend to favour bigger brains and greater intelligence – to make for better tool-makers. But we are getting ahead of ourselves. This was still a long way off 7 million years ago. Back to the evolutionary tree.

The Australopithecines

We do not have the space to cover every hominin species in the fossil record. So we jump to the Australopithecines, a genus of hominin with relatively small bodies and brains that inhabited parts of Africa between about 4.2 and 2 million years ago. They were adapted for upright walking, though perhaps not over long distances and they retained a facility for tree-climbing. They had good hand grip, strong jaws and large teeth. There is growing evidence that they were at large in varied environments – open savannah, wooded savannah and gallery forest.

Though the discovery was made a while ago, in 1974, the almost complete skeleton of a small female of the species *Australopithecus afarensis* – dubbed 'Lucy' in honour of the Beatles' hit playing in the palaeo-anthropologists' campsite! – remains of huge significance. What really mattered was Lucy's vertebrae, pelvis, femur (thigh bone) and tibia (shinbone), because these proved her to have been an efficient upright walker.

Lucy was found at Hadar in Ethiopia's Afar Depression. A few years later, at another East African site, Laetoli in Tanzania, a trail of fossilized footprints was uncovered, 70 in all, extending for nearly 27m (89 ft), representing a small group of hominins on the move. These, too, like Lucy were of the species *Australopithecus afarensis* and of approximately the same date, about 3.7 million years ago. Upright walking was dramatically confirmed.

We have moved on three million years from *Sahelanthropus tchadensis* and we are bound to ask that big question: had hominins got the hang of tool-making yet?

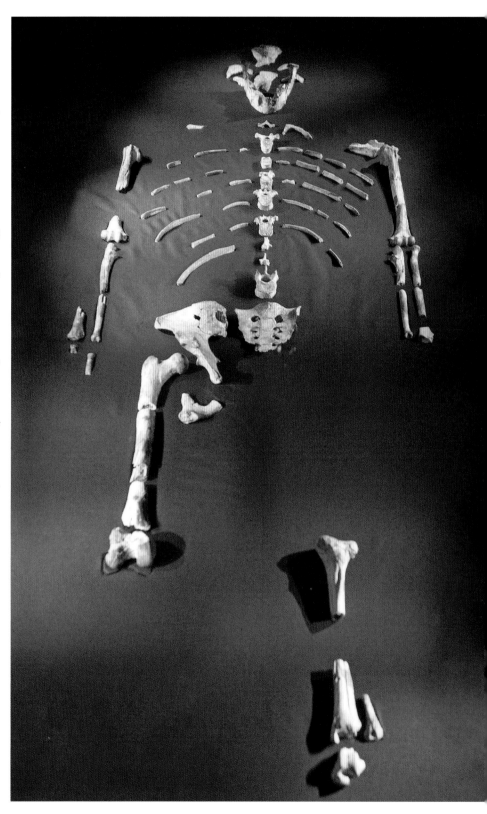

ABOVE: The skeleton of Lucy, an *Australopithecus afarensis*, discovered by the American palaeoanthropologist Donald Johnson in 1974.

The Earliest Tools

The debate about exactly what it is that makes us human runs and runs. In truth, there is no sharp dividing line between the genus *Homo* and the genus *Australopithecus* (discussed previously) or *Paranthropus* (discussed below). The lines are fuzzy. But this is not surprising: we are talking about an evolutionary process involving gradual incremental changes. There are tipping-points, of course, but they result from the drip-drip of slow change. Take tool-making as an example of the problem. It is often considered a clear marker of the animal–human transition, but things are not so simple.

We now know that the palaeo-anthropological evidence of the fossils and the archaeological evidence for stone tools does not match up. The earliest known stone tools predate the earliest *Homo* fossils by well over a million years! These were found at Lomekwi in Kenya, where large pieces of volcanic rock had been chipped to create cores, flakes and perhaps anvils; they date from around 3.3 million years ago.

A different tradition of tool-making is represented by finds at the Olduvai Gorge in Tanzania. Dating from around 2.6 million years ago, these tools were made by chipping bits off smaller pebbles.

We have to assume that these Lomekwian and Oldowan tools were made by species of *Australopithecus* or *Paranthropus*, not *Homo*. Only with the development of a third 'industry' – the Acheulian (named after a French site) – is it safe to assume that the tool-maker was an archaic form of human. Acheulian tools are typically hand-axes and the earliest date from around 1.7 million years ago.

RIGHT: A handaxe found at Olduvai Gorge in Tanzania. The Oldowan tools were made of pebbles of quartz or basalt and could be used for several purposes.

ABOVE: A series of Acheulian bifaces. These would have been used for tasks such as digging, chopping and butchering.

Hand-axes were made from cores (from which flakes had been chipped off to create the right shape) and they tend to be tear-drop shaped and to fit neatly in the hand. It is easy to imagine them being used for butchering carcasses, including smashing bone to access marrow; and in fact associated animal-bone fossils often display tell-tale butchery marks.

All three of these industries belong to the Lower Palaeolithic phase of the Old Stone Age – that is, they date from the period 3.3 million to 300,000 years ago. Note that in each case the same basic technology remained in use for hundreds of thousands of years. Cultural evolution was a very slow process indeed during this period!

Paranthropus

The Australopithecines may not have been the only early tool-makers. Another genus of hominin, around between 2.6 and 1.3 million years ago, may have been responsible: *Paranthropus*. The first fossil found was a massive lower jaw with large molars unearthed at Omo in Ethiopia in 1967. The second only came two decades later, at West Turkana in Kenya, but this time it was an almost complete cranium, dubbed 'the Black Skull' because of its blue-black appearance.

Further examples suggested other species of the same genus, but all with a distinctive *Paranthropus* look. These included, in addition to large chewing teeth with thick enamel, flaring, forward-projecting cheek bones, giving *Paranthropus* a disc-shaped face and sometimes a pronounced sagittal crest (on top of the skull). Both the check bones and the sagittal crest provided muscle attachments – to help power that massive jaw. A fair guess is that *Paranthropus* was dependent on a diet of grasses and sedges – rough, fibrous plant foods of low calorific value, so you needed lots of it and strong jaws to grind it down.

Paranthropus fossils also display marked sexual dimorphism, where the male is much bigger than the female, implying male competition over sexual access. Despite this, *Paranthropus* was preyed upon by other animals. The skull of a young *Paranthropus* found in a collapsed cave system at Swartkrans in South Africa bore the unmistakable puncture marks of a leopard's lower canines on the back of the head!

Paranthropus became extinct around 1.3 million years ago: the genus proved to be an evolutionary dead-end. But there can be no doubt that several species of *Australopithecus*, *Paranthropus* and *Homo* were around at the same time in both eastern and southern Africa. We can guess that they encountered each other occasionally, but that they were not necessarily in competition, for their distinctive physical adaptations may have equipped them to exploit different ecological niches.

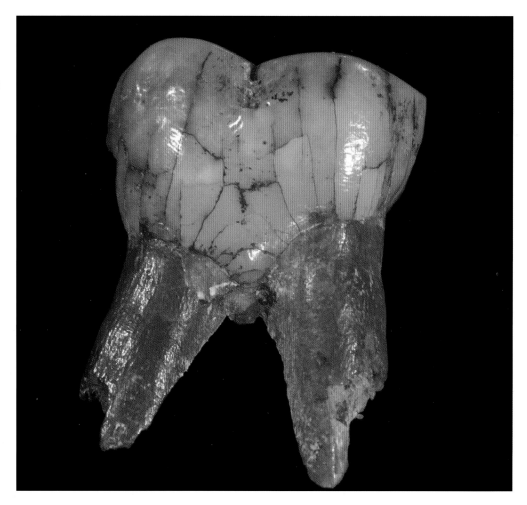

RIGHT: A 1.8-million-year-old molar tooth from a *Paranthropus*, found in Gauteng, South Africa.

Out of Africa

When the world-famous palaeo-anthropologists Louis and Mary Leakey excavated some unusual hominin fossils at Olduvai Gorge in Tanzania in 1960, they were at first unsure how to classify them. They did not look like *Australopithecus* and certainly not *Paranthropus*: the front teeth were too large, the back teeth too small, the skull bones too thin, the brain case too large. Only four years later, though, did they publish a paper claiming a new species: *Homo habilis*.

The name means 'Handy Person' – chosen because they assumed an association with the oldest known tools on the site. Both the fossils and the tools date from around 1.9 million years ago. Here is the genesis of humanity.

Unfortunately, the overall picture around this time is very hazy. There are too many fossils of too many species for us to be confident about lines of evolution. *Homo habilis* may have evolved into *Homo erectus*, the earliest examples of which date from between 1.9 and 1.6 million years ago, but we cannot be sure. What we are certain of is that *Homo erectus* was the first hominin to leave Africa and colonize other parts of the world (an event sometimes dubbed 'Out of Africa I').

BELOW: A replica of a *Homo habilis* skull found in the Olduvai Gorge, dated to approximately 1.8 million years ago.

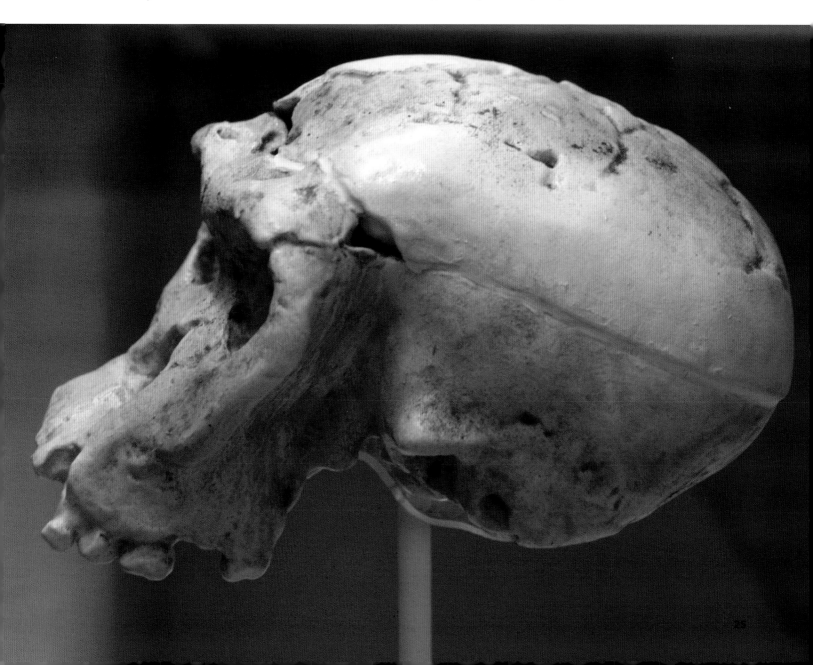

Fossil Hunting

The evidence for early hominins is heavily skewed by what palaeo-anthropologists and archaeologists call 'taphonomic processes', a term that within archaeology relates to how sites form and change over time, whether because of human, animal or environmental influences. These processes impact both the fossils and the tools we are looking for.

While the first hominin remains are found exclusively in Africa, some species left their homeland to range further. The oldest known are represented by the Dmanisi fossils (1.7 million years ago) in Georgia, currently classified as a form of *Homo erectus*. Does this mean that early hominins were confined to these areas? Or is it that we just do not find fossils elsewhere? Absence of evidence is not necessarily evidence of absence.

Another problem is that material moves around. Many fossils are recovered in collapsed cave systems. These are often difficult to find and difficult to access. In one case, excavation of a deep chamber in the Rising Star system near Johannesburg had to be carried out by a team of women slender enough to squeeze their way in! And there is often uncertainty about how the fossils got there. Were these places where early hominins were actually living? Or had they fallen through a hole in the ground and got trapped? Or had their bodies been dragged there by predators? Or were their bones washed in at some point?

Perhaps some of the find spots are places where remains from different periods somehow collected together and got jumbled up. Then there can be uncertainties about which bones belonged to the same individual and which can be associated with animal bones and stone tools found in the same location.

It is likely that the fossils we recover are far from being a wholly representative sample. This compounds the problem of the 1,000-piece jigsaw where we have only 50 of the pieces. We may not even have a good spread of pieces in our small sample.

RIGHT: Bones discovered by the expedition to the Rising Star cave system near Johannesburg, South Africa. How did they get there?

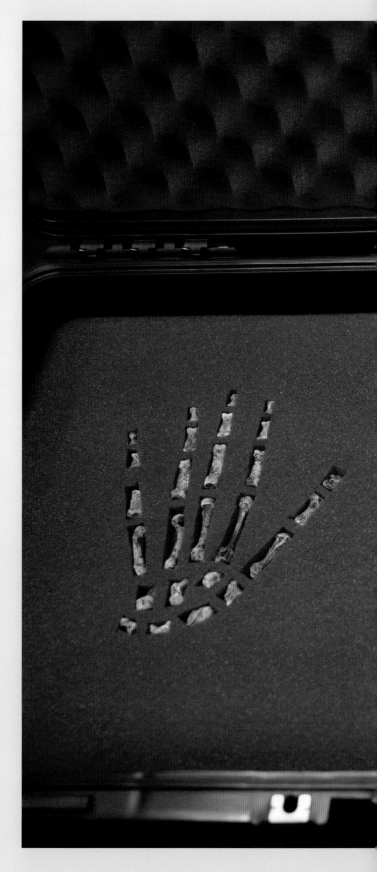

RIGHT: Excavations underway at Gran Dolina. At the bottom of the image, underneath the plank is the site where the first remains of *Homo antecessor* were discovered.

Erectus was about the same size and shape as modern humans, but was stockier, had a smaller brain and was distinguished by a large face with pronounced brow-ridge and a chinless lower jaw. Wanderlust seems to have been characteristic of the species from the get-go, for it arrived in Indonesia as early as 1.6 million years ago and in China between 700,000 and 500,000 years ago. *Erectus* fossils have also been recovered in the Middle East and across much of Europe.

Again, however, there is overlap with other species and the evolutionary relationships are unclear. Spanish palaeo-anthropologists have identified a species called *Homo antecessor* ('Pioneer Person') at Gran Dolina in northern Spain and dated it to about 850,000 years ago. Does it represent another 'Out of Africa' movement? Is it perhaps the common ancestor of *Homo heidelbergensis*, *Homo neanderthalensis* and *Homo sapiens*? Are we beginning to see a separate hominin line that evolved over a million years in parallel with that of *Homo erectus*?

Much more widespread, mainly across Europe, are remains of *Homo heidelbergensis*, which we can date to between 600,000 and 300,000 years ago. Spectacular evidence for this species was discovered at Boxgrove in southern England in the 1990s. The site is that of a fossilized shore-line where butchery was practised around 500,000 years ago. In addition to a human shinbone and two incisor teeth, excavators found plentiful hand-axes and large mammal bones displaying butchery marks. Such was the preservation, it was even possible to observe the position of a flint knapper's legs as he or she sat to manufacture an Acheulian hand-axe! This, incidentally, confirmed the idea that stone tools were disposables: they could be made quickly when and where needed, with no expectation they would last very long.

The Neanderthals

Banish all thoughts of clumsy, stooped, shuffling, knuckle-dragging brutes communicating in grunts and bashing each other with clubs. That is the old stereotype of *Homo neanderthalensis*. The new thinking is hyper-charged with a battery of scientific techniques that are creating a radically new picture.

Teeth are examined for daily growth lines, for dietary evidence in 'micro-polishes' and even for hearth smoke incorporated into dental calculus. Sites are picked apart teaspoon by teaspoon, with every artefact and ecofact three-dimensionally logged and separately bagged, so we can work out what a Neanderthal knapper was making 100,000 years ago.

BELOW: A Neanderthal burial site. New archaeological techniques are radically changing our understanding of the species.

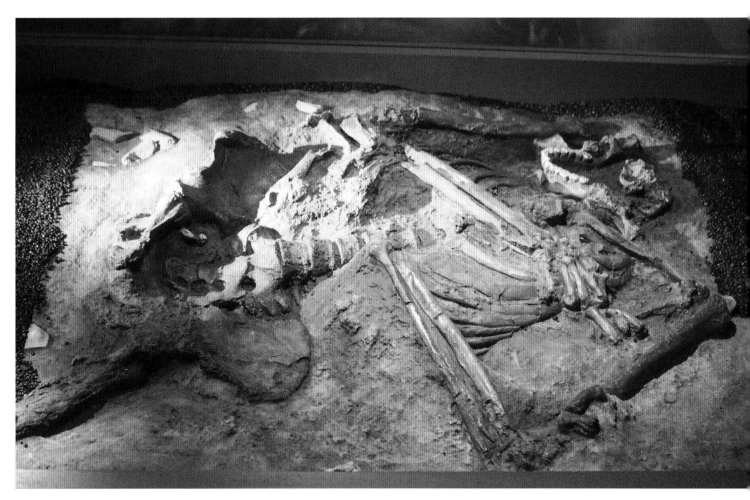

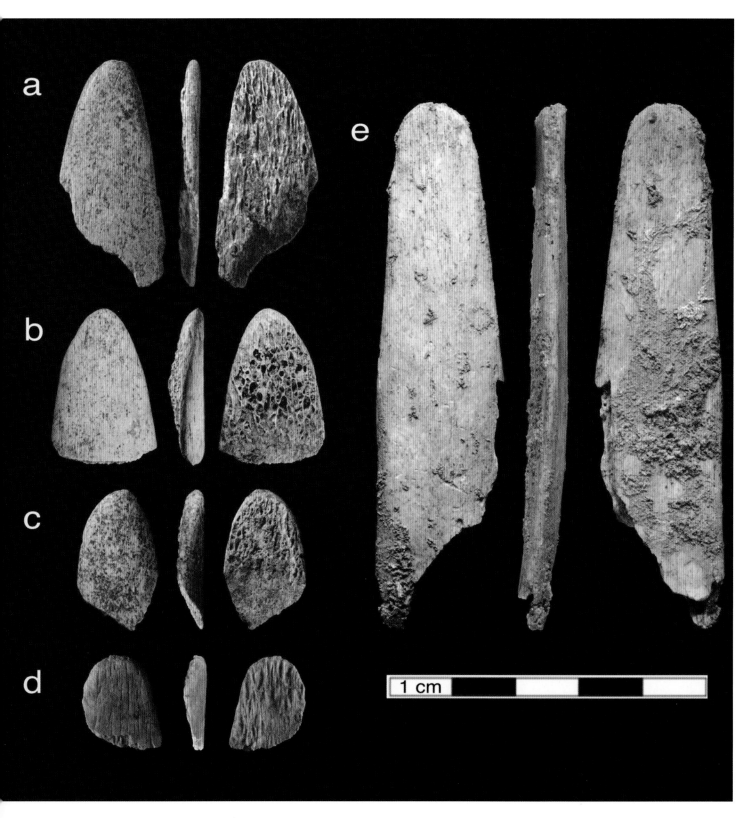

ABOVE: Neanderthal bone tools found in southwest France. These tools were
lissoirs, specialized tools designed for working animal skins.

These postage-stamp images then get slotted into ever more refined macro-reconstructions of palaeo-ecology and palaeo-climate. Another battery of scientific techniques here: ice cores, ocean-sediment samples, pollen sequences in lake beds, dust accumulations from ancient tundra, flowstone in caves and chunks of coral reef. To zero in on just one of these techniques, ice cores drilled deep into the Greenland ice sheet and into Antarctic ice are now producing accurate records of the climate extending back at least 800,000 years. Together, these techniques provide a minutely calibrated record of the past climate, with its changing cold and warm periods.

The result is that none of the old stereotypes work anymore. We imagine Neanderthals smothered in furs against the northern cold, their heaving breath clouding the frosty air, spears at the ready to fell Ice Age mega-fauna like woolly mammoth. It is a vision reinforced by what turn out to be hoary old myths about 'Arctic-ready' adaptations such as stocky bodies to conserve heat and big noses to deal with thin air.

In fact, Neanderthals were as likely to be hunting straight-tusked elephants in balmy forests, collecting seafood on estuarine sand or scurrying through sheets of rain, as to be hunched against bitter snow flurries. The climate fluctuations and the Neanderthal range mean there was nothing especially 'Arctic-ready' about the species.

They emerged around 450,000 years ago and the last of them perished perhaps 45,000 years ago. In that time of great fluctuations, of advance and retreat by the glaciers, of smaller oscillations of cold and warm, they ranged from Central Asia to the Iberian Peninsula, from the Baltic to Gibraltar. Adaptation was, as ever among the hominins, as much cultural as physical, a matter of clothing, shelters, tool-kits and food strategies than bone and muscle.

The Neanderthals depended on their tools and no doubt furs and other garments, as well as fire, for warmth. Arguably, indeed, it was hardly physical at all. Narrowly functional explanations of evolutionary form are giving way to a more nuanced understanding of how species develop. Evolution, we now realize, can be weirdly idiosyncratic; it is not always ultra-adaptive.

We think of Neanderthals as very much 'other'. But we are pretty weird, too, with all kinds of peculiarities of form; it is just that we have got used to ourselves. But all those differences between us and 'them' – our tall globular heads, our pinched faces tucked under great domes, our little piggy eyes, our pointy noses and stuck-out chins – are just a different way of 'being human'.

The physical differences were real, of course. With their squat shape, big chests and short, thick, bandy legs, the Neanderthals would have been good long-distance hill-walkers but rotten sprinters. On the other hand, there was nothing 'stooping' about them. They walked fully upright, had dextrous hands and were intelligent, innovative tool-makers.

They were not alone: they shared their world with other species of hominin. Early on, with *Homo erectus* and *Homo heidelbergensis*, for example and later with *Homo sapiens* and with such newly discovered species as Siberia's Denisovans and Indonesia's *Homo floresiensis*, a diminutive island hominin dubbed 'the hobbit' in the popular press.

Then, quite suddenly, there was only one. All other hominin species seem to have been extinct by around 45,000 years ago. Only *Homo sapiens* ('Wise Person') survived. And it just so happens that this date coincides with the eve of a cultural explosion amounting to an Upper Palaeolithic revolution. It is time to meet ourselves.

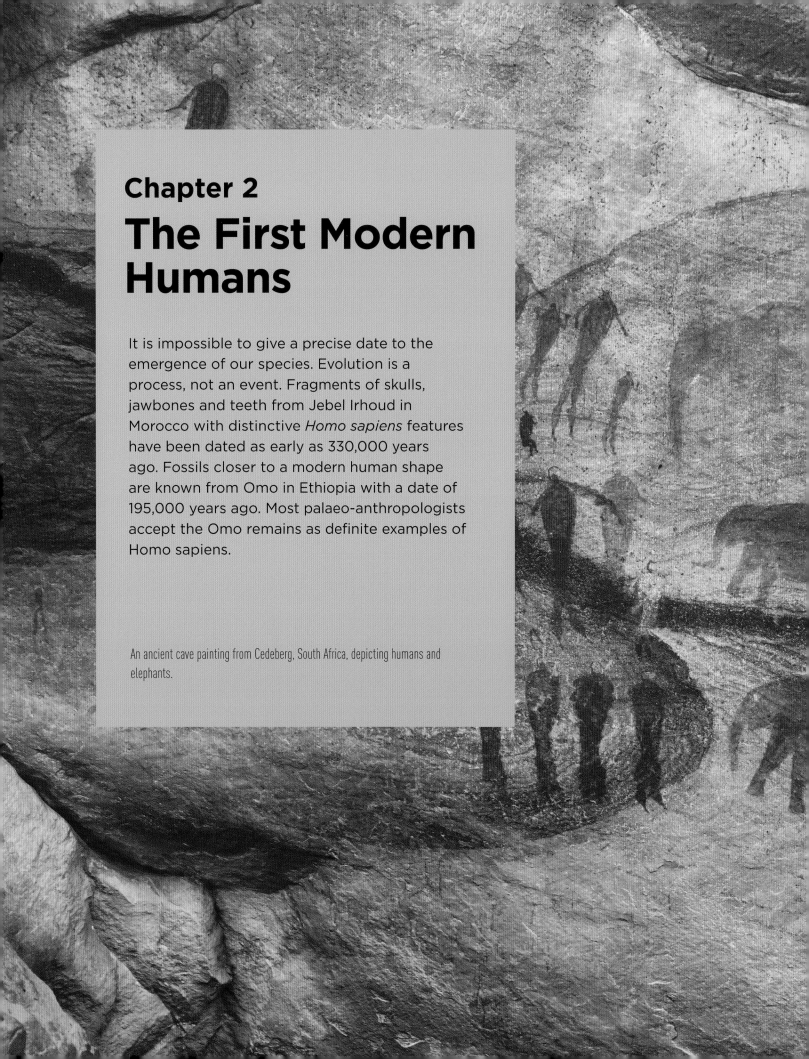

Chapter 2
The First Modern Humans

It is impossible to give a precise date to the emergence of our species. Evolution is a process, not an event. Fragments of skulls, jawbones and teeth from Jebel Irhoud in Morocco with distinctive *Homo sapiens* features have been dated as early as 330,000 years ago. Fossils closer to a modern human shape are known from Omo in Ethiopia with a date of 195,000 years ago. Most palaeo-anthropologists accept the Omo remains as definite examples of Homo sapiens.

An ancient cave painting from Cedeberg, South Africa, depicting humans and elephants.

These African fossils long predate the earliest examples of *Homo sapiens* known from elsewhere. Fossils from two caves at Skhul and Qafzeh in Israel seem to represent somewhat primitive forms of *Homo sapiens* and these date from around 100,000 years ago. Additional recent discoveries from further afield include fossils from western, southern and eastern Asia that have been dated to round 80,000 years ago; but the remains are minimal, mainly isolated teeth and it may be that all of them represent an evolutionary branch of primitive *Homo sapiens* that died out. Most palaeo-anthropologists believe that the main 'Out of Africa II' dispersal did not occur until about 60,000 years ago.

But this was explosive. In the space of just 20,000 years – a mere flicker of time in evolutionary terms –

ABOVE: This body of an adolescent, sex unknown, was found in 1971 in Qafzeh cave, with deer antlers clasped to their chest.

RIGHT: Fossilized human footprints found in White Sands National Park, New Mexico, dating to approximately 23,000 years ago. A total of 61 footprints were uncovered at the site and the presence of seeds embedded in the footprints themselves allowed researchers to use radiocarbon dating to discover their age.

the new species seems to have spread across Europe, Asia and Australia. After another 20,000 years, *Homo sapiens*, had also begun the colonization of the Americas.

Various strands of data are pushing back the occupation of America to a far earlier time than previously realized. The old theory, based on the Clovis culture, assumed the first settlement occurred around 12,000 years ago. However, we now know that humans were in the Americas far earlier. Clues have emerged from across the region, from the Yukon River in the far north, where human settlement has been dated to about 24,000 years ago, right down to the Andes and Chile in South America. The most recent evidence to hit the headlines has been a series of ancient human footprints found in the White Sands National Park, New Mexico. These prove that humans were in the region by 23,000 years ago.

This eruption across the world coincided, as we have seen, with the extinction of all other hominin species. How are we to explain the extraordinary success of this new super-species?

The Upper Palaeolithic Revolution

Acheulian hand-axes were in use for about 1.5 million years. Throughout the Lower Palaeolithic (3.3 million–300,000 years ago), tool-making technology was effectively static. During the Middle Palaeolithic (300,000–40,000 years ago), early humans made a wider range of tools, using a new Levallois technique, whereby the knapper would shape the core in such a way that, with a single blow, he or she could strike a flake of the required shape and size. The Mousterian industry associated with the Neanderthals, for example, included knives for cutting, scrapers for preparing hides, points for making clothes, spearheads for mounting on wooden shafts and many more.

But this again was a long-lived technology that changed little over hundreds of thousands of years. Cro-Magnon fossils (as *Homo sapiens* remains tend to be known in European archaeology) are, by contrast, associated with a range of sophisticated Aurignacian blades. These were flakes longer than they were wide, having the form of thin, fragile but super-sharp cutting tools. Aurignacian blades were part of a diverse and dynamic culture that would, [continued on p. 38]

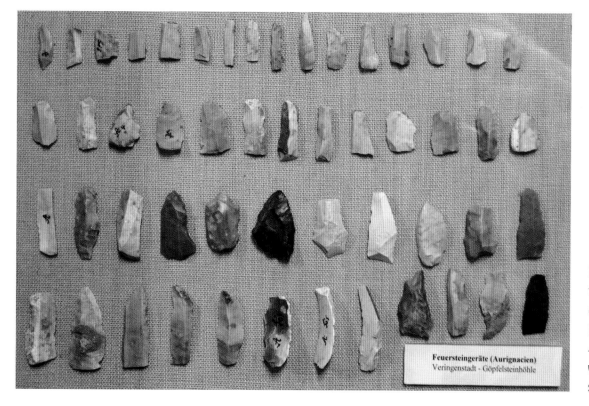

Feuersteingeräte (Aurignacien)
Veringenstadt - Göpfelsteinhöhle

LEFT: Aurignacian tools tended to be characterized by sharp blades, emerged around 40,000 years ago and were particularly well-suited to cutting.

What Makes Us Human?

We cannot define ourselves in terms of a tick-box checklist. Evolution does not work that way. We draw lines – families, genera, species – so that we can classify fossils, but what we are observing is a slow process of continuous change over hundreds of thousands of years.

Nonetheless, incremental changes can accumulate to the point where they reach a sort of tipping-point and it becomes meaningful to talk about a new species, with its own distinctive repertoire of attributes and capacities. Australopithecines made simple stone tools. Neanderthals made clothes of fur and leather. All archaic humans were social animals who moved around the landscape in groups, must have had common rules of behaviour and probably used some sort of language to communicate. But none of them achieved the rapid globalization that started around 60,000 years ago.

We are entitled to speak here about 'progressive' evolution – in the sense that humans were becoming more intelligent and creative. Crucial to this was brain capacity. Hominin brains got bigger over time. Modern human brains typically range between 1130 and 1260cm^3 (69 and 77 cubic inches). By contrast, that of *Australopithecus afarensis* was around 450cm^3, that of *Homo erectus* around 950cm^3/58 cubic inches (though note that Neanderthal brains were similar in size to ours, if not a little larger).

Natural selection for this characteristic was a serious matter. Brain tissue is more expensive than other kinds: the brain accounts for only 2 per cent of our body weight but no less than 20 per cent of food-energy consumption. It is also high risk. Humans are adapted for upright walking, which requires a narrow pelvis, yet have a large brain-case,

BELOW: The skull of a *Homo erectus*.

RIGHT: A reconstruction of an elderly neanderthal man.

which imposes a strain on the woman's pelvis at childbirth; the result is slow, painful and sometimes dangerous birth trauma.

But the advantages are considerable. Large brains enable modern humans to create and sustain complex social relationships, typically with about 150 others, by means of shared language and common culture. Humans are not just social animals, but social animals to an extreme degree, with brains especially enlarged and sophisticated for this purpose.

Sociability confers enormous evolutionary benefits. Human hunter-gatherer bands were probably very small – perhaps 30 or 40 people. But they would have had links with other groups, perhaps half a dozen of similar size, with whom they shared mates, resources, labour, information, ideas. Sociability, cooperation and culture are closely related and achieving them requires high levels of intelligence: in biological terms, brain tissue.

This brings us to a hard answer to that question 'what makes us who we are?' The answer is culture. This means everything we create, from the simplest of tools, like stone hand-axes, to the most complex, like modern robots, from the language by which we communicate to the political institutions by which we are governed, from the 'low culture' of TV game shows to the 'high culture' of classical music and artistic masterpieces.

Homo sapiens has this unique characteristic: unlike all other animals, including other hominins, it is not restricted by biology to a limited range of environments. Thinking it through, talking it over, working together, creating new forms of culture, *Homo sapiens* was able to adapt to life almost anywhere. Biological evolution was therefore superseded by cultural evolution. While other animals adapt to nature, modern humans transform it.

in the course of time, produce the spear-thrower, the harpoon and the bow, as well as domesticating the dog, helping to turn the people of the Upper Palaeolithic (40,000–10,000 years ago) into highly versatile, ultra-efficient hunters.

Gough's Cave in Cheddar Gorge in England is a classic *Homo sapiens* site. It has yielded human remains, animal bones, thousands of stone tools and artefacts made of bone and antler. These date to around 14,000 years ago and belonged to a community of horse hunters. The cave offered shelter and a vantage point overlooking a gorge through which herds of horses and deer regularly passed. Here was a community of *Homo sapiens* adapted to a very specific ecological niche: a natural funnel on

BELOW: Gough's Cave is the site of an array of artefacts from an early *Homo sapiens* site, dating to approximately 14,000 years ago.

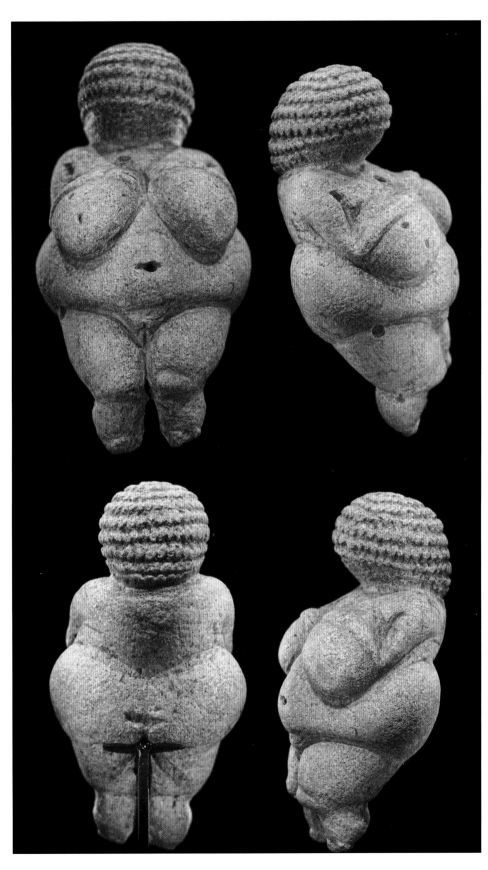

the migration routes of wild animals during the later part of the last great glaciation.

The people of the period were not only providing themselves with a full toolbox. They were also creating art. One of the earliest known examples came to light during excavations at Willendorf in Austria in 1908: an 11cm (4.3in)-tall figure carved from oolitic limestone and tinted with red ochre, she had huge breasts, tummy and thighs, making the 'Venus of Willendorf', dating from around 25,000 years ago, unmistakable as some sort of fertility goddess. Many other examples of 'fat lady' figurines have been discovered.

More spectacular still is the growing corpus of Upper Palaeolithic cave art. Among the earliest examples were those discovered in 1994 at Chauvet Cave in the French Ardèche. Hundreds of animal paintings have been catalogued here, representing 13 different species – aurochs, bears, bison, deer, horses, leopards, lions, mammoths and rhinos among them – and they have been dated to two separate periods, 37,000–33,500 years ago and 31,000–28,000 years ago.

LEFT: The 'Venus of Willendorf', a 25,000-year-old figurine found near Willendorf, Austria. Such figurines have been found across Upper Palaeolithic Europe.

ABOVE: A stunning example of the cave art at Chauvet Cave, depicting horses and lions. These are some of the oldest examples of art anywhere in the world.

Here and elsewhere, Upper Palaeolithic paintings have remained hidden and been preserved for so long because they were executed in the deepest recesses of cave systems, in flickering artificial light, yet by artists of astonishing accomplishment. Why? Archaeologists are fond of debating such questions. There is always a jostle of competing theories. But the correct answer is almost certainly the most obvious: we are witness to the magic of fertility ritual, where the representation is a means to conjure the reality and we can imagine

groups of hunters visiting the caves periodically to perform holy rites, a mix of dancing, singing and chanting, perhaps led by a shaman.

The range of Upper Palaeolithic art is huge. It includes rock carving, engraving and sculpture in stone, bone, antler, ivory and clay, inscribed and painted plaques and decoration on tools, ritual objects, musical instruments and other artefacts. This art gives us an insight into the minds and beliefs of Upper Palaeolithic people that is, of course, impossible for all earlier hominins. And when we view it, we know that we are in the company of people very like ourselves, for we too have our sacred objects and magic rituals, our flags, anthems, costumes and ceremonies.

The Upper Palaeolithic Crisis

By the end of the Upper Palaeolithic, around 10,000 years ago, there was a problem. The hunters were just too efficient and while human groups grew in size, the big game on which so many of them depended were dying out: mammoths, giant deer, wild horses and other mega-fauna were being hunted to extinction.

At the same time, the earth was warming at the end of the last glaciation of the last ice age and the open grasslands across which the big game had roamed were disappearing beneath regenerated forest. The biomass of animals available to the hunters was reduced by about 75 per cent. A shift to a more omnivorous diet, with a higher proportion of plant foods, became essential to survival. Here was a supreme test of *Homo sapiens'* evolutionary fitness, the species' ability to adapt and survive.

In the newly forested northern regions, most humans now settled by rivers, lakes, deltas, estuaries and seashores, where food was both abundant and varied. Around 7500 BCE, Star Carr in Yorkshire in northern England was the site of a seasonal camp used in late spring and summer each year. The Mesolithic (as opposed to Palaeolithic) people who used it hunted wild cattle, elk, red deer, roe deer and wild pig, but also smaller animals like pine martin, red fox and beaver. Stalking and close-range ambush was their chosen method. Their toolkit now included a range of specialized weapons, like barbed spearheads and very small flakes, known as 'microliths', to create arrowheads or to be glued with others into a wooden shaft to create composite tools like harpoons.

Refined techniques of hunting, gathering and scavenging enabled the Mesolithic people of the temperate zone to exploit the new food resources of a wet and wooded landscape. But further south, the crisis was far more serious. Here, in the newly arid regions of Asia, the effects of global warming required a much more radical response from our uber-adaptable new breed of hominin: a shift from food *gathering* to food *production*. The nature-culture transition was about to be moved onto a whole new level.

BELOW: Microliths like this represented an important development in stone tool technology as they could be used effectively for a multitude of purposes, they were small and easily portable and dull or broken microliths could quickly and easily be replaced.

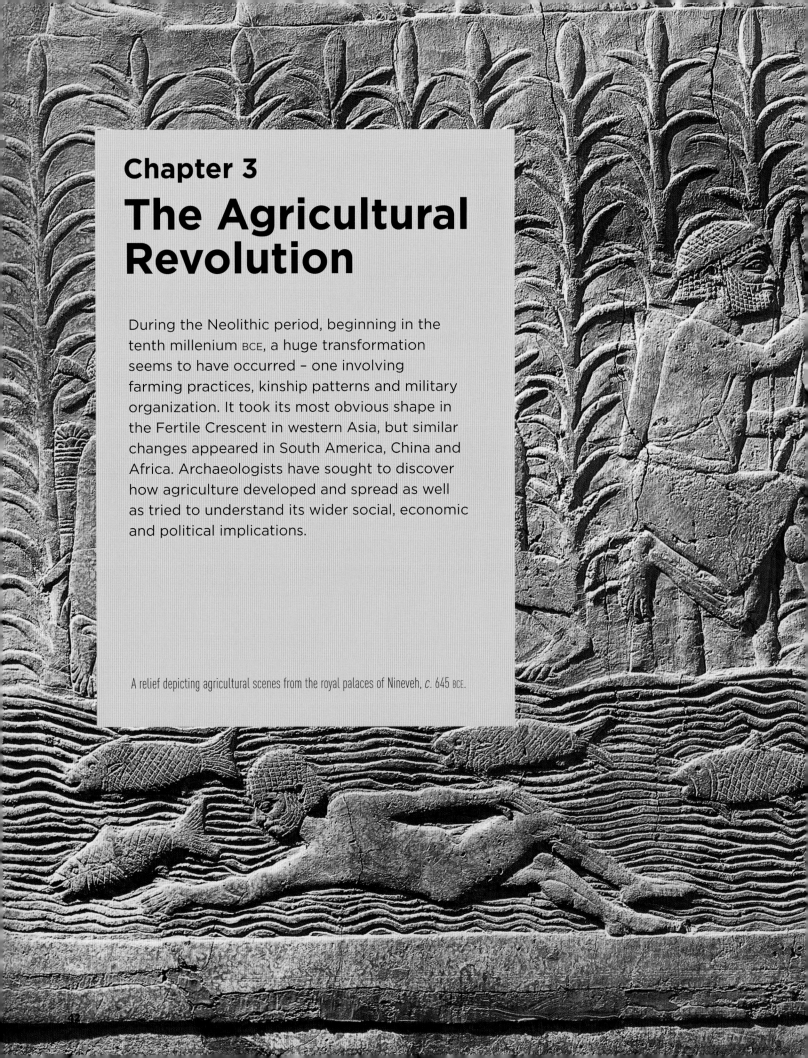

Chapter 3
The Agricultural Revolution

During the Neolithic period, beginning in the tenth millenium BCE, a huge transformation seems to have occurred – one involving farming practices, kinship patterns and military organization. It took its most obvious shape in the Fertile Crescent in western Asia, but similar changes appeared in South America, China and Africa. Archaeologists have sought to discover how agriculture developed and spread as well as tried to understand its wider social, economic and political implications.

A relief depicting agricultural scenes from the royal palaces of Nineveh, *c.* 645 BCE.

An Early Neolithic Village

Petra in southern Jordan is one of the most famous archaeological sites in the world, renowned for its long, winding sandstone canyon by which visitors enter its thousand or so rock-cut tombs, including the monumental, elaborately carved burial places of Nabataean Arab kings and its giant temples ranged along either side of a central colonnaded street. But right beside it, almost entirely forgotten and hardly ever visited, lies another archaeological site whose world-historical importance dwarfs that of Petra. Known by its Arabic name of El-Beidha, it is one of

ABOVE: The remains of the Neolithic village of El-Beidha, which was inhabited from *c.* 7200 BCE to 6500 BCE.

the earliest known agricultural settlements ever found.

A community of Early Neolithic farmers lived here around 6500 BCE. They occupied little family houses of stone, mud and thatch, ground grain on simple saddle-querns and manufactured many and varied flint tools, including arrowheads, knives and scrapers.

Why here? That is easily explained, for the village lies in the lee of one of Petra's sandstone mountains, while stretched out before it is an extensive wadi formed of alluvial (water-deposited) soil. The mountains both absorb and channel winter floodwater, creating streams, springs and pools: Petra is an oasis. The Nabataeans later created artificial canals and giant cisterns to capture this valuable resource for use in the dry summer months. Their Early Neolithic predecessors – when the environment was wetter and greener – probably made do with the natural supply to irrigate their crops and water their animals.

El-Beidha is situated in the Fertile Crescent, an arc of land which stretches from the Levantine coast (now Israel and Lebanon), across Syria, into Mesopotamia, the 'Land Between Rivers' (modern-

day Iraq). Archaeologists once believed that agriculture originated here and later spread to other regions. While we know that agriculture practices and domesticates certainly diffused over wide regions, we also know that it developed independently in different places at different times – for example, there were independent centres in South America, in China and

BELOW: A map showing the spread of farming through western Eurasia, 9600–4000 BCE. From its emergence in the fertile crescent, the spread of agriculture westwards through Europe and eastwards across the Iranian plateau can be traced through the archaeological evidence – though there were several other locations where agriculture emerged independently.

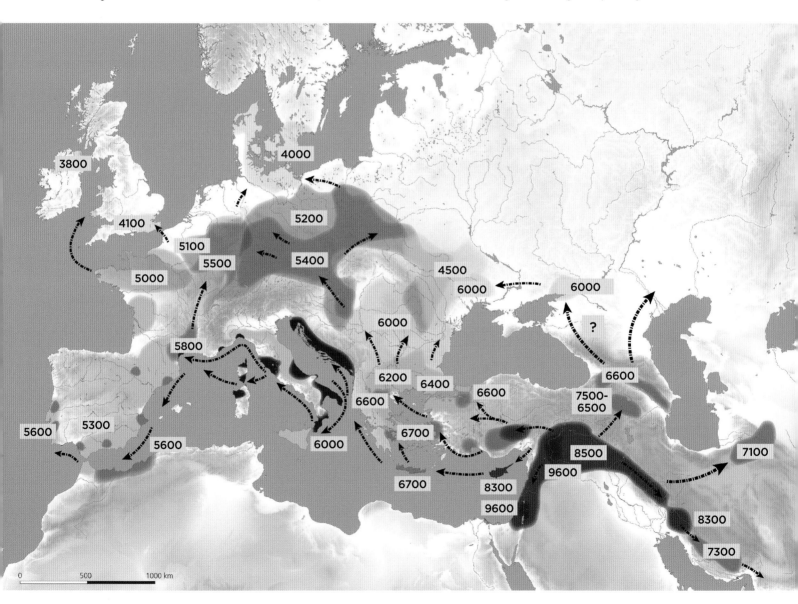

in the Horn of Africa. In other words, a monolithic theory of 'diffusion' has been displaced by ideas of 'independent evolution'.

There is no doubt, though, that the earliest agricultural settlements lay in sub-tropical regions, whereas people continued to make a living as hunter-gatherer-scavengers in the temperate zone with its deciduous forests. The first farmers had no choice. Global warming in the sub-tropics meant desiccation and a reduction in natural resources of wild animals and plants. For existing populations to survive, they had to start producing their own food.

A New Way of Life

The leap from hunting and gathering to herding domesticated animals and cultivating crops was less abrupt and absolute than once believed. Hunters had long existed in a symbiotic relationship with their prey. They created clearings, channelled movement, provided food, warded off predators and spared

the young. The transition from this sort of animal management to animal husbandry was easily made. Pastoralism evolved out of managed hunting.

Equally, it was a matter of simple observation that plants grew from seeds and an obvious deduction that people might collect and plant seeds. No barrier of ignorance prevented people from cultivating crops at an earlier stage. But farming is hard work: it requires long, repetitive, back-breaking toil – cutting down forests, draining wetlands, breaking the sod, hoeing

the ground, protecting crops from weeds and vermin, harvesting and storing the crop once ripe. It also involves the risk of drought, flood or blight. Then the same again, year after year.

Unsurprisingly, there is growing evidence for mixed regimes, with the same communities practising cultivation and herding side-by-side with hunting and gathering for hundreds, even thousands of years. This was facilitated by the 'slash-and-burn' techniques of early farmers: they would create garden-plots, work them for a few years, then, when the soil was exhausted, move on, allowing the old plots to merge back into the wilderness.

But there was no going back. Farming may have been a reluctant choice at first, but it meant higher output able to support larger populations, increasing the gap between what nature could provide and what was necessary to survive. Humanity was soon yoked to toil by its own success.

The agricultural 'package' varied from place to place. The staples in the Fertile Crescent were wheat, barley, pulses, cattle, sheep, goats and pigs. In South-East Asia, it was rice, bananas, yams, water buffalo, pigs and chicken. In Central America, it was maize, beans, sweet potatoes, tomatoes, avocados and cocoa.

Each time, the social impact was enormous. The agricultural revolution was one of only two all-embracing transformations in human history (the other would be the industrial revolution). It meant that people became sedentary or at least semi-sedentary. It meant they had collective property to defend – their fields, their granaries, their flocks and herds, their water supplies. It meant larger populations, more complex social organization, more sophisticated cultural achievements. Nomadic hunter-gatherers had to carry all they possessed. Settled farmers could afford to accumulate a clutter of household utensils, farming tools and ritual objects.

LEFT: The results of modern slash-and-burn techniques in Bolivia. This approach dates back to the origins of agriculture.

Bloody Stone Age

The Talheim death-pit in south-west Germany is one indication of what could happen when the pressures spilled over. Three-metres wide, it contained the bodies of 34 people, half of them children. Two of the adults had been shot in the head with flint arrows. Twenty others, including children, had been clubbed. The bodies had then been unceremoniously dumped in the pit. The archaeologists who uncovered it in 1983 were in no doubt that it was a massacre site.

Dating to around 5000 BCE, the Talheim killings took place at the very beginning of the European Neolithic period. This evidence of Stone Age violence is far from exceptional. A number of bodies were found unceremoniously dumped in the ditch of a Neolithic enclosure at Schletz in Austria. The causewayed enclosure at Crickley Hill in Gloucestershire in Britain was attacked on two occasions; over 400 flint arrowheads were littered around the perimeter, with particular concentrations at the gaps between the ditches. Also in Britain, an adult male was excavated with a flint arrowhead lodged in his chest region at Hambledon Hill in Dorset.

The growing evidence for Neolithic warfare has prompted some archaeo-osteologists to re-examine museum collections of human bones from old barrow excavations. The results have been startling. At least 26 among 350 skulls examined by one research team displayed evidence of traumatic injury.

Social distance largely precludes warfare. Small bands of roaming hominins with plenty of space and ready access to food were unlikely to fight one another even on the rare occasions when they come into contact. But the Early Neolithic world was filling up with people who were settling down to farm and acquiring assets – homes, tools, fields, animals, grain-stores – that needed safeguarding. We know they were marking out territory, because they were constructing huge barrows and monumental enclosures. Social distance was clearly shrinking. Life was at subsistence level, with only narrow margins in hard times and the neighbours were close by. Things could easily turn nasty.

So warfare – organized group violence – came as part of the Neolithic 'package'. And that had implications for social organization. It meant the empowerment of warrior males. A new kind of society – more violent, more patriarchal, more hierarchical – was beginning to emerge.

OPPOSITE: The skull of a man killed in the Talheim massacre, c. 5100 BCE, showing evidence of traumatic injury.

The Neolithic way of life was expansionary. More and more land was turned into fields and pastures. Populations continued to grow and became ever more dependent on cultivation and herding. Farming spread across much of the sub-tropical and temperate world.

But Early Neolithic techniques were primitive and wasteful and society lacked the reserves to see it through natural disasters and hard times. In places where there was much virgin land still available for colonization, the pressures were manageable. But in others, where land was in short supply and population was still growing, something had to give.

Australia

Yet the Neolithic revolution did not occur in the same manner everywhere. In some places, older strategies of hunting and gathering remained in place, while new approaches were adopted to make the most of the local environment. The entire continent of Australia, along with the islands of the largest ocean in the world, remained populated by hunters, fishers and gatherers using a Stone Age toolkit until European explorers first reached them in the late 18th century. There were perhaps half a million Aboriginals in Australia at this time. Their ancestors had arrived around 40,000 or 35,000 BCE, but rising sea-levels had later cut off the continent from continuing contact with the wider world and Aboriginal culture had therefore gone its own way. Change was slow, but change there was and this has been tracked by archaeologists. Shell middens at settlements around coastal estuaries and lagoons attest the former presence of seafood-based communities from about 3000 BCE. Grinding stones at settlements beside major rivers of the interior indicate a subsistence strategy based on the harvesting of wild millet. A new class of hafted stone tools, sometimes to be found in even the harshest of desert and mountain terrains, imply improved hunting techniques. Later again, from around 1000 BCE, there is evidence for settled villages of up to 700 people and for long-distance exchange networks, with fine-grained stone

RIGHT: An ancient Aboriginal petroglyph of a kangaroo from Bundeena, New South Wales, Australia.

ornamental shells and red ochre being moved across hundreds of miles.

Archaeology also records a rich culture of myth, ritual and ancestor worship. Petroglyphs – paintings and carvings on rock – are found throughout Australia and in some cases may date to the beginnings of

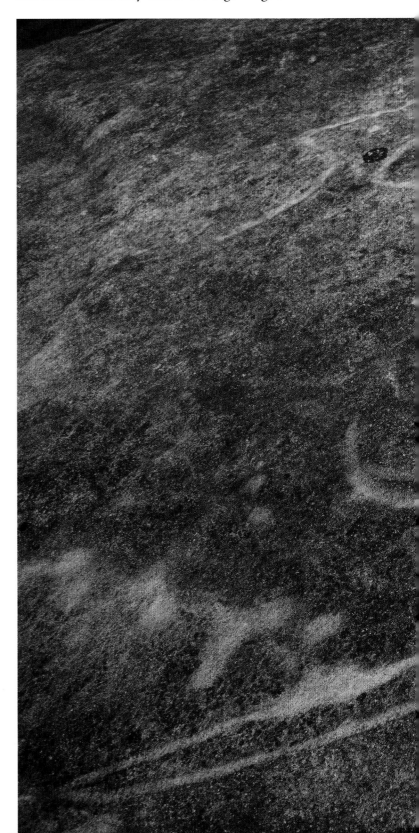

human colonization, for they sometimes depict extinct megafauna. The Australians also decorated bark, basketry and textiles. The artworks include depictions of animals, scenes of hunting, representations of spirit beings, fertility symbols and jagged geometric designs. These images can be related to sites of sacred ritual and burial, such as Roonka Flat, located on a winding flood-plain of the Murray River in Victoria. Twelve early graves, dated 5000–4000 BCE, were vertical interments placed in narrow shafts, the deceased buried with pendants of bone and shell. Another 70 burials date from *c.* 2000 BCE and now the rite involved horizontal placement in

the extended or crouched position, accompanied by food offerings, everyday objects of bone or stone and, in some cases, elaborate clothing and jewellery; around the skull of one man was found a headband of two rows of wallaby incisor teeth. Interpretation of the archaeological evidence is well-informed by anthropological studies. We learn that 'the Dreaming' – a primeval period when ancestor-spirits created earth, water, sky, animals and humans and were themselves incorporated into their own creation, so that the material world remains suffused with a divine presence – is common to all Aboriginal groups.

Primitive Matriarchy

When it comes to interpretation – our concern in this book – one should never assume that the latest research is necessarily the best guide. Academic disciplines are accumulations of knowledge and understanding and invariably there are stand-out seminal studies that scholars are obliged to return to again and again. Now we turn to Neolithic social organization as it seems to have developed over several thousand years, where we will see how strongly this is the case.

Our approach must be cross-disciplinary. Just as Palaeolithic archaeologists are bound to draw on the work of palaeo-anthropologists who study fossil remains – as we saw in Chapter 2 – so Neolithic archaeologists need the insights of both social anthropologists (who study small-scale societies) and ancient historians (especially those who specialize in the study of archaic societies).

We begin, then, with one of the great works of early social anthropology, Lewis Henry Morgan's *Ancient Society* (1877). During fieldwork among the Iroquois Native Americans of New York State, he made a surprising discovery about kinship patterns. The Iroquois man called not only his own children his sons and daughters, but also all the children of his brothers; and they called him father. The children of his sisters, on the other hand, he called nephews and nieces; and they called him uncle. In parallel, the Iroquois woman called her sister's children as well as her own her sons and daughters and they called her mother. Whereas the children of her brothers she called nephews and nieces and they called her

ABOVE: Lewis Henry Morgan (1818–1881) was an American anthropologist who examined Iroquois kinship patterns in detail.

aunt. Nor was this mere affectation. The kinship terms in use reflected Iroquois feelings of nearness or remoteness to their respective relations.

When he extended his researches to other societies – both past and present – Morgan discovered the same basic pattern again and again. His radical conclusion was that the earliest forms of marriage were polygamous group marriages, not monogamous pair marriages; and something equally radical that flowed from this, namely that early social organization must have been essentially matriarchal, where people tended to live with their mother's family and to trace their descent in her line.

Another pioneering social anthropologist, Bronisław Malinowski, found ample confirmation for Morgan's theories during fieldwork among the Trobriand Islanders of the Western Pacific during the First World War. He discovered that the Trobriand kinship system was matrilineal (descent was traced through the female line), but marriage was patrilocal (wife and children lived among the father's family). Malinowski interpreted this dichotomy as a struggle between 'mother-right and father-love'; in other

words, it represented a transitional phase in the development of the Trobriand kinship system.

I shall venture one more digression into a complementary discipline before returning to the material evidence of archaeology. The eminent German classicist Johann Jakob Bachofen published his *Mother Right* in 1926 – around the same time that Malinowski was publishing his Trobriand monographs. Studying Greek and Latin texts, he uncovered a wealth of evidence that the ancient world had once been matriarchal in character. In archaic Lycia (in south-western Turkey), for example, the status of children had been taken from the mother, not the father; property had been inherited by daughters, not sons; and decision-making power rested with women, not men.

What do archaeologists say about all this? It is certainly an area of huge debate among prehistorians, but the balance of evidence still favours the idea that the earliest farming communities were essentially egalitarian and matriarchal.

While there may have been a division of labour, including some specialists like shamans or healers, there seems to have been no social stratification or hierarchy. Take the *Linearbandkeramik* culture of Early Neolithic Europe around 5000 BCE. People lived in large villages of two or three dozen timber longhouses, up to 30–40m (98–131ft) long and 5m (16ft) wide. Building them would have required collective effort – perhaps involving the whole community – and they were so big that each must have accommodated an extended

(as opposed to nuclear) family group. Neither houses nor burials give any indication of social differentiation by wealth. The impression we have is that everyone contributed and everyone consumed on an equal basis according to their ability; and perhaps that groups of siblings lived together with their children in each longhouse.

The existence of a more or less universal earth-mother cult in the Early Neolithic might also be taken as evidence for archaic matriarchy. Marija Gimbutas, whose *The Language of the Goddess* (1989) is a superb collection of prehistoric mother-goddess representations, certainly believes so. In her view, an Old European culture that involved matriarchal organization, developed agriculture, sedentary residence, great works of art, an absence of violence and a harmonious relationship with nature was superseded between 4300 and 2800 BCE by an intrusive 'Proto Indo-European' culture originating in the Central Asian steppes that was patriarchal and militaristic. Her argument is controversial and details may be wrong. But the evidence she presents for the prevalence of the earth-mother cult is overwhelming.

ABOVE: A model of a typical Linearbandkeramik longhouse. Longhouses would have housed whole family groups and imply a fairly unstratified society.

There seems to be no good basis, then, for assuming that Early Neolithic society was male-dominated. Because women spent much of their lives either pregnant and suckling – with high mortality rates in child-birth and relatively low life expectancy overall – there was almost certainly a sexual division of labour. Women probably performed somewhat different roles in Upper Palaeolithic/Mesolithic and Early Neolithic societies – more gathering than hunting in the former,

more hoe-cultivation than herding in the latter – but that is no reason for assuming that women's work was looked down upon or that women's voices were marginalized in decision-making.

From Mother-Right to Patriarchy

They were nothing more than thin lines of darker soil scratched across the exposed surface of the excavation. But they were by far the most spectacular discovery made during a ten-year University of Glasgow excavation at the village of Dunning in Perthshire, Scotland. They dated from the 38th century BCE (3800–3700 BCE) – Neolithic – and they were associated with hundreds of sherds of prehistoric pottery. They represented the movement of a hand-held ard – a primitive wooden plough. The Glasgow team had uncovered some of the earliest evidence for farming in the Scottish archaeological record.

Ards may well date back even further in other parts of the world, perhaps as far back as the 6th millennium BCE. They would usually have been pulled by two oxen, while the ploughman guided the ard, ensuring it cut the sod, by pushing on a handle at the rear and also kept the animals moving using a goad or whip.

Hoe cultivation usually involved a 'slash-and-burn' technique (explained above). Ard cultivation tended to come as part of a package of new techniques that included fertilization of the soil using animal (and human) manure; this kept the land 'in good heart' and fields became more permanent.

Hoe cultivators were often women, since the garden plots were close to the home base, the labour was relatively light and babies could be managed in slings suspended from the body. Ard cultivators were almost invariably men. The fields tended to be larger and more distant and the work was strenuous and would have been hard to manage carrying a baby.

It was already the case that men tended to be the herders, moving animals to and from pasture,

LEFT: A Neolithic mother figure idol, approximately 15cm (6in) tall. Marija Gimbutas was influential in her argument that the culture of Old Europe was strongly matriarchal, as evidenced by the widespread representations of a mother goddess.

essentially owing to their greater mobility; the role of women in the bearing and suckling of infants had already determined this sexual division of labour, just as previously, in hunter-gatherer society, it had determined their role as gatherers more often than hunters. But the advent of the plough seems to have pushed human society to one of those periodic tipping-points.

Heavy labour at a distance (men's work) came to predominate over light labour around the home (women's work). Men were now responsible for the bulk of food production. The plough and the herd; grain and meat: this was now man's domain. And this clashed in a very obvious way with matriarchal kinship systems.

In a matriarchal system, the fruits of a man's labour – in the fields and at pasture – belonged to his wife's family. The pressure was therefore now on to overturn mother-right and assert father-right. More broadly, the pressure was on to redefine agricultural wealth, no longer to be seen as a common store from which a group may draw, but to be recognized as the private property of one man and his immediate family.

We have already noted another potent factor in the mix: the beginnings of organized warfare.

Fantasy fiction aside, only in the most exceptional circumstances can prehistoric women have played any role in warfare, except that of victims. They would have spent a large part of their often brief adult lives either pregnant or nursing dependant infants. Warfare involved traversing the landscape and wielding weapons – bows, spears, axes, clubs – in combat with other bands. It was men's work.

Marija Gimbutas may be wrong to believe that patriarchy was introduced by invaders from the outside. All the ingredients of a major transformation could have developed inside Neolithic society. The plough and the herd; organized warfare; private property and patriarchy: here was a new cultural package and a new social order.

Rooted in this new order, of course, was the oppression of women. Denied control over private property, they became dependants of men and subject to the authority of fathers and husbands. But they were not the only losers. An end to communal production and goods held in common, the development of private holdings of wealth, created the basis for differences in wealth and the emergence of social classes.

BELOW: A diagram of an ard plough. The ard plough remained in use across much of the world until the Middle Ages.

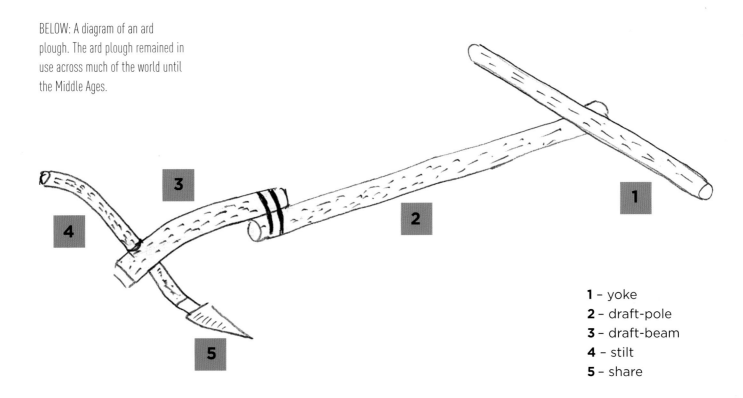

1 – yoke
2 – draft-pole
3 – draft-beam
4 – stilt
5 – share

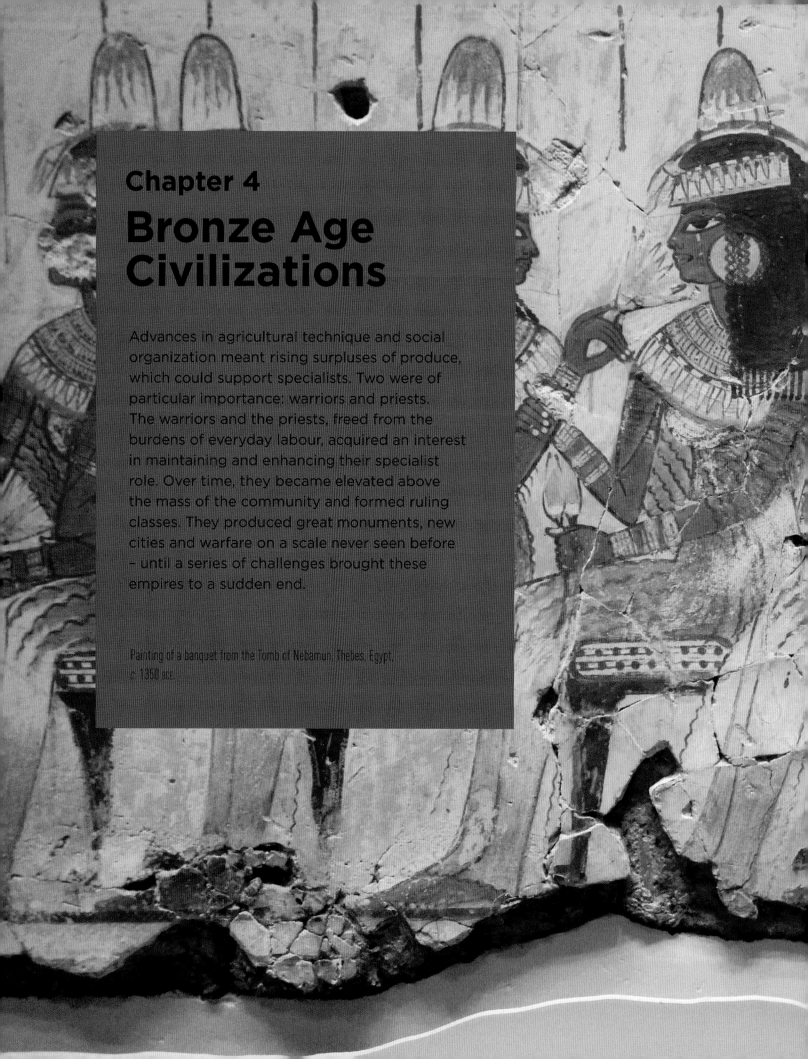

Chapter 4
Bronze Age Civilizations

Advances in agricultural technique and social organization meant rising surpluses of produce, which could support specialists. Two were of particular importance: warriors and priests. The warriors and the priests, freed from the burdens of everyday labour, acquired an interest in maintaining and enhancing their specialist role. Over time, they became elevated above the mass of the community and formed ruling classes. They produced great monuments, new cities and warfare on a scale never seen before – until a series of challenges brought these empires to a sudden end.

Painting of a banquet from the Tomb of Nebamun, Thebes, Egypt, c 1350 BCE.

The First Social Classes

The recent discovery of two skeletons of a man and a woman together in a huge ceramic jar dating from the mid-17th century BCE at the site of La Almoloya in Murcia in Spain confirms the highly stratified character of Early Bronze Age society.

The El Argar culture controlled an area the size of Belgium in the south-eastern part of the Iberian peninsula between 2200 and 1500 BCE – broadly contemporary with Minoan Crete. La Almoloya is a key site for investigation of this little-known culture.

The couple, buried around the same time, were accompanied by 29 prestige objects, most of them assumed to belong to the woman, aged between 25 and 30 years of age. These included bracelets, rings, ear-plugs and a diadem, mainly silverware, with some gold. Similar diadems have been found in other female burials of the El Argar culture.

Archaeologists from the Autonomous University of Barcelona have been working at the site since 2013, keen to learn more of the first civilization in Spain to use bronze, build urban centres and create

ABOVE: A person buried inside a jar, a ritual practice of the El Argar culture of southern Iberia. These bodies of the deceased were often accompanied by valuable grave goods, indicating that this was the practice of an elite.

an advanced class society and state structure. The impression is of a militaristic society of male warriors.

The La Almoloya burial tells the same story as thousands of other Bronze Age sites: this was an age dominated by a social elite. In marked contrast to the Early Neolithic, when the social structure seems to have been flat, we now have unequivocal evidence for hierarchies of wealth and power.

We will shortly take a close look at an Early Bronze Age society where surplus accumulation and social stratification made possible such concentrations of wealth that a quantitative leap to urban civilization became possible. Before we do this, however, let us give some thought to the metalworkers who, in some sense, define this period.

The Bronzeworkers

We still use what is really a rather old-fashioned term: the Bronze Age. It was coined in the mid 19th century, when antiquarian scholars focused their attention on the materials from which archaeological artefacts were made. The Bronze Age dates from around 3000 BCE or a little earlier to around 1200 BCE or a little later.

This was not the earliest use of metals. Copper had occasionally been used to make ornaments for some thousands of years before it was mixed with other metals to make a harder and more serviceable alloy. Bronze, strictly speaking, is an alloy of copper and tin, but copper could also be mixed with other metals – like zinc to make brass – and archaeologists tend to use the term 'copper-alloy' to describe all copper-based objects.

But 'Bronze Age' is something of a misnomer. The metals are relatively rare and hard to come by; we have ample evidence of Bronze Age elites going to great trouble to access supplies of copper and tin. The alloy is also relatively soft, so not really durable enough for the tools of everyday life. Bronze artefacts – often highly crafted and of great artistry – were essentially elite items, typically arms, armour ornaments and trinkets. Bronze Age farmers continued to use tools of stone, wood and bone for working the land.

Unsurprisingly, perhaps, hoards of buried Bronze Age metalwork are relatively common discoveries. The largest ever discovered in London has just been unearthed in Havering. Among 453 bronze objects were axeheads, spearheads and fragments of swords, daggers and knives, all dating between *c.* 900 and 800 BCE, at the very end of the Bronze Age in Britain.

As usual in such cases, the archaeologists were unable to decide whether the hoard was a ritual offering – to an unknown deity at an unknown sacred site – or what is sometimes called a 'founder's hoard' – a cache of metalwork buried for safety by an itinerant bronzeworker.

Bronzeworkers were a special breed. They were masters of an arcane craft. Their services were in high demand. Their occasional visits were eagerly anticipated. Like the wandering craftworkers of later history, they were ever on the move, seeking commissions wherever they might be had, for only the greatest of Bronze Age lords could be expected to maintain a full-time metalworker.

RIGHT: Fragments of a Bronze Age sword discovered in Havering. Hundreds of bronze weapons were uncovered at the site.

The Land of Shinar

He lived more than 4,000 years ago, at the dawn of civilization. He was war leader, high priest, hydraulic engineer and first minister – all rolled into one – of the Sumerian city-state of Lagash from 2144 to 2124 BCE. His name was Gudea and we know of him because some two dozen statues of him have survived along with a wealth of inscriptions recording his achievements.

Let us set him in context. Ancient Sumer – the Biblical 'Land of Shinar' – lay astride the Tigris and Euphrates river system of Lower Mesopotamia (today's Iraq). In the mid 4th millennium BCE, it was a region of vast swamps, of slow, sluggish, muddy rivers and streams, of towering reeds and date palms. Compared with the desert wastes on either side, this watery jungle teeming with foodstuffs was a veritable Garden of Eden – perhaps, indeed, it was *the* Garden of Eden. But let it once be tamed, let the waters be canalized and the swamps drained and the result would be fields of alluvial soil of exceptional richness.

This was the transition carried out in the final centuries of the 4th millennium. It required massed labour to achieve – to straighten and deepen channels, to build protective banks, to divert and manage the waters. It required continuing massed labour to maintain – to dredge channels, restore banks, repair flood damage. But the result was unprecedented agricultural wealth. And such bounty allowed the transition to be made from Copper Age villages to Bronze Age cities.

But later standards, for sure, Sumerian civilization was small in scale. Sumer as a whole was about the size of modern Denmark and even the larger cities might extend across only one or two square miles. Records for Lagash – city and countryside – imply a population of about 36,000 adult males, so perhaps 100,000 people in total.

But by comparison with everything that had gone before, this was an urban revolution – a massive leap in the scale and complexity of human social organization. And it created the basis for a cultural explosion. This included writing, measurement, arithmetic, geometry, time-keeping and money. Much

RIGHT: A statue of the Sumerian official Gudea, *c.* 2090 BCE. He was responsible for restoring the temples of Lagash and installed several statues of himself in them.

of what we know about this civilization we owe to the invention of writing, the keeping of records and the existence of a city-state bureaucracy. The town clerks of ancient Sumer not only created official documents: they also filed them in the form of baked clay tablets – for archaeologists to find 4,000 years later.

These innovations were not necessarily good news for the peasant farmers of Mesopotamia. Many of the surviving documents are records of who owed what to whom. We learn, for example, that the goddess Baü – one of 20 deities with holdings in the territory of Lagash – owned 44km² (17 square miles) of land. In the absence of Baü herself, this property was managed on her behalf by temple priests. They were well rewarded for their efforts. While tenant-farmers on her estate might hold as little as a third of a hectare, one senior temple official held more than 14ha. As for the city governor – who was also the high priest – he held no less than 246ha (608 acres). Thanks to the meticulous record-keeping of the Sumerian bureaucracy, we can say more. The tenant-farmers on Baü's estate paid a seventh or an eighth of their produce to the temple in rent. These rents enabled the priests to employ 21 bakers, assisted by 27 female slaves, 25

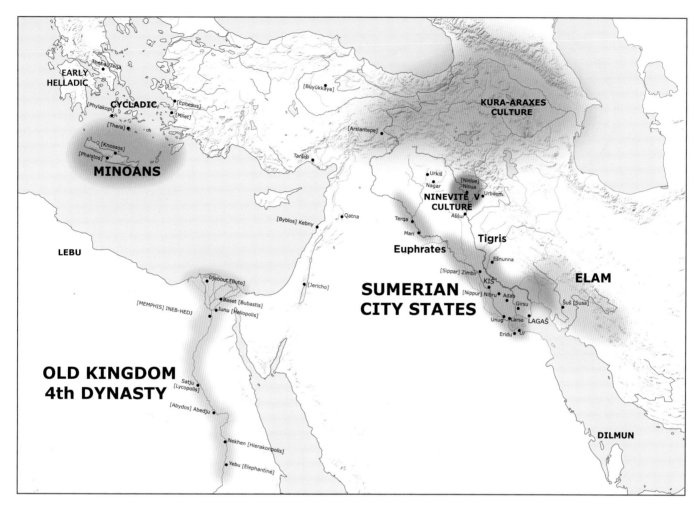

ABOVE: A map showing the major cultures of the Near East, *c.* 2600 BCE. The Sumerian civilization occupied a narrow strip of territory along the Tigris and Euphrates Rivers and consisted of a series of city-states rather than a single centralized empire.

brewers, with six slaves and 40 women textile workers.

As well as investing in grand living, the Sumerian ruling class used the wealth it controlled to build great monuments and to wage war. The greatest monuments were the large temples and artificial mounds known as 'ziggurats'. An early ziggurat at Erech, for example, was 10m high, built of sun-dried bricks, faced with thousands of pottery goblets and topped by an asphalt platform.

As for war-making, our most precious piece of evidence is perhaps the gorgeous Standard of Ur. Found during excavations of the Royal Tombs at Ur in the 1920s and dating from around 2600 BCE, it is

ABOVE: A bas-relief of the Goddess Baü, *c.* 2120 BCE. Baü was one of several deities worshipped in Lagash and was regarded as a divine mother by several rulers of the city.

LEFT: The original structure of the ziggurat at Erech (known today as Uruk) was built *c.* 4000 BCE and expanded on in 3500 BCE.

a small hollow box decorated with scenes executed in shell, limestone, lapis lazuli and bitumen. On one side, the so-called 'Peace Panel' depicts the ruler and his courtiers seated and drinking in the top tier, with two lower tiers depicting lesser mortals apparently bearing gifts, booty or tribute. On the opposite side, the 'War Panel' shows the ruler in battle. Four-wheeled chariots and phalanxes of spearmen are seen crushing their enemies and, on the top tier, a forlorn procession of captives being paraded before the leader. So this was a class society – and a slave society – dominated by an elite of war leaders and high priests. It was a complex society that required an elaborate literate bureaucracy to be manageable. It also required connection with the wider world, for whatever

the abundance of Mesopotamia's irrigation-based agriculture, Sumer lacked many of the raw materials her advanced civilization required – timber, metals, stone for tools, precious stones for decoration and also gold and silver.

The wood may have come from Iran or Syria, copper from Oman, tin from Iran, Syria, Asia Minor, even Europe, lapis lazuli from Afghanistan and mother-of-pearl from the Persian Gulf. These are long-distance connections and we must imagine the implications – the caravans and desert trading posts, the merchant ships and ports, the diplomatic arrangements and the payments of protection money to local tribal leaders.

So Sumer's vast surpluses not only sustained an urban civilization and a ruling elite; they gave rise to a merchant class and a web of trade lines extending for thousands of miles. As well as giant grain-stores, there must have been warehouses full of precious imported commodities.

BELOW: The peace panel from the Standard of Ur. Made during the First Dynasty of Ur, it tells us much about the nature of Sumerian society, yet the original purpose of the Standard itself remains a mystery.

A Global Transformation

We have looked at Ancient Sumer in detail. This must serve as our main case-study in Bronze Age civilization. But two other river-valley systems also experienced an urban revolution in the Early Bronze Age.

Menes, the legendary first pharaoh, united the Nile Delta (Lower Egypt) and the Nile Valley (Upper Egypt) in *c.* 3200–3000 BCE, creating a single centralized state with himself as autocratic god-king. The early pharaohs, like the city governors and high priests of Sumer, fostered the cultural prerequisites of an urban revolution in Egypt.

The most important of these were irrigation works. Control of the waters of the Nile ensured abundant harvests, large surpluses and a healthy workforce. Official trade missions secured the raw materials needed for arms manufacture, monumental architecture and luxury consumption. A literate and numerate bureaucracy managed the tribute and labour services on which state power depended.

The most striking archaeological remains of Old Kingdom Egypt (2700–2250 BCE) are, of course, the pyramids of Giza. These were not temples – like the ziggurats of Sumer – but royal tombs. They are masterpieces of architectural design and social organization, but they are also monuments to exploitation, dictatorship and waste.

The elite also created these monuments to demonstrate their semi-divinity and to link themselves to the gods. After all, the gods gave life and they took it away and the pharaohs were the all-important intermediaries between this world and the gods. The gods were everything: they made the sun rise and they made the Nile flood.

BELOW: The Pyramids of Giza are the iconic emblems of ancient Egypt. They reflected a strongly hierarchical society, which devoted immense resources to honouring royal ancestors.

For the Egyptians, the Nile was their lifeblood. The great river slashed through the otherwise arid land like a blue arrow. Most everyday Ancient Egyptians lived in villages dotted along the length of the river. Ancient Egypt is sometimes called the 'civilization without cities' and indeed relatively few ancient cities are known. This was unlike the situation in contemporary Mesopotamia. There, the land was fed and watered by the Euphrates and the Tigris River. The people ranged more widely between the two rivers, irrigating the

ABOVE: The ruins of Harappa, in the Indus Valley, suggest a very different type of society, with minimal differentiation between the residential houses discovered.

region between and satelliting around multiple great municipalities. Regardless of their different settlement patterns, both Egypt and Mesopotamia were heavily hierarchical societies.

This was in sharp contrast with another contemporary urban civilization based on rich riverine agriculture which emerged in the Indus Valley of today's Pakistan around 2600 BCE. The great monuments and residential suburbs of Mohenjo-daro cover 2.6km² (1 square mile). The walled perimeter of Harappa is 4km long. Inscribed seal stamps and standard weights and measures indicate complex bureaucratic administration. It was also a highly developed society. The sanitation at Mohenjo-daro was of a type not seen until Roman times and later – including individual 'flush'-style toilets (the oldest in the world), shower cubicles and drainage systems that passed through the city. The houses were carefully built and yet, each was almost the same. The Indus Valley, unlike the great civilizations of Mesopotamia or Egypt, seems to have been a classless society or at least there was no class differentiation among the city dwellers. Fascinatingly archaeologists have also failed to find any good evidence for religion and zero evidence for warfare or violence, again in complete contrast to its two contemporaries. Thus, the Indus cities had none of the usual temples, boastful statues or elite art. Indeed, among the only human representations that exist from Mohenjo-daro are those of a young 'dancing girl' and the bust of a 'priest-king'. However, there is no evidence that the man was a priest or a king – his eyes are half closed as if in meditative, perhaps yogic, contemplation. It is quite possible that this was a peaceful, non-hierarchical society. And yet it was also wealthy and well-connected, its tentacles reaching as far as Arabia. Perhaps once the elusive script of the Indus Valley Civilization has been deciphered, we will know more about this ancient civilization, the polar opposite of Egypt or Mesopotamia.

RIGHT: The 'priest-king' of Mohenjo-daro. The Indus Valley civilization rarely expended its resources on producing elite monuments and we cannot be sure who this figure was – and whether he actually was even a priest or a king.

Basket-makers and Olmecs: the First Civilizations of the Americas

No clear break separates hunting and foraging from farming in the prehistory of the Americas. Many cultures – most famously perhaps, the big-game hunters of the Great Plains – eschewed farming right up to the 19th century. Others seem to have adopted farming as early as 7000 BCE in South America and 3000 BCE in North America; or perhaps more often, a mixed regime in which hunting and foraging were combined with horticulture.

The evidence is patchy and therefore skewed. We owe our first clear glimpses of North American horticulturalists to the arid conditions of the South-west, where the dry climate has preserved organic plant remains and also basketry containers for foraging, storage and winnowing. Archaeologists have therefore dubbed this culture 'the Basket-makers' (1500 BCE–750 CE). The early Basket-makers seem to have remained on the move, but between 1 and 500 CE permanent hamlets with ten or so houses were established beside valleys irrigated by winter rains and filled with fertile alluvial soil. Even so, there is little evidence for cultivation at this stage; it seems that food was still hunted or gathered. A bigger change came after 500 CE, when villages were built on terraces beside flood plains and maize, beans and squash were cultivated. Archaeologists estimate that around 50 per cent of the food intake was now supplied in this way. The settlements of this phase (Basket-maker III) were larger. Villages of up to 50 dwellings have been excavated, each a shallow pit-house with sunken floor varying from 2m (6.5ft) to 7m (23ft) across, surrounded by grain-storage pits. One well-preserved example excavated at Shabik'eschee in New Mexico comprised a rectangular sunken room with hearth and small pits used for grinding corn and other household tasks linked by a short, raised passage with a circular antechamber (for storage?). Stone slabs lined the walls and these were plastered with a mix of adobe and ashes. A framework of poles and beams supported the brushwood panels forming the roof.

In Mesoamerica, the first clue that an ancient civilization had developed in the area was a colossal carved basalt head, found protruding from the ground

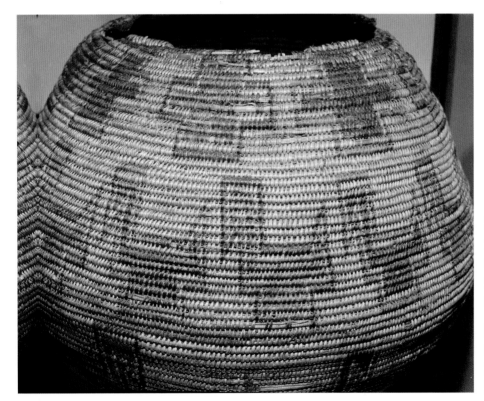

LEFT: A coiled basket from the Basket-maker culture. The Basket-makers inhabited a large area of the American Southwest and mostly relied on hunter-gatherer techniques for subsistence.

OPPOSITE: A colossal Olmec head, *c.* 1200–900 BCE found in San Lorenzo Tenochtitlán. The largest stone head measured more than 3m (9.8ft) high and weighed 28 tons.

by a sugar-cane worker in Mexico's Veracruz region in 1862. But it was only in 1925 that archaeologists discovered another. Even then, despite careful study of artefacts in similar style held in various private collections and the coining of the term 'Olmec' to define the culture group, the identity of the people who had created these objects remained a mystery. The critical breakthrough came with the development of radiocarbon (C-14) dating. This is based on the fact that radiocarbon – a radioactive isotope of carbon – which is present in all organic matter, decays at a known rate, so that, by measuring the amount of radiocarbon remaining, the age of an excavated object containing organic material can be ascertained. The application of C-14 dating to organic material found in association with Olmec pottery allowed the culture

to be dated to the period *c.* 1200–300 BCE, making it the oldest civilization in Central America. Few Olmec settlements have been excavated. Among those that have is the ceremonial centre at San Lorenzo. Situated on a natural plateau 50m (164ft) high and measuring 1.25km (0.8 miles) north–south, the upper layers comprise 7m (23ft) of deliberate dumping, presumably to level the site. Some archaeologists

believe that finger-like extensions of the plateau may have been intended to represent a bird. At the heart of the complex were courtyards defined by platforms of earth, perhaps used for ritual bathing, a sacred ball game and other religious activities. A network of underground drains was dug to remove excess water. Basalt sculpture – the stone brought from mountains 80km (50 miles) away – included eight colossal heads up to 2.85m (9ft) high in distinctive Olmec style, with thick lips, flat noses, large eyes and helmets of the kind worn in the sacred ball game, making Olmec figures look like archaic baseball players. Some 200 house mounds have also been excavated at the site, bearing testimony to the agricultural productivity of this hot, wet, tropical region.

But San Lorenzo is dwarfed by Teotihuacán – a site still shrouded in even greater mystery than Olmec civilization. A short distance from Lake Texcoco in central Mexico, only 40km from modern-day Mexico City, it was, at its zenith around 500 CE, the sixth largest city in the world at the time, home to an estimated 200,000 people, the heart of a mini empire of 25,000km². Laid out on a grid pattern which extended across 20km² (8 square miles), it centred on a vast ceremonial complex whose main north–south axis, the Avenue of the Dead, was 5km (3 miles) long and lined with 75 temples – each one a flat-topped mound of adobe, earth and stone, painted red and white, many decorated with polychrome murals. Dominating all were the Pyramid of the Moon, at the far end of the Avenue and the Pyramid of the Sun, the greatest temple of all, a 70m (230ft) high monument formed of an estimated million tons of soil and rubble.

LEFT: The Avenue of the Dead at Teotihuacán as seen from the Pyramid of the Moon. At its zenith around 500 CE, Teotihuacán was one of the largest cities in the world.

The Chavín

The sacred stone known as the Lanzon at the heart of the temple was 4.5m (15ft) tall. It was carved with a human-like creature, but with the fanged teeth of a cat and twisting snakes for hair. The whole temple had been built around this cult image of the deity in about 800 BCE. The structure had a U-shaped form ranged around a sunken courtyard. An underground gallery was packed with ceramics, brought from far

BELOW: The archaeological site of Chavín de Huántar, which was occupied c. 1200–500 BCE. The site contained a fabulous array of artefacts that has shaped our understanding of the Chavín culture.

and wide and then ritually broken as offerings to the divine. This was Chavín de Huántar and its discovery and excavation by Peruvian archaeologists proved the existence of an ancient civilization with its roots in the Andes dating back to 1200 BCE. Little is known of belief and ritual, but Chavín art, on stone, gold and ceramics, including a fabulous range of stirrup-spouted bottles, was dominated by animal deities – jaguars, eagles, caymans, snakes and, as in the case of the Lanzon, anthropoid forms with animal attributes. This first flourishing of Peruvian civilization ended around 200 BCE.

RIGHT: The statue known as Lanzon de Chavín, which lays within the temple of Chavín de Huántar, is believed to represent the deity of the people who lived there.

Akrotiri, Troy, Knossos and Myceanae

There can be no doubt that the major centres of civilization had an impact on surrounding societies. There was an interaction between 'core' – advanced metropolitan areas – and 'periphery' – less-developed areas economically dependent on them. We shall take as an example four famous Bronze Age sites in the Eastern Mediterranean.

'Wonderful things' was Howard Carter's answer to Lord Carnarvon's question of whether he could see anything. It was 25 November 1922. The first of the stones sealing the entrance had been removed. The interior was packed with the richest imaginable grave-goods. Carter had found the intact tomb of a New Kingdom pharaoh: the Tomb of Tutankhamun.

In the century since, the contents of the tomb have become probably the most famous archaeological treasures ever found. The alabaster statues, busts, chests and jars; the animal sculptures and golden goddesses; the jewellery of gold, chalcedony, cornelian, feldspar, lapis-lazuli and turquoise; the delicate furniture finished with gold plate and inlaid with ivory, ebony, glass-paste, glazed terracotta

and semi-precious stones; above all, the sequence of mummy cases and the fabulous golden death-mask. And so much more: 5,000 objects in all. Virtually all these objects were of composite manufacture and incorporated imported raw materials. Not the least significance of the Treasures of Tutankhamun is the evidence with which they provide for Egypt's international trade.

The mercantile connections of the New Kingdom pharaohs of the Late Bronze Age – Tutankhamun ruled from 1334 to 1325 BCE – extended across the

RIGHT: The death-mask of Tutankhamun and an alabaster jar found in his tomb. Tutankhamun's grave goods provided evidence of an interconnected world, as the resources used in their manufacture were imported from several different locations.

whole Eastern Mediterranean and deep into Africa. They obtained wood from Lebanon, copper from Cyprus and gold from Sudan. The city of Byblos in the Lebanon grew rich on the timber trade and local merchants employed clerks who could read Egyptian. The city of Enkomi in Cyprus was equally successful as a copper-trading emporium, with archaeological evidence for smelting on the site and strong defensive walls constructed in the second half of the 2nd millennium. Northern Sudan, on the other hand, was annexed by Egypt and forced to pay tribute in gold.

The demands of trade encouraged merchants, sea captains and shipbuilders. Longboats powered by rowers were used in the Aegean from *c.* 3000 BCE onwards. Spectacular evidence comes from the Middle Bronze Age small town of Akrotiri on the island of Thera in the Cyclades. Destroyed by a volcanic

eruption in the 16th century BCE, it was buried in ash and pumice and exceptionally well-preserved, a sort of Bronze Age Pompeii. One long fresco depicts a flotilla of boats sailing along the coast in front of a harbour and small town, the boats ranging from small rowing boats to medium-sized vessels, some with banks of oars, some with mast and sail, up to large galleys with as many as 20 oars on either side and a central mast. These vessels look very similar to those depicted on much later ancient artworks. The technology of long-distance maritime trade was already well advanced. The site of Troy also throws light on Bronze Age commerce. Antiquarians and archaeologists were first

BELOW: A Minoan fresco from Akrotiri *c.* 1550 BCE, shows a procession of ships. This fresco is 6m (20ft) long and has been exceptionally preserved due to a volcanic eruption which buried the city in ash.

drawn to it during the 1870s because of its potent association with Homer's epic poems. It is located near the mouth of the Dardanelles Straits, a key trade route linking the Mediterranean and the Black Sea and, though some distance inland now due to silting, it was originally on the sea and possessed of a good harbour.

Troy has the form of a tell – an artificial mound formed by thousands of years of accumulation of rubble and mudbrick – and excavation has revealed a long history extending from *c.* 3000 BCE to the 6th century CE. Archaeologists recognize 11 main phases in all, but only in Greek and Roman times (Troy VIII onwards) could the site be described as a town. During the Bronze Age (Troy I to VI), it was a fortified palace complex overlooking the harbour, less than 200m (656ft) across. But there can be no doubt that it owed its existence – and its relative importance – to trade. The example of Crete is even more clear-cut. The Thalassocracy (sea power) of Crete rose to prominence in the Middle Bronze Age (*c.* 2000–1600 BCE) on the basis of the island's central location in the

Eastern Mediterranean and the islanders' revolutionary design of deep-hulled, high-capacity, sail-powered cargo ships.

The rulers of Minoan Crete lived in sprawling stone palaces laid out in strictly symmetrical fashion, creating dense labyrinths of narrow corridors and small rooms. The 'royal apartments' and 'house chapels' were richly decorated with frescoes, including figured scenes which offer us a vivid glimpse of the former residents. Annexed to the palaces were storerooms packed with giant ceramic containers, where, one assumes, the tribute levied on subject peasants and the tolls levied on merchant traders were accumulated. Round about 1450 BCE, Minoan Crete was overrun by invaders from the Greek mainland: the Mycenaeans. Archaeological interest in the Mycenaeans was triggered by the excavation of immensely rich assemblages of grave goods among 19 bodies found in six shaft-graves at Mycenae itself in the 1870s. Not until the 1950s, however, with the decipherment of the Linear B script on baked clay tablets

BELOW: A fresco of a bull leaping, found in the Minoan palace of Knossos, dating to *c.* 1550 BCE. It is believed that this may have reflected the actual practice of bull sports in Minoan culture.

LEFT: A rock crystal flagon found in the Zakros palace on Crete, *c.* 1500 BCE.

FOLLOWING PAGES: The ruins of Troy were discovered by the archaeologist Heinrich Schliemann in 1871. Before its discovery, it was believed to have been a legendary invention of the Greek poet Homer.

from Mycenaean sites, was it confirmed that these people were indeed, as long suspected, actually Greek speakers.

The assumption is that they were invaders from the north, a warrior aristocracy that swept over Greece and established themselves as a new ruling class during the Middle Bronze Age. They seem to have achieved their own local urban revolution in the 16th century BCE, creating a highly stratified society dominated by chariot-borne nobles (somewhat akin to Homer's heroes). These nobles built themselves palaces – centred on a *megaron* or feasting hall – which were later girt with massive walls of 'Cyclopean' masonry.

Mycenaean palace civilization was underpinned by imported raw materials – metals, ivory and glass – and perhaps oil, wine and wool were exported in exchange. There is obvious evidence of connectedness in the spread of Mycenaean artefacts across much of the Eastern and Central Mediterranean, from Sicily to the Levant and in the fact that the Mycenaeans were obviously aggressive sea-rovers: we know they seized Minoan Crete in the mid 15th century BCE, we have the Homeric tradition of them mounting a major expedition against Troy in the mid 13th century and we may have references to them as pirates in both Hittite and Egyptian records around this time.

The great lords and urban centres of the Bronze Age 'core' – Mesopotamia and Egypt in the case of the Mediterranean – triggered a growth of long-distance trade and the emergence of new civilizations on the 'periphery'. So much so that by the end of the Bronze Age, the world had become a crowded and fractious place, with rival elites competing for wealth and power. In fact, a slow motion arms-race was underway and the Bronze Age civilizations were heading for cataclysmic crisis and collapse.

LEFT: The Lion Gate of Mycenae, an example of Cyclopean masonry. This was the entrance to a Mycenaean citadel built in *c.* 1250 BCE.

A Late Bronze Age Arms Race

It was an age of hubris – of great empires, autocratic warlords and predatory violence. Right across the Late Bronze Age Mediterranean, the archaeological evidence bears witness to growing militarization – a slow-motion arms race.

One of the great cities of the era was Boğazköy, ancient Hattusha, in north-central Anatolia, capital of the Hittite Empire. Around 1500 BCE, it consisted of a central citadel and a walled lower city to the north-west. A century later, it had doubled in size, with the construction of a new upper city. Some decades later again, there was further expansion, until the Hittite capital extended 2.5km (1.5 miles) in one direction, 1.5km (0.9 miles) in the other. This unified kingdom, in control of most of today's Turkey, was forged around 1650 BCE. The growing wealth and power of the empire was reflected in the development of Boğazköy. By now, it was filled with monumental architecture, above all the substantially rebuilt royal palace inside the citadel. Here was a pillared audience chamber of 32m² (345ft²) and two royal archives from which the excavators recovered some 3,000 baked-clay cuneiform tablets. No less than five temples have been identified in the city, along with a major religious sanctuary about 3.5km (2.2 miles) outside it. The main gateways into the city were also constructed on a massive scale. Many fragments of stone sculpture depicting deities, kings and warriors, some in the round, some in relief, often larger than life-size, have been uncovered at Boğazköy and also at other Hittite sites. The defences of the city, reaching completion during the 13th

LEFT: The Sphinx Gate at Hattusha, a symbol of the emerging power of the Hittite Empire in the mid-2nd millennium BCE.

century, made the Hittite capital one of the strongest fortresses in the region. In the southern part of the circuit, the upper wall was built on top of a stone-faced rampart, with a lower wall beyond as an outer defence. It was further reinforced with regular projecting bastions (to allow defenders to enfilade attackers with shot) and the city gateways were guarded by massive twin towers.

Especially valuable were the hauls of cuneiform tablets. Cuneiform was a script developed in the Middle East around 3200 BCE and then used to represent a wide range of regional languages over the next three millennia. It was formed by impressing a wedge-shaped pen (*cuneus* is Latin for wedge) into a soft clay tablet. Many of these survive in the archaeological

LEFT: A Hittite cuneiform tablet. Tablets such as these provide a wealth of information about the politics, society, religion and international relations of the Bronze Age.

BELOW: Large-scale pottery found at the ancient Hittite capital of Hattusha.

ABOVE: A relief depicting the Battle of Kadesh of 1274 BCE at the Egyptian temple of Abu Simbel. It shows Rameses II personally slaying an enemy during the battle, one of the largest military engagements of the era.

record either because they were deliberately fired for permanent archiving or because they were baked in an accidental conflagration. Along with the evidence of Egyptian hieroglyphic inscriptions, they provide us with all sorts of clues about international tensions in the Late Bronze Age. One event for which we have especially vivid written and artistic evidence is the Battle of Kadesh in perhaps 1274 BCE (the precise date is uncertain). The Hittite Empire and New Kingdom Egypt were engaged in a centuries-long struggle for control of the Levant. In this latest clash, we hear that Pharaoh Rameses II commanded 2,000 chariots and 20,000 infantry, his opponent, the Hittite King Mutawallish, 2,500 chariots and 15,000 infantry. It was probably the biggest chariot battle in history. It certainly represented a massive investment of resources in armaments on the part of these imperial rivals. But it ended in a draw. The Late Bronze Age arms race had become a stalemate.

Bronze Age System Failure

A century later, the picture was radically different. The Eastern Mediterranean in the 13th century had been dominated by great empires – the Hittites, the Egyptians, the Mitanni, the Assyrians, the Babylonians, the Mycenaeans. During the 12th century, these empires struggled to defend their borders against the incursions of 'barbarian' peoples coming by land and sea, apparently from all directions, to raid, plunder and eventually settle.

Our knowledge of who they were is hazy in the extreme. Many of them are referred to by the portmanteau term 'Sea Peoples'. This is rather like the later term 'Viking'. It does not indicate a clearly identified ethnic and linguistic group, but an amalgam of sea-raiders, essentially pirates, but operating on a massive scale. We might, for example, class Homer's Achaeans (the Mycenaean Greeks), whom he describes mounting a massive seaborne operation against the city of Troy, with the Sea Peoples. It seems certain that the Philistines (*Peleset* in the Egyptian sources), who settled in the Levant in the 12th century BCE and gave their name to Palestine, were also among the Sea Peoples, for they are depicted on the famous relief sculptures at Medinet Habu (1185–1152 BCE), which celebrate Pharoah Rameses III's victory over seaborne raiders from the north. Other raiders, however, came overland. This is especially clear in the Egyptian evidence, where we have depictions of both Sea Peoples (shown with distinctive feathered headdress) and Libyans (with thick black hair). What is beyond doubt are the consequences of this century of storm and strife. Major urban centres were destroyed, notably Mycenae in Greece, Troy at the Dardanelles, Hattusa in Asia Minor and Ugarit in the Levant. The Hittite Empire fell apart, its territory overrun by northern barbarians in the west and by the emerging power of Assyria in the east. New Kingdom Egypt collapsed in on itself, its ruling class of courtiers and priests riven by faction, the country entering a long period of decline and eclipse. The Mycenaeans vanished and Greece entered a 'Dark Age' destined to last several centuries.

What had brought about this spectacular collapse of Late Bronze Age civilization? This sort of question is always exceptionally difficult for archaeologists to answer. The material evidence of burnt, ruined and abandoned settlements is unequivocal; even more so when supplemented with the evidence of documents

BELOW: The victory of Rameses III against the Sea Peoples, in a reproduction of an engraving at Medinet Habu.

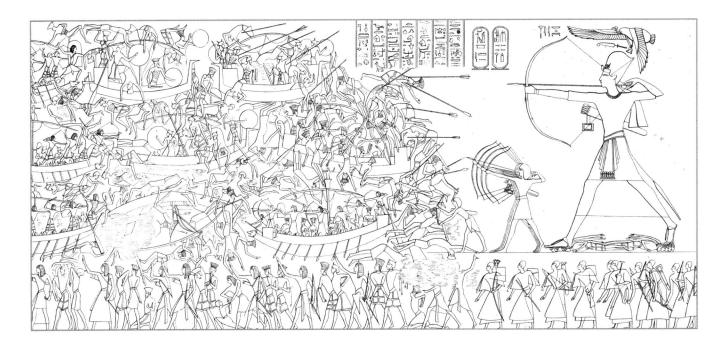

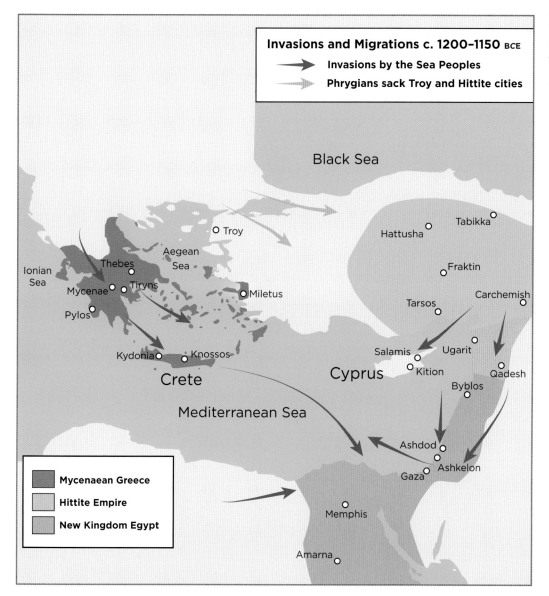

LEFT: The invasions of the Sea Peoples and the migrations that triggered the collapse of the empires of the late Bronze Age, *c.* 1200 BCE.

Black Sea

Troy

Aegean Sea

Ionian Sea

Thebes

Mycenae   Tiryns

Pylos

Miletus

Kydonia   Knossos

Crete

Mediterranean Sea

Tabikka

Hattusha

Fraktin

Carchemish

Tarsos

Salamis   Ugarit

Cyprus   Kition   Qadesh

Byblos

Ashdod

Ashkelon

Gaza

Memphis

Amarna

■ Mycenaean Greece
■ Hittite Empire
■ New Kingdom Egypt

and artworks that attest a period of chaos and violence. But none of this provides direct evidence for causation. Perhaps, though, the wider evidence for Late Bronze Age militarization holds the answer. We know that Bronze Age society was top-heavy: it empowered and enriched a relatively small class of warrior nobles, high priests and their retinues; it enabled them to accumulate resources for investment in grand living, monumental architecture and military competition with their rivals. We bear witness to mounting levels of fortification at Late Bronze Age sites. Mycenae was undefended in the 16th century BCE. It was girt with walls formed of massive blocks

of masonry by the 13th century. This effort rested on a modest base of Bronze Age agriculture, essentially unchanged for hundreds of years, as farmers continued to toil with simple tools of wood, stone and bone. It seems likely that the growing weight of empire – of the politico-military infrastructure – was too much for this base to bear. A diminished, impoverished, sullen peasantry may lurk behind the storm and strife of the 12th century, rotting Late Bronze Age civilization from within, making it vulnerable to the waves of invaders who seem to have overwhelmed it in the space of a few decades. We do not know. We can never be sure. But it seems a reasonable working hypothesis.

The Collapse of Indus Civilization

What of the wider Bronze Age world? We noted above that irrigation-based civilizations developed in both the Indus Valley of Pakistan and the Yellow River of China. What was their fate?

Indus civilization, centred on great cities like Harappa and Mohenjo-daro, seems to have been relatively short-lived. A slow process of decline and abandonment began as early as *c.* 2000 BCE and

nothing comparable was to be seen in the Indian Subcontinent for around a thousand years. But the reasons for this remain one of archaeology's great mysteries.

During one of a series of major excavation campaigns at Mohenjo-daro during the 20th century, the remains of 37 people were uncovered in part of the lower town. Many of the skeletons were fragmentary or contorted, as if cast down and left

without any attempt at formal burial. This has given rise to speculation, supported by references to India's oldest known book, the Sanskrit *Rig-Veda*, that Aryan invaders from the north, whose principal god Indra was 'a destroyer of cities', may have been responsible for the collapse of Indus civilization. As it happens, some scholars think a date of around 1900 BCE is likely for the composition of the *Rig-Veda* (though others put it several centuries later), which would

tie in closely with the archaeological evidence for the crisis of Indus civilization. Many archaeologists are highly dismissive, claiming the Aryan invasion theory to be mythical, essentially on the basis that there is no direct archaeological evidence in the form of weapons, burning, tumbled walls and so on. This argument is very weak. Absence of evidence is not evidence of absence and there are numerous examples of large-scale military upheavals recorded in written sources which nobody would dream of questioning despite a complete lack of archaeological evidence. The conquests of the Huns in the 5th century CE or the Mongols in the 13th century, for example, would be completely unknown to us without the historical records.

The Aryans – horse-nomads from the Central Asian steppes? – may well have played a role in the collapse of civilization in India akin to that of the Sea Peoples in the Mediterranean. The debate cannot be closed down by dogmatic assertions that there is no evidence. But either way, other factors were surely at work. The agricultural basis of the urban revolution may have been undermined by ecological change – changes in the river system, large-scale flooding, salination of the soil, breakdown in irrigation systems. Mohenjo-daro eventually extended across 60ha (148 acres) and may have been home to 40,000 people. Building and supplying an urban settlement on this scale would have required control over very large agricultural surpluses. Given the primitive nature of Bronze Age technology, relatively small shifts in the ecological balance could easily have reduced productivity to the point where cities became unsustainable.

Whatever the explanation, we have another example of Bronze Age system failure and relapse into an essentially pre-urban way of life.

LEFT: The remains of the great city of Mohenjo-daro, which was inhabited from *c.* 2600 BCE to 1900 BCE. The reasons for its fall are unclear – it is possible Aryan invaders are to blame, but equally environmental change could be responsible.

The Shang Dynasty and its Overthrow

At Anyang, in the Yellow River region of northern China, there are remains of an unwalled complex measuring almost 10km (6.2 miles) in length by 4km (2.5 miles) in width. This was probably the capital of the Shang Dynasty (1523–1027 BCE). Excavations have revealed rich royal tombs, great caches of decorated bronzes and tens of thousands of cracked and inscribed 'oracle bones'. So successful was the Shang Dynasty of Late Bronze Age China that the original centre of civilization along the Yellow River of northern China was extended to the Yangtze River of north-central China during the second half of the 2nd millennium BCE. In control of vast agricultural surpluses, the Shang ruling class founded numerous cities, built themselves elaborate tombs and patronized a wide range of luxury crafts. Especially notable are the great variety of huge and elaborately decorated bronze vessels and the evidence for lacquer surfacing of walls and ceilings in high-status buildings.

The gap between rich and poor was huge. One Shang queen went to her grave at Anyang accompanied by 16 sacrificed humans, six sacrificed dogs, more than 440 bronzes, some 590 jades, 560 bone artefacts and 7,000 cowrie shells. Another elite Shang burial contained no less than 165 human victims. They may have been household slaves or war captives. Either way, the grotesque rituals represented bear testimony to a highly stratified society. This may help us to understand the collapse of the Shang Dynasty in the 11th century to Zhou invaders from the north. This did not mean the end of Chinese civilization. It meant a change of masters and even though the Zhou Dynasty (c. 1027–221 BCE) proved to be highly fractious with frequent civil wars, the basic form of Chinese society endured and evolved, though it became more decentralized and feudal in character.

Shang power had rested on control of grain surpluses to sustain military forces. Horses, chariots and bronze were the essentials of contemporary Chinese warfare. The cost – along with that of cities, elite tombs and luxury expenditure – was borne by the Chinese peasantry. This pattern broadly endured for thousands of years, despite periodic changes of dynasty and protracted interludes of chaos and strife. The Zhou would be followed by the Han (206 BCE–220 CE), the Sui (581–618 CE), the Tang (618–907 CE), the Song (960–1126 CE), the Yuan or Mongol (1279–1368), the Ming (1368–1644) and the Manchu (1644–1912). Each dynasty, whatever its origins, quickly adapted to the established forms of the Chinese imperial state. The pattern of Chinese history has therefore been likened to a revolving door.

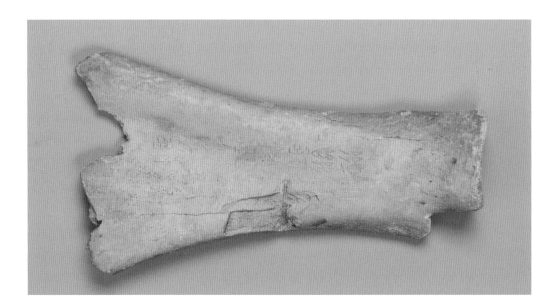

RIGHT: An 'oracle bone' from the Shang Dynasty, with characters inscribed on the cracked bone.

ABOVE: A chariot burial at Anyang. The elites of the Shang Dynasty were buried with an array of goods demonstrating their status and often slaves were sacrificed to accompany them in the afterlife.

The imperial state was a ruthless, powerful and successful exploiter of the Chinese peasanty. It was capable of accumulating massive surpluses, of supporting a huge controlling bureaucracy and of creating powerful armies usually well able to protect the national territory. But bitterness accumulated in the Chinese countryside and would occasionally flare into popular revolt against officials, landowners and merchants. Sometimes these rebellions would be powerful enough to bring down a dynasty, perhaps in combination with civil war and foreign invasion, but the peasants would be satisfied with replacing a 'bad' emperor with a 'good' emperor and the old order would soon re-establish itself after the rebels had dispersed to their villages. We can guess – though we cannot be sure – that peasant resistance, well-known from later Chinese history, may have been a factor in the collapse of Shang power before the Zhou onslaught of the 11th century BCE.

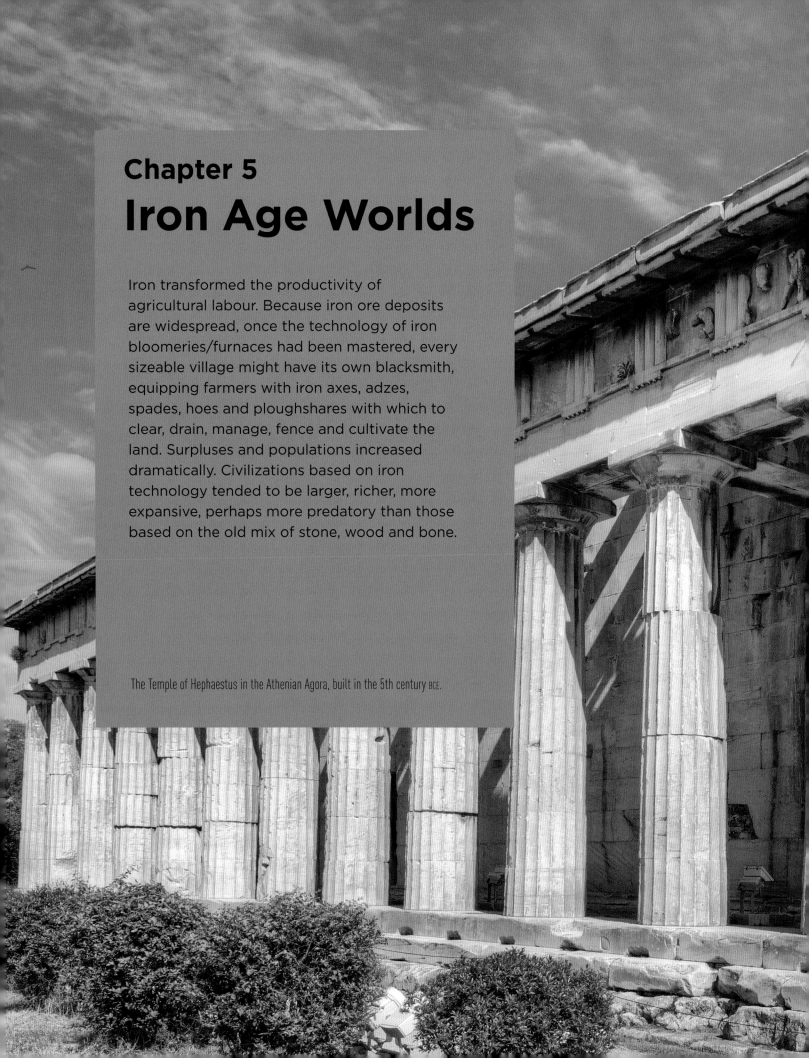

Chapter 5
Iron Age Worlds

Iron transformed the productivity of agricultural labour. Because iron ore deposits are widespread, once the technology of iron bloomeries/furnaces had been mastered, every sizeable village might have its own blacksmith, equipping farmers with iron axes, adzes, spades, hoes and ploughshares with which to clear, drain, manage, fence and cultivate the land. Surpluses and populations increased dramatically. Civilizations based on iron technology tended to be larger, richer, more expansive, perhaps more predatory than those based on the old mix of stone, wood and bone.

The Temple of Hephaestus in the Athenian Agora, built in the 5th century BCE.

The First Industrial Revolution

Can you imagine trying to chop down a forest with a stone axe? This is how it was done pretty well everywhere until around 1200 BCE. Metalworking had been known for thousands of years, but gold, silver, copper, bronze and brass had been used mainly for ornaments and weapons. These metals were too expensive for making farm tools, even if they had been hard enough for heavy-duty work.

ABOVE: A relief from the palace of the Assyrian king Ashurnasipal, *c.* 883–859 BCE.

Iron, on the other hand, was potentially cheap and widely available, for deposits of the ore existed all over the world. But there was a major technological barrier to its adoption. Bronze can be smelted at around 900°C, iron only at around 1100°C or more.

THE FIRST INDUSTRIAL REVOLUTION

The first great industrial revolution – based on iron technology – was dependent on the development of efficient smelting furnaces capable of reaching very high temperatures.

There is growing archaeological evidence for some iron smelting in parts of Africa and Asia long before 1200 BCE, but none for large-scale industrial production until after this date. So the Iron Age began around 1200 BCE and its first mass production coincided with the great crisis of the Late Bronze Age empires. These two developments were connected.

Bronze had been the preserve of elites: iron was in the hands of all. Bronze Age warfare had centred on chariot-borne noble warriors of the kind described in Homer's *Iliad*. But the local blacksmith could put an iron-tipped spear in the hands of every able-bodied

LEFT: Four iron spearheads, *c.* 550 BCE. The availability of iron changed the nature of warfare.

man. If he did this, the villagers could form a phalanx – a bloc of spearmen – and challenge the power of the local lord. Iron not only transformed agricultural output: it also democratized warfare and eventually helped to overturn the entire Bronze Age social order.

It was in this way that iron cut its own path to global supremacy. The old civilizations – dominated by conservative elites who wasted resources on monuments and luxuries and who were resistant to change – had often blocked the adoption of new technology for fear it would destabilize the status quo (though the Hittite Empire seems to have been a partial exception). When the Late Bronze Age civilizations collapsed, their place was filled (for a while at least) by a mosaic of smaller polities. Ironworking flourished in this new, more open, less top-down world. The new technology created a new economy, new social relationships, new political forms.

African Ironworking

With some evidence from West and Central Africa of ironworking as early as 2000 BCE, there is debate about whether the technology was imported from the north or developed locally. Archaeologists are often involved in this kind of debate – between 'diffusion' (new ideas spreading out from one or two original centres) and 'independent innovation' (where societies at similar levels of development come up with similar ideas independently). What is certain, however, is that Africa has produced evidence for an extraordinary range of furnace types and iron artefacts.

An iron-smelting bloomery typically comprised a clay chimney into which were packed layers of charcoal and broken-up ore. The open top of the chimney permitted the release of gas and top-ups of raw material and fuel. At the base of the chimney were two openings, one (known as a tuyere) to allow air to be pumped in by bellows, the other to permit slag run-off. Over a period of many hours, with regular use of the bellows to maintain an internal temperature in excess of 1100°C, a 'bloom' of iron and slag would form at the base of the furnace. This could be removed once the furnace had been allowed to cool. The smelting process was followed by a smithing process – essentially a combination of heat and hammering to beat slag out of the bloom. The resulting lump of iron could then be 'wrought' into a wide array

BELOW: A drawing depicting the use of bellows to pump air into an iron-smelting bloomery. The air helped to maintain the temperature inside and the iron and slag collected at the bottom.

1 Carthage
2 Naukratis
3 Mogador
4 Akjoujt
5 Walalde
6 Do mini
7 Afunfun
8 Dekpassanware
9 Fitola
10 Taruga
11 Opi & Lejja
12 Daima
13 Fundong
14 Batalimo
15 Napata
16 Meroe
17 Dimam
18 Kwale
19 Kabacusi 1
20 Rwiyange 1
21 KM2&3
22 Kapwirimbwe
23 Kalundu
24 Benfica
25 Imbonga
26 Divuyu & Ngoma
27 Great Zimbabwe
28 Matola
29 KwaGandaganda
30 Rooiberg
31 Wadi Dara
32 Badari
33 Nagada
34 Jenne Jeno
35 Buhen
36 Mahilaka

RIGHT: A map showing some of the most important metalworking sites in Africa. Ironworking spread widely across the continent and evidence for it can be found in every region.

of artefacts in a secondary smithing process. In practice, the smelting and smithing processes might be combined in a single workshop or they might be performed by separate specialists at different locations. Archaeologists look for the tell-tale traces of both smelting and smithing at sites they are working on.

The earliest reliably dated bloomeries in sub-Saharan Africa date from around 450 BCE. The technology remained in use into the 20th century across much of the continent. Furnaces range from little more than tiny slag-pits scooped out of the ground, to metre-wide shafts with multiple bellows and 5m (16ft) tall chimneys employing natural draft. This range is testimony to the ingenuity of African ironworkers in adapting the technology to regional variables – the availability of wood for making charcoal, the quality of local ores and the skill and experience of local specialists.

Bantu Expansion

Eurasia is a gigantic east–west thoroughfare extending across almost 10,000km (6,200 miles) from the Atlantic to the Pacific. Africa, by contrast, runs north–south for 6,500km (4,000 miles). As it does so, it passes across great barriers and through several climatic zones: from north to south, coastal plain, desert, savannah, tropical forest, savannah, desert and coastal plain again. Both desert and forest are barriers to movement – of animals, people, technologies, ideas.

This is one reason that Africa leaps from Stone Age to Iron Age, without any intervening Bronze Age. Earlier metallurgies lacked the leverage to achieve an agricultural revolution and create imperial civilizations in the face of Africa's formidable ecological barriers. It was the rapid spread of ironworking during the 1st millennium BCE that equipped Bantu-speaking Africans (originally from West-Central Africa) with the weapons and tools they needed to expand southwards, through and beyond the tropical forests of Central Africa, at the expense of local communities of hunter-gatherers. Between 500 BCE and 500 CE, farming, metalworking and Bantu culture advanced in tandem through the southern part of the continent.

Great Zimbabwe is a monument to this process. Founded in the 11th century CE, abandoned in the 15th century CE, it was the capital of a Bantu-speaking African empire, a great stone-built city spanning almost 8km² (3 square miles) and housing up to 20,000 people. The Great Enclosure at its heart – presumably the royal residence – was with the largest building in sub-Saharan Africa at the time, comprising a wall 250m (820ft) long, 5m (16ft) thick and 10m (33ft) high. The wealth of the rulers of Great Zimbabwe was based on cattle and trade in gold, iron, copper and tin.

LEFT: An aerial view of the Great Enclosure and Valley complex of Great Zimbabwe, which is believed to have been the capital of a kingdom at some point in the country's Late Iron Age.

Sacred Metal

Iron was the basis of power in several Nigerian kingdoms in the second half of the first millennium BCE. Ogun was the local god of iron. Credited with having introduced the metal, he was a hunter, a warrior, a clearer of forests, a builder of roads and a founder of royal dynasties. The iron sword of Ogun was symbolic of both his civilizing mission – hacking farmland from the wilderness – and his imperial mission – creating new warrior-based polities.

Furnaces, forges and iron objects often carried a potent sacred charge. The anvil might function as an altar for swearing oaths or making sacrifices. Ironworkers were both revered and feared, for their specialist knowledge and skill was believed to bring them into close proximity with divine powers. They were often itinerants, moving from place to place, a way of life that enhanced the sense that they were somehow outsiders. Even so, their assumed knowledge of the divine and the sacred meant that tribal leaders would seek their counsel when major decisions were to be made.

All iron objects, even everyday artefacts, carried something of the magical charge. But in addition to tools and weapons, African blacksmiths also created regalia, protective amulets, sacred staffs and other iron objects with special ritual significance. *Bamana* staffs, for example, known as 'iron women', were long ceremonial spears carried by people of high rank and displayed at shrines and altars. *Bamana* staffs – combining a phallic form with female representation – echoed another prevalent idea: that anvils were female and the blacksmith was 'the husband of the forge'. Thus were iron and ironworking – a revolutionary technology that was the very basis of agricultural productivity and political power – suffused with fertility symbolism.

RIGHT: An ivory statuette in the Phoenician style from the 8th century BCE, found in the Assyrian palace of Nimrud. The Iron Age saw the rise of several new powerful states in the Levant.

New Civilizations

I have suggested that the Late Bronze civilizations of the Mediterranean and the Middle East collapsed in large part under their own weight: the military infrastructures of rival states competing for territory and engaging in an arms race became too much to bear for the agricultural system on which they were based. These weakened empires were then vulnerable to both popular revolt and external aggression. The Late Bronze Age world imploded in storm and strife during the 12th century BCE.

This was the very time when iron was first introduced to the Mediterranean. The Hittite Empire had been working iron from *c.* 1500 BCE. It is uncertain whether they developed the technology themselves or learned it from others, but there is no doubt they were using iron weapons in war during the Late Bronze Age. The technology then became

widespread amid the chaos of the 12th century – perhaps because rival states felt compelled to gain every advantage they could in a desperate military situation.

War was probably the mother of innovation. But once iron-working technology became widespread, it was adopted by farmers and became the basis of huge increases in agricultural output. The modest surpluses available to Bronze Age rulers were dwarfed by the massive surpluses available to Iron Age rulers. Empire and civilization acquired a much stronger economic platform during the 1st millennium BCE.

In this chapter, we range across the Iron Age world to explore the diversity of human cultural achievement in this period.

BELOW: An illustration of the southwestern entrance to the palace at Nimrud, contemporary with Layard's expeditions to the site.

Mesopotamia: the Assyrian Empire

The crisis of the Late Bronze Age caused major states to collapse or shrink and a plethora of minor states to emerge in their wake. The Phoenicians established a string of mercantile cities along the Levantine coast and founded a network of trading outposts across the Mediterranean. The Israelites established a new kingdom in Palestine with its capital at Jerusalem. The Armenians also created their own kingdom, in the mountains around Lake Van, known as the Kingdom of Urartu. But these minor states of the early 1st millennium BCE would eventually be absorbed by new imperial systems.

During the 9th century BCE, a new empire emerged in the Upper Tigris Valley, one that inherited the rich agricultural traditions of Ancient Mesopotamia, now hyper-charged by Iron Age technology. This was the empire of the Assyrians.

Around 880 BCE, the Assyrian capital was transferred from Ashur to Nimrud, where it would remain for most of the next two centuries (before transferring again to Khorsabad and finally to Nineveh). Nimrud comprises a vast enclosure beside the Tigris, some 360ha in extent, with massive mud-brick defences. Relatively little of this vast site has been excavated, even though explorations were begun as early as 1845, when the famous antiquarian scholar Austen Henry Layard first drew attention to Nimrud's phenomenal richness and interest. Further large-scale excavations were then undertaken by the British School of Archaeology in Iraq in the 1950s. These were led by Max Mallowan, the husband of crime novelist Agatha Christie, who invariably joined the excavation seasons, where she worked on finds (restoring ancient ivories with face cream!), managed the catering, maintained standards (napkin holders were included in the camp equipment!) and otherwise spent her time writing in the dig house; a number of Christie's mysteries are, of course, set on archaeological sites.

Excavators have focused their attention on the ancient citadel; the rest of the city, where an estimated 80,000 people once lived, has yet to be investigated. The 20ha (50 acre) citadel is dominated by a 60m (197ft)-high ziggurat in the south-west corner and it was here that the Assyrian kings built a succession of temples, palaces and administrative buildings. In the south-east corner lies a second complex, Fort Shalmaneser, with ranges of buildings around open courtyards, including a stepped throne, a raised dais, reception rooms, residential quarters, a royal treasury, barracks, magazines and workshops.

Here and at other Assyrian sites, the reception halls and throne rooms of the royal palaces were decorated with relief sculptures depicting the Assyrian kings in all their majesty. We see them hunting, leading military expeditions, supervising

RIGHT: A relief from the Kingdom of Urartu in Armenia. Urartu lasted from the 9th to the 6th centuries BCE.

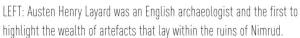

LEFT: Austen Henry Layard was an English archaeologist and the first to highlight the wealth of artefacts that lay within the ruins of Nimrud.

building works, receiving subjects bearing tribute and meeting with senior courtiers and foreign ambassadors. Of special value are the closely observed and finely executed depictions of the Assyrian army – on the march, in pitched battle and during siege operations. These include unashamed representations of atrocities, with prisoners shown beheaded, impaled and flayed alive *en masse*. The Assyrian sculptures provide the most comprehensive set of contemporary artworks we have for any ancient army: an invaluable resource. Meantime, monumental gateways and entrances were guarded by huge, winged, human-headed lions. The Assyrian kings were predatory military imperialists. These images were designed to inspire fear and compliance among both Assyrian subjects and foreign emissaries.

Such, indeed, was the military power of the Assyrian kings that they built an empire that eventually encompassed the whole of Mesopotamia and Syria, much of the Levantine coast, the island of Cyprus and the Taurus Mountains of south-eastern Anatolia. This gave them control over immense resources: the grain-fields of Syria, the trading wealth of the Phoenician cities, the metals – iron, copper and lead – of Cyprus and the Taurus and much more.

BELOW: A relief of an Assyrian battle from *c.* 730 BCE, found at the palace of Nimrud. Reliefs such as these are our main source of information on the Assyrian military.

OPPOSITE: Max Mallowan (bottom left, facing away from the camera) supervises the excavations at Nimrud. Mallowan took a more scientific approach, using stratigraphic excavation methods and systematically surveying the terrain to build up a portrait of the ancient city.

Persia: the Achaemenid Empire

In the 5th century BCE, had you wanted to see a great imperial centre, you would not have travelled to Nimrud, Khorsabad or Nineveh. The Assyrian cities lay in ruins following an uprising of the empire's subject-peoples – Babylonians, Chaldeans, Medes, Persians, Scythians, Cimmerians – in the late 7th century. Two of these peoples, the Medes and the Persians, were united by conquest in 550 BCE. The Medes were nomadic horsemen of the steppe-lands of the Caspian region. The Persians were settled farmers of the rugged mountain valleys of Iran. Within two generations, Mesopotamia, Egypt, Anatolia, the Indus Valley and a large part of Central Asia had been overrun in campaigns of conquest by three great Achaemenid kings: Cyrus, Cambyses and Darius.

Nothing on this scale had ever been seen before. By the end of the 6th century BCE, the Persian 'Great King' or 'King of Kings' controlled three of the four original centres of civilization – the Nile, Tigris/ Euphrates and Indus river valleys – and everything in between. Eventually, the Persian Empire would extend from Thrace (Bulgaria) in the west to the Indus (Pakistan) in the east and from the Caucasus Mountains in the north to the Nubian Desert of Sudan in the south.

The empire was bound together by a network of roads and an official postal system. The Royal Road, for example, extended from Sardis in western Turkey to Susa in western Iran. It was ruled by provincial viceroys (known as 'satraps'), but there was no attempt to create a uniform culture; each of the distinct subject-peoples of the Great King retained their own ethnic and religious identity, their own economic and social organization, their own political structures. What mattered was that they obeyed the law and paid their taxes. The wealth accumulated by the Persian

RIGHT: An overview of the ruins of the ancient city of Persepolis, the capital of the Achaemenid Empire.

royal elite was stupendous. When Alexander the Great captured the royal capital at Persepolis in 331 BCE, it contained treasure equal in value to the annual income of Athens, the richest of the Greek city-states, for 300 years.

The royal palace at Persepolis stood on a terrace measuring 500m (1,640ft) by 300m (984ft). It comprised a complex of cavernous audience-chambers, the ceilings supported on high columns, with associated residential quarters, storerooms and barracks, the whole surrounded by a massive defensive wall. A sprawling town lay beyond the palace and, a few miles away, a cemetery with the rock-cut tombs of the Achaemenid rulers. Persepolis, moreover, was only one of several royal residences: there are known to have been others at Susa, Babylon, Hamadan, Pasargadae and we may suspect more at sites as yet undiscovered. In addition, of course, each satrap maintained a palace at his provincial capital, where he lorded it as a semi-independent local ruler, such were the distances across the Persian Empire and the time taken for news and orders to travel to and fro.

The ceremonial stairways leading to the Apadana, the principal audience-chamber of Darius I at Persepolis, was decorated with relief-sculptures depicting 23 different subject-peoples bearing tribute to the Great King, including textiles and clothing, metal vessels, gold, elephant tusks, horses and camels and such exotic animals as antelope, lions and okapi (for, we might guess, the royal hunting-park). Inscriptions at Persepolis list the principal peoples of the empire, while thousands of burnt-clay tablets record disbursements of food or silver to royalty, officials and workmen. Thus does archaeology reveal critical evidence for reconstructing the internal workings of the greatest empire the world had ever seen.

LEFT: The stairs leading to the Apadana at Persepolis. The Apadana was where the Great King received official visitors. It measured 60m (197ft) on each side and contained 72 columns.

India: Warlords and Hindus

Archaeologists sometimes name entire periods after a dominant class of artefact. A very broad-brush version of this is the traditional tripartite division into Stone Age, Bronze Age and Iron Age. But there are many examples of far more refined chronologies based on 'culture-history'.

Let us recall the controversial idea that the Indus Valley civilization was terminated by Aryan invaders from the north early in the 2nd millennium BCE. Some scholars who base themselves on ancient writings prefer to describe India's Late Bronze Age and Early Iron Age as the 'Vedic period' – by which they mean the period when Aryan invaders from the steppes of Central Asia, having crossed the mountain passes of the Hindu Kush, first spread out across the Indus Valley (of Pakistan), then the Northern Plain (of India) and the Ganges Valley (of Bangladesh) and finally the Deccan (of southern India). During this centuries-long process, a new language (Sanskrit), a new religion (Hinduism) and a new social structure (the caste system) became dominant. Note that some scholars date the earliest known Aryan-Hindu text, the *Rig-Veda*, as early as 1900 BCE (though it seems more likely that, rather like Homer's *Iliad* and *Odyssey*, it originally took the form of oral epic and was first written down only many centuries later).

We might speculate, then, that Iron Age India was ruled by a class of Aryan-Hindu lords who

introduced horses, chariots and later iron-working and that over time they imposed a caste system backed by religious authority. They defined themselves as warriors (*kshatriyas*), priests (*brahmins*) or landowners (*vaishyas*) and they recognized a class of peasants as forming a fourth caste (*shudras*). The bulk of the indigenous population were eventually integrated into the social order as members of various sub-castes, except for those wholly excluded from the tribal system, who were classed as 'outcasts' or 'untouchables'. This rigid hierarchy was mirrored in the Hindu religion, which is notable for its conservatism, elaborate ritual and fearsome power-deities. The social order was assumed to be natural and divinely approved. Those who conformed would be reincarnated in a higher caste; those who did not could expect relegation in the next life.

Iron technology filled the Ganges Valley with highly productive farms based on irrigation and rice cultivation. Large agricultural surpluses made it possible to construct new princely states and urban centres. By 600 BCE, around 16 small states had come into existence in the Ganges Valley. When Chandragupta Maurya usurped the throne of Magadha in 321 BCE, he turned it into a base for a campaign of conquest that over the next two decades made him the master of the Ganges Valley, the Northern Plain and the Indus Valley. His successors, notably the great Ashoka in the mid 3rd century BCE, then extended the empire even further, across the Deccan of southern India.

This huge imperial edifice was not built to last. Much like Alexander the Great's near-contemporary empire in the west, the Mauryan Empire was pulled apart by internal conflict within two generations of Ashoka's death. One of the fatal fracture lines seems to have been a religious conflict between Hindu and Buddhist.

LEFT: A silver coin from the reign of Ashoka.

India: Merchants and Buddhists

The Mauryan capital at Pataliputra near Patna is reported to have extended some 14km along the banks of the Ganges. It contained palaces with columned halls in the Persian style and was defended by an earth rampart laced with timber. Many other cities were founded in northern India before, during and after the Mauryan period. The fall of the unified empire does not seem to have impeded this second urban revolution; indeed, a dramatic expansion in trade in the final centuries of the 1st millennium BCE brought the process of urbanization to a new peak. Major trade routes ran (continued on p. 112)

BELOW: A column top from the Mauryan capital of Pataliputra.

ABOVE: The excavation of the ruins of Pataliputra in 1912.

Culture-History

Culture-history is a key archaeological concept. Where historical sources are non-existent, limited or questionable, archaeologists seek to divide up the past, both chronologically and geographically, by identifying, dating and mapping characteristic types of settlement and associated assemblages of artefacts. We have met with some notable examples already, like the *Linearbandkeramik* (Linear Banded Pottery) culture of Early Neolithic Europe, with its villages of huge longhouses and its distinctive way of decorating home-made pottery vessels.

The prehistoric Iron Age of the Indian Subcontinent is studied through the lens of culture-history. Two main cultures are recognized, the Painted Grey Ware culture (*c.* 1300–300 BCE) and the Northern Black Polished Ware culture (*c.* 700–200 BCE).

More than a thousand PGW sites have been discovered, though the great majority are modest Iron Age farming villages; only a few dozen sites are large enough to be considered small towns and only a handful

LEFT: Fragments of Northern Black Polished Ware pottery from *c.* 500 BCE.

of the largest merited simple defences of ditch, rampart and wooden palisade. In other words, despite the example of the Indus Valley civilization of 2600–1900 BCE, this was not an urban society, but one more akin to contemporary Celtic Europe (see below). This is one reason that archaeologists use classes of pottery to define sites of this period: there are no great cities or spectacular monuments to provide alternative markers.

The pottery – in a fine grey fabric with linear geometric decoration applied in black paint – is associated with other evidence to form a cultural 'package'. Of particular importance was the use of the domestic horse and the working of iron to make weapons and tools. This characteristic assemblage informs our speculations about the origins of PGW culture.

BELOW: An example of Painted Grey Ware culture pottery.

overland to the Hindu Kush and Central Asia, down the Ganges to the Bay of Bengal and beyond and, in the case of the Deccan, across the Indian Ocean to Africa and Arabia following the discovery of the monsoon wind system.

Symbolic of the connectedness of the new Indian cities is the remarkable archaeological site of Arikamedu on the east coast of the Deccan. Located and excavated in the late 1940s, it was identified as the emporium of a place called 'Podouke' in ancient Roman writings. Excavations produced great hauls of Roman amphorae, fine-ware pottery, ceramic lamps, glassware, precious stones, glass and stone beads, and coins. Pottery and coins permit close dating and the excavators concluded that the site was occupied from the late 1st century BCE to the early 3rd century CE. It was probably founded by Greek merchants (the Greek-speaking world having by this time been absorbed into the Roman Empire). A remarkable testimony to ancient globalization, Arikamedu reflects the vitality of Indian maritime trade in this period.

Commerce and cities promoted the spread of a new religion: Buddhism. The Buddha ('Enlightened One') was a Hindu warrior-prince called Siddhartha Gautama (*c.* 563–483 BCE) who had broken with his caste, undergone a profound religious experience and spent the rest of his life preaching a new philosophy. The essence of his teaching was that true happiness arises when one accepts the natural and social orders, recognizes that everything is in a state of flux and achieves a spiritual peace of mind above the froth of everyday life.

Buddhism's radicalism lay in its universalism and its marginalization of property, rank and status. It enjoined a way of life that was purposeful, ethical and open to all. It appealed especially to merchants, artisans and townspeople – the makers and shakers of the new India – because, in sharp contrast to Hinduism, which legitimized the socially rigid caste system, it implied that everyone should be free to carve out their own place in the world. The famous Silk Road – the great Eurasian trade route that linked China with the Middle East – was, unsurprisingly, given its unending flow of merchant caravans, one of the primary mechanisms

for the spread of Buddhism. But the maritime trade routes were equally important, carrying the message to Ceylon, Malaysia and Indonesia.

The Mauryan emperor Ashoka had promoted a form of Buddhism – a social ideal known as *Dhamma* that stressed toleration, harmony and live-and-let-live. Buddhist principles were inscribed on stone pillars and smooth rock surfaces during his reign and the

ABOVE: The city of Arikamedu in southern India is a testament to the extent of globalization in the ancient world. Excavations have uncovered large quantities of Roman artefacts and established that it was likely established as a Greek trading colony.

distribution of these provide an indication of the extent of his territory in the mid 3rd century BCE.

Around this time, the earliest of the great Buddhist monuments appear in the archaeological record: temples, reliquaries and monasteries. These early monuments survive only as buried remains and most are inaccessible to archaeologists for they are overlain by the more stupendous monuments of later periods.

The golden age of Buddhist art and architecture was during the first half of the 1st millennium CE, when the *stupa* (a domed mound covering holy relics) and the *pagoda* (a multiple-roofed tower adorning

BELOW: The Ashoka pillar at Vaishali, built *c.* 250 BCE. Many such pillars were built during his reign and 20 survive to the present day.

temples and monasteries) became characteristic features of major religious complexes. Sanchi in central India was founded by Ashoka in the mid 3rd century BCE, but it continued to develop until the 12th century CE, becoming one of India's greatest Buddhist sites. The Great Stupa (with a diameter of 37m/121ft and a height of 16m/52ft) is adorned with a Pillar of Ashoka. Two smaller *stupas* were added later, along with monasteries, temples and lesser shrines, and the whole complex was surrounded with a monumental enclosure wall.

ABOVE: The *stupa* at Sanchi is one of the oldest in India. It was established by Ashoka in the mid-3rd century BCE and quickly became one of India's most important Buddhist sites.

Ajanta in central India comprises a ring of rock-cut temples and monasteries ranged around a horseshoe-shaped cliff. The site dates from the late 2nd or early 1st century BCE, but it reached its peak in the later 5th century CE, when most of the caves were cut, with no less than 21 separate monastic units, each with colonnaded halls and verandahs, some on two levels, all richly decorated with relief sculptures and wall paintings depicting the life of Buddha – the model to be followed by the faithful.

Long before, the Mauryan Empire had collapsed. There were tensions between Hindu and Buddhist fractions of the ruling class, subjugated states were in revolt and external enemies seized fragments of territory on the borders. The Mauryan state had remained a hastily assembled amalgam of smaller polities onto which a top-heavy military superstructure had been imposed. The essential glue of a broad-based ruling class united by common culture, good communications and effective mechanisms for social integration and political cohesion was lacking.

Perhaps it was just as well. The Mauryan military elite would have drained resources from civil society and wasted them on war. The collapse of the centralized imperial state allowed farmers, traders and urban communities to flourish. It was this relative freedom, surely, that underpinned the golden age of Buddhism.

RIGHT: The *stupa* in the Ajanta cave 26, built during the 5th century CE.

China: the First Emperor

Yang Zhifa was digging a village well when, on 23 March 1974, he uncovered a circle of clay that looked like the top of a pot. In fact, it was the neck of a life-size model of a soldier who had somehow lost his head. Digging down, Yang discovered that he was standing on the brick floor of an underground chamber. Clearly, he had stumbled upon something of great significance – perhaps something to do with the local legend that nearby Mount Li was the burial place of Qin Shihuangdi, the First Emperor of China, who had died in 210 BCE.

So it proved. Decades on, we now know that Pit 1, first revealed by Yang Zhifa, contains more than 6,000 terracotta soldiers – archers, crossbowmen, spearmen, cavalrymen, charioteers – wearing padded jerkins and scale armour. They occupy a floor space of more than 25,000m² (270,000ft²), paved with some 250,000 clay bricks and this vast chamber was originally roofed with huge pine and cypress trunks. The soldiers were fired to a very high temperature (*c.* 800°C/1472°F), giving them a grey surface colour, but the figures were subsequently painted. Though the bodies were standardized, each face was different, in both form and expression and the 25 styles of beard and moustache may imply that all the various racial-ethnic groups forming the Chinese Empire were somehow represented.

But this was not all. In 1976, archaeologists discovered two further pits immediately north of Pit 1. Another 1300 terracotta men and horses and 80 wooden chariots were deployed in Pit 2 and 68 warriors, four horses and a chariot in Pit 3; one suggestion is that the latter represented a group of commanders, staff and personal guardsmen.

Are there more pits yet to be found? Quite possibly; so much so, in fact, that estimates of the total number of model warriors forming the Terracotta Army range from 10,000 to a million! This is based on the fact that the three pits are dwarfed by Mount Li, the fabled final resting-place of the First Emperor. This was an ancient sacred site dedicated to the goddess Nüwa. The story goes that the Emperor was obliged to perform a long penance after being afflicted by the goddess with a malignant growth for the outrage of importuning her for sexual favours. He earned a reprieve and managed to cleanse himself by bathing in the hot springs that sprang from the sides of the mountain. And here his mortal

RIGHT: A 19th-century depiction of the Emperor Qin Shihuangdi, the first ruler to unite the whole of China under a centralized state.

LEFT: A mural of the goddess Nüwa, the deity responsible for the creation of humankind in Chinese mythology.

Let us put Emperor Qin Shihuangdi (221–210 BCE) into context. He is known as the First Emperor because he conquered the whole of China and created a unified state. The Zhou Dynasty (1027–221 BCE) which had replaced the Shang (1523–1027 BCE) had never established a stable centralized state. Civilization had advanced, with the expansion of rice cultivation, the digging of a network of canals for long-distance communications and a multiplication of walled administrative cities. But regional warlords were powerful, civil wars were frequent and in the 4th and 3rd centuries BCE, during 'the Age of Warring States', China fell apart completely. In this bloody climax of Zhou chaos, it was the King of Qin, on the wild frontier of China, who emerged supreme.

Armies of Qin chariots, crossbowmen and horse-archers defeated their Zhou rivals one by one. The human cost was colossal. After one victory, it is reported, 100,000 prisoners were beheaded. After the final victory, 120,000 of the 'rich and powerful', the old Zhou ruling class, were deported. And henceforward the King of Qin ruled as the Emperor of China, master of a territory five times larger than that of his Shang predecessors.

remains are reputed to lie, beneath the great mass of the mountain, at the centre of a vast sculpted representation of his empire, stretching from the northern wilderness beyond the Great Wall down to the forests of the south coast, with the Chinese rivers represented in mercury running down to the ocean and the ceiling above encrusted with jewels in the pattern of the constellations. Here, too, it is reputed, lie hundreds of human sacrifices – the unfortunate tomb-builders and the Emperor's harem of concubines.

FOLLOWING PAGES: The massed ranks of soldiers of the Terracotta Army in the mausoleum of China's first Emperor, Qin Shihuangdi.

Here was the culmination of the Chinese Iron Age. Vast agricultural surpluses supported a centralized military-bureaucratic elite of unprecedented power. The road system became longer than that of the Roman Empire. The canal system was without parallel. Weights and measures, road and wagon gauges, even the forms of agricultural tools were standardized. Above all, there was the Great Wall of China, the greatest construction project in human history, built by the First Emperor as a barrier against the Xiongnu, the horse-nomads of the steppes, the ancestors of the Huns and the Mongols. Some 3,600km (2,200 miles) long, the Wall was more than 7m (23ft) high and wide enough for eight men to march abreast along the top. At varying intervals along its length were 25,000 projecting towers. It took 12 years to build and involved the conscription of hundreds of thousands of forced labourers and the appropriation of the grain surpluses of millions of peasants.

Little wonder that the mausoleum of Qin Shihuangdi dwarfs in its monumental ambition even the Great Pyramid of Cheops at Giza. Here was Iron Age civilization unmatched in grandeur, brutality and waste; a civilization hard-wired for enduring conservative resilience despite the churn of dynasties to come. What an extraordinary contrast it presents to the radically different Iron Age civilization of Classical Greece – to which we now turn.

LEFT: The Great Wall of China was begun by the First Emperor and expanded on and restored by subsequent dynasties. This section, Mutianyu, was built in the 6th century by the Northern Qi dynasty and then rebuilt during in the 15th century by the Ming Emperors.

Classical Greece

Tucked away in the delightful little Agora Museum in Athens are some of the most extraordinary artefacts ever found on an archaeological excavation. They are so easy to miss, but nothing like them is to be seen anywhere else in the world and they are packed with historic significance. They are the earliest known material remains of a working democracy.

Fifth-century BCE Athens was a participatory democracy. For sure, it was restricted to adult male citizens. Women, slaves and foreigners did not have political rights. Ancient Athens was no paradise: it was a patriarchal, militaristic, slave-owning society. But, unlike just about everywhere else in the world at the time, it was not run by a dictator or warlord or cabal of oligarchs, but by the adult male citizen-body as a whole (the Greek word for which was *demos*). This was around 30,000 people, the great majority of them ordinary working farmers. They were all entitled to attend the *Ekklesia*, an open-air general assembly where all major decisions were taken, with full speaking and voting rights. Any of them might be selected for jury service in the law courts, which were themselves general assemblies, with anything between 201 and 2,001 jurors sitting in judgement, depending on the seriousness of the case. Any of them might be elected to the *Boule*, the 500-strong council that oversaw the day-to-day running of the city-state between meetings of the *Ekklesia* or to one of the supreme high offices of state, becoming one of the ten annually elected *Strategoi*.

Back to those special artefacts in the Agora Museum. The Agora, where they were found, was the ancient market-place, which then became the main centre of public life, with council chambers, law courts and open spaces for large meetings. Here was found part of a stone allotting device. This was used to select men on the jury roster to hear a particular case. The idea was to prevent plaintiffs or defendants identifying jurors in advance and trying to bribe or intimidate them. Each juryman was issued with a bronze ticket inscribed with his name (*pinakion*) and on the day of a trial these were placed in the slots on the allotting device. A rather elaborate contraption (described in ancient sources but for which no archaeological evidence has been recovered) involving black and white marbles, a funnel and a crank was then used to determine which rows of tickets (and therefore jurymen) had been selected for service.

Also unearthed were a number of circular bronze ballots. Each jurymen was issued with two, that with a solid axle for innocent, that with a hollow axle for guilty. These were placed in a stone ballot box at the end of a trial – and this, too, was found, still *in situ*, inside the law court in the north-east corner of the Agora! And because long-winded lawyers could be very tiresome, speeches were limited to approximately six minutes, using ceramic water-clocks – fragments

BELOW: A bronze *pinakion* from the 4th century BCE, inscribed with the name of the juror, found at the Agora of Athens.

ABOVE: These bronze discs from *c.* 300 BCE were used to cast jurors' votes in Athenian legal cases.

of which can also be seen in the museum. There is even grim evidence of the fate of those judged guilty on capital charges: a number of small, black, ceramic medicine bottles were found in the state prison on the south-west edge of the Agora and we can guess they once contained hemlock, for this was the relatively humane, self-administered form of execution favoured in democratic Athens. This, of course, was how poor Socrates, the founder of the Western philosophic tradition, met his end following condemnation for dishonouring the gods and misleading the youth.

Mention must also be made of the many *ostraka* on display in the museum. These are potsherds crudely inscribed with the names of leading politicians. An ostracism was a sort of reverse election, where citizens voted to send an unpopular figure into exile for ten years; it was designed to reduce ongoing factional strife in the political life of the city-state. If anyone received more than 6,000 votes against him, he had ten days to pack his bags! The haul of *ostraka* from the Agora excavations includes virtually all the famous names of Athenian politics during the 5th century –

Aristeides, Cimon, Miltiades, Themistocles, Pericles and many others.

Towering over the Athenian Agora is the Acropolis. This was once the city's fortified citadel, but in the Classical Age it was exclusively a religious sanctuary, dedicated mainly to Athena, the patron goddess of the city-state. Persian invaders had destroyed the sanctuary in 480 BCE, but Athens had ejected the invaders and gone on to build a maritime empire spanning the Aegean Sea. Part of the tribute from her empire, combined with the wealth of silver mines in southern Attica, was used to rebuild the sanctuary. The ruins seen by the visitor today – the Parthenon, a huge new temple to Athena, the Erechtheion, a reconstruction of the original temple and the Propylaia, the monumental entrance to the sanctuary – can be interpreted as symbols of the wealth and power of imperial Athens during the 5th century.

ABOVE: Several *ostraka* against Themistocles from 482 BCE. Themistocles was one of the leading Athenian politicians during the wars with Persia and was ostracized *c.* 472 BCE.

RIGHT: The theatre of Dionysus had a capacity of approximately 17,000 at its height and remained in use until the 6th century CE.

On the opposite side of the Acropolis from the Agora lie the tumbled remains of another monument rich in symbolic significance: the Theatre of Dionysus. Here, 2,500 years ago, the dramas of Aeschylus, Sophocles and Euripides were first performed. Attic tragedy is one of the greatest cultural achievements of the Athens' golden age. It owes its enduring power to the freedom of expression and buzzing spirit of enquiry under Athens' democratic constitution – so different from the dreary propaganda of autocratic regimes then and since.

The archaeology of 5th century BCE Athens bears testimony to a cultural explosion rarely matched in human history: here we see the full creative potential of Iron Age humanity unleashed.

FOLLOWING PAGES: The Acropolis of Athens houses a number of monumental temples demonstrating the strength of the Athenian state.

The Macedonian Empire and the Hellenistic World

In 1961, the King of Afghanistan was out hunting in the north of his country, close to the Soviet border, when he came upon a Corinthian capital and a small stone pillar. He was 2,500 miles as the crow flies from Greece, far beyond the Himalayas, in the very heart of Central Asia. Yet, as a French archaeological team soon confirmed, the King had stumbled upon a lost Greek city. We know it today as Ai-Khanoum, which is the name of the nearest village, meaning 'Lady-Moon' in Uzbek.

Located on the banks of the River Oxus, where it guards the approach to Bactria from the north, it was founded in the late 4th or early 3rd century BCE, perhaps by Alexander the Great himself. Though there are strong eastern influences – a temple in the Mesopotamian style, for example – we should not be surprised at this, for Alexander and his Hellenistic successors adopted a deliberate policy of 'orientalizing' designed to integrate local elites into the new order. Further evidence of this is a group of six coins of the Hellenistic-Bactrian ruler Agathocles (*c*. 275 BCE) with an inscription in Greek on one side and the local Brahmi script on the other.

But much about the city is distinctly Greek. The site is dominated by a defensible high point, an acropolis. In the city centre is a peristyle courtyard with an attached administrative block on the southern side that one entered through a vestibule with 18 Corinthian columns. A little to the north of this is a *heroön*, a mausoleum honouring a legendary founder, a very common feature of Greek cities. Here was found an inscription recording how one Clearchos went all the way to Delphi to make a copy of its moral maxims and bring them to Ai-Khanoum. The whole city – modest in size as one might expect on this wild frontier of Hellenistic civilization – was encompassed by a defensive wall. That wall was badly needed, but seems to have failed in its purpose, for

RIGHT: A disc from Ai-Khanoum, dating to the 3rd century BCE, shows the Greek deities Nike and Cybele.

Ai-Khanoum was burnt towards the end of the 2nd century BCE and never recovered.

Ai-Khanoum pales by comparison with the great cities of the Hellenistic East – Aphrodisias, Ephesus, Miletus, Pergamum and Priene in Anatolia; Antioch, Apamea, Baalbek and Jerash in the Levant; Alexandria in Egypt. But it is a measure of one of the greatest campaigns of conquest in history, that of Alexander the Great between 334 and 326 BCE, which saw the complete destruction of the Persian Empire and carried the Macedonians all the way to India.

Almost certainly, there are other lost Hellenistic cities waiting to be found, especially in the regions beyond Syria, where the Macedonian hegemony was shallow and short-lived. In Anatolia, the Levant and Egypt, however, Hellenism endured; though Alexander's empire broke up after his death, Greek-speaking kings continued to rule and many more cities were founded. (We use the term 'Hellenistic', by the way, for the period following the conquests of Alexander the Great and preceding the conquests of the Romans.) A strong Greek urban civilization now stretched all the way from Alexandria in Egypt and Jerash in Jordan to Paestum and Tarentum in southern Italy, Agrigento and Selinunte in Sicily and even as far as Marseilles on the south coast of France

LEFT: A coin of King Agathokles from Ai-Khanoum.

and Ampurias on the east coast of Spain. These Western Greek cities were the result of earlier waves of colonization, but they were substantially rebuilt in the Hellenistic period.

Archaeological investigation of the Hellenistic cities is complicated by two factors: first, many of the Greek cities evolved into medieval and modern cities and are largely built over to this day; second, even where this is not the case, they tended to be remodelled in the Roman period, especially during the 2nd century CE, when huge numbers of new monuments were constructed in provincial cities. Nonetheless, there are still spectacular Hellenistic remains to be seen in many places, representing colossal investment of resources in temples, council chambers, marketplaces, gymnasia, theatres, libraries and sports stadia, often laid out in a regular grid-plan of streets extending for a kilometre or more.

Who paid for all this? It is a question we should always ask when viewing the great architectural and artistic monuments of the past. For the great majority of people living in the Hellenistic world were not Greek at all. The Greek-speakers were a minority of administrators, landowners and townsmen. Most of the country people were native to the region, speaking their own language, worshipping local gods, with customs and a way of life predating the arrival of the Greeks. They probably viewed their foreign overlords much as the English people viewed the Normans in medieval times or the diverse peoples of India viewed the British during the Raj. Let us keep in mind that the great achievements of Hellenistic urbanism rested on the backs of a native peasantry required to perform labour services and pay rents and taxes to make it all possible.

BELOW: The temple of Hera at Agrigento in Sicily. Greek cities could be found across the Mediterranean by the Hellenistic period.

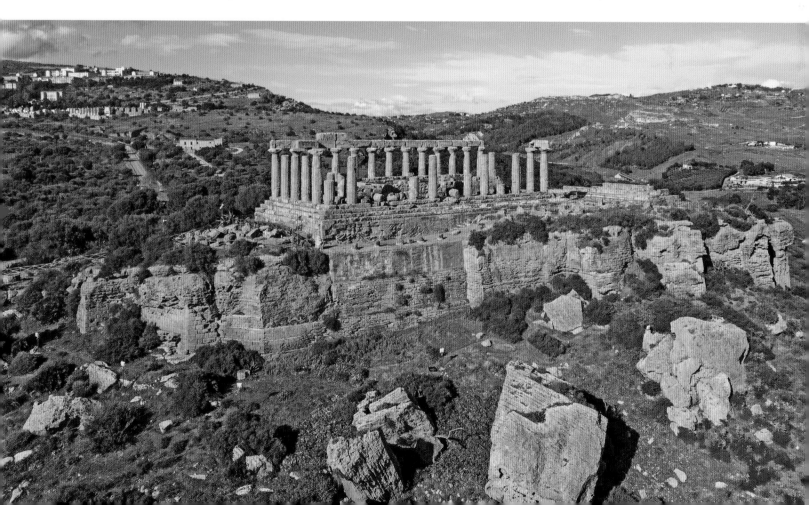

The Scythians

The Yenisei River Valley in the Altai Mountains, located on the western edge of Mongolia, seems to have been the incubator of a distinctive Iron Age culture destined to become dominant across Central Asia: that of the Scythians.

Several campaigns of excavation since the 1970s have revealed a series of royal *kurgan* or mound burials of exceptional sophistication. The first to be exposed, labelled Arzhan 1, dating to the late 9th century BCE, comprised a log-built grave chamber 8m across and a surrounding latticework of logs extending across much of the 110m (360ft) extent of the mound. Some

6,000 tree-trunks were employed in the construction, involving an estimated 10,000 person-days of labour.

The central chamber had contained an old man and a young woman, buried in finery of gold, turquoise and coloured fabrics. Nearby were the bodies of eight others, presumably retainers, sacrificed to accompany the dead leader into the afterlife and also six horses, their bridles decorated in gold. Among other grave offerings interred around the central chamber were some 150 horses with saddles and bridles.

Kurgans have been a special focus of Russian archaeology from as far back as the 18th century. Many contain sumptuous artworks, often executed in solid gold, with vivid depictions of the Scythians themselves. They wear pointed hats, long-sleeved tunics and tight-fitting trousers. And, from the

BELOW: An aerial photograph of the Kurgan at Arzhan. It was created in the 8th century BCE and rich grave goods, like this pectoral plate, were found within.

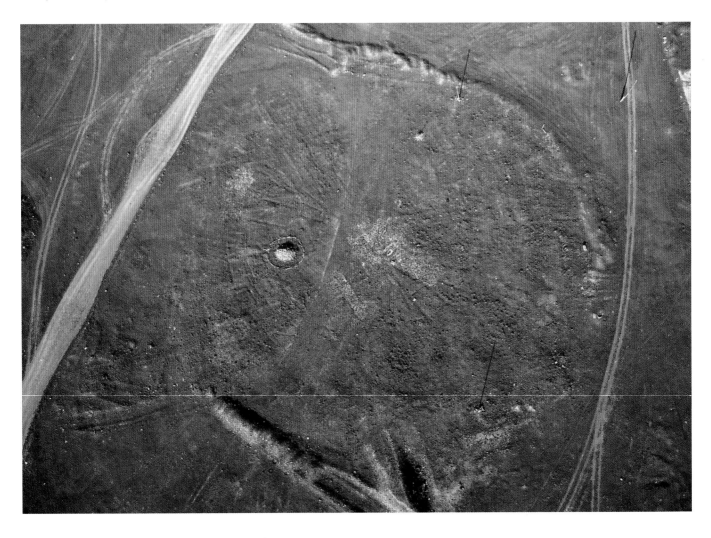

LEFT: A Scythian pommel from the 6th century BCE.

evidence of textiles preserved in frozen tombs, we know that these were made of felt, fur and soft leather, and that fabrics were often elaborately decorated with embroidered designs and gold and tin foil. The mummified corpses are sometimes covered in intricate tattoos, a complex interlacing of swirling animal motifs; perhaps these provided magical protection against the blows of the enemy in battle.

Art and artefact combine to reveal the equipment of the nomadic steppe warrior. He carried a composite 'recurved' bow for long-range shooting; his quiver, often highly decorated, hung at his side. He was armed with a lance, either a close-range missile or a thrusting spear for use in the melee. He had a sword for hand-to-hand fighting. A helmet, homemade or perhaps a Greek import, body armour of metal scales sown onto a leather jerkin, and a shield, perhaps of close-woven wicker, provided personal protection.

The Scythians ornamented their bodies, clothing and metalwork with riots of curling, twisting, fighting beasts. We see recumbent deer, coiled felines, winged griffins and birds of prey. We see predators tearing at sheep, deer and horses; and sometimes predators fighting each other. We see human hunters in action, running down and spearing ferocious wild beasts, whether life-like lions or mythic horned felines. And these images seem to blur into depictions of war, where human fights human, as if the battling beasts should be read as metaphors.

Here is yet another kind of Iron Age culture, one specially adapted to life on the Eurasian steppe, a belt of grassland several hundred miles wide which extends from the Pacific Ocean to the Hungarian Plain. To the north lie forests, to the south deserts and the steppe has traditionally been home to nomadic herders of horses, cattle and sheep. Nine thousand, six hundred kilometres (6,000 miles) in length east–west, it functions as a 'corridor' of movement and the generally lusher grasslands towards the west (the 'steppe gradient') have tended to encourage movement from east to west in moments of ecological or social crisis.

Such crises have been relatively frequent, for modest fluctuations in climatic conditions can have a profound impact on the delicate balance between people, animals and grazing on the steppe. It is an unstable equilibrium at the best of times, with the relative abundance of summer pasture contrasting with dependence on the reeds of rivers and marshes for animal feed during the bitter winters. A subtle shift in ecology can trigger successive shockwaves of folk movement across the steppe as whole communities trek west in search of fodder.

So the steppe peoples were always warriors, ever-prepared to fight for their place in the world – or rather, for a new place further west where the grass grows taller. And these shock-waves have sometimes sent the steppe peoples barrelling beyond the steppe, colliding with more sedentary societies of cultivators to the south. Then they explode onto the historical stage and we hear of them as Scythians, Cimmerians, Sarmatians, Huns and Mongols. All these are *portmanteau* terms to describe agglomerations of otherwise disparate tribes thrown together in moments of turmoil.

The Celts

Hoards and hillforts dominate Iron Age archaeology north of the Alps. Let us consider an example of each.

The Snettisham Hoard was recovered in a series of investigations at an exceptionally rich sanctuary site near the coast of north-west Norfolk in England between 1948 and 1973. Among the many objects unearthed were no less than 70 complete and a further 80 fragments of gold, silver and bronze torcs dating from around 70 BCE. These were neck-rings worn as marks of status in life and often deposited as ritual offerings to the gods. Many of them are works of craftsmanship and artistry of exceptional accomplishment, involving the weaving together of bands of metal, each composed of multiple threads, with the heads decorated in a distinctive 'La Tène' style of curves and loops, stylized plant motifs and confronting animal heads.

Maiden Castle in Dorset is Britain's biggest hillfort. Cut into chalk downland, it is the size of 50 football pitches and was once home to hundreds of people, presumably followers of the great lord who presided

BELOW:The Snettisham Hoard from *c.* 70 BCE consisted of many lavish gold and silver pieces of jewellery.

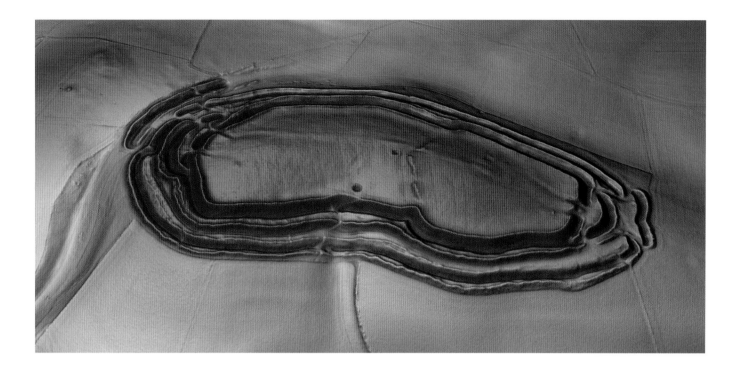

ABOVE: A digital 3D model of the terrain of Maiden Castle in Dorset.

there. It reached its finished form during the 1st century BCE, when its defences came to comprise no less than four separate ramparts separated by ditches, some 6m high, which would once have been surmounted by timber palisades, combined with elaborate multi-angled gateways. Many Iron Age landscapes are studded with such monuments, often located only a few miles apart, implying a world characterized by political fragmentation and military insecurity.

What sort of people deposited the Snettisham Hoard and built Maiden Castle? The Greeks described the people of Northern and Central Europe as *Keltoi*. The Romans called them *Galli*. Many modern archaeologists are dubious about such lump-all terms; some would argue that 'the Celts' never really existed. This seems to go too far, because there is little doubt that across a huge swathe of Europe during the Late Iron Age we seem to have a multiplicity of tribes who shared language, customs and beliefs, as if they all had a common cultural origin.

During the 6th century BCE, a distinctive warrior aristocracy – members of what archaeologists now call the 'Hallstatt culture' – controlled a group of territories north of the Alps. The Hallstatt lords spoke Celtic, lived in hillforts and were buried with funerary carts, bronze cauldrons and drinking horns. At first their numbers were few and the territories they controlled small and scattered, but during the 5th century BCE the archaeological evidence shows a marked spread of Celtic-style artefacts. A new style – the 'La Tène culture' – was adopted by an increasingly numerous aristocracy. Drinking sets and fire-dogs, gold and silver torcs, elaborate horse fittings and weaponry, especially iron swords in decorated scabbards, became essential status-symbols across much of Central Europe.

From the evidence of hoards, hillforts, burials and chance finds, and from the descriptions of Greek and Roman writers, we can imagine an elite of chieftains and warrior retinues who wore helmets and sometimes body-armour, fought on horseback or in chariots and were expert in the use of long slashing swords. Though the warrior ethos affected the whole of Celtic society, such that military service as infantry equipped with spear and shield was an obligation on all free men, military achievement was a particular mark of

noble status. The standing of a chief was measured by the size of the retinue of followers he was able to attract through success in war and raiding. As for the numerous sanctuaries revealed by archaeology – on hilltops, in forest clearings, on the banks of lakes, rivers and marshes – we know that the Celtic priests who presided over holy rites at these places were called 'druids'.

In the late 5th century BCE, this Celtic warrior culture seems to have burst the bounds of its original homeland and flooded across Europe in a succession of violent waves. In this age of migrations (c. 400–200 BCE), the Celts reached the furthest fringes of the Continent and beyond: across France and into southern Britain and eastern Spain; eastwards to the lower Danube and the shores of the Black Sea; from there into Greece and across the Aegean to Turkey; and over the Alps into the Po Valley, where, in the fullness of time, they would clash with the Romans.

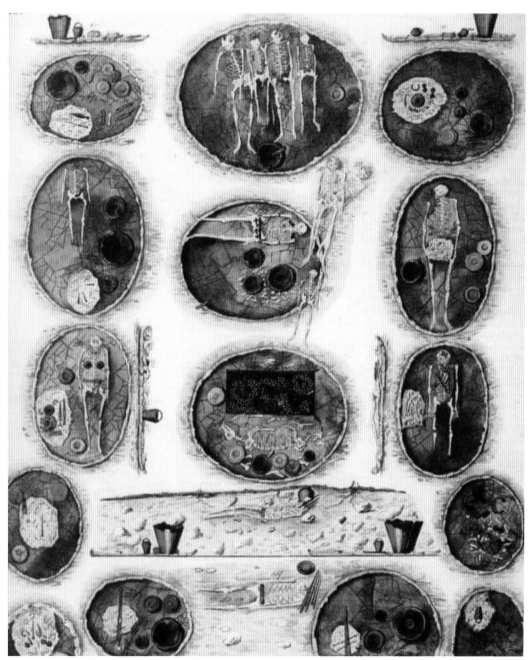

OPPOSITE: A Celtic helmet in the La Tène style, c. 350 BCE.

LEFT: An illustration of a cemetery dig at Halstatt commissioned by the archaeologist Johann Georg Ramsauer, showing the arrangement of the graves at the site and the items buried with each corpse.

Animal Power

Humans use animals for food, raw materials, transport, traction and
warfare. Animals are a source of meat, milk, eggs, wool, hides/leather,
furs, horn, ivory and more. But they are also used in transport, to move
both people and goods, in traction to pull heavy loads and in warfare to
pull chariots, as cavalry mounts and to carry supplies. The Standard of
Ur, dating from *c.* 2500 BCE, depicts what are assumed to be onagers –
Asiatic wild asses – pulling four-wheeled Sumerian chariots, each with
a crew of two, a driver and a warrior. Egyptian art shows donkeys being
used as pack animals as early as *c.* 3000 BCE, mules from around 1500
BCE (the mule, a hybrid of male donkey and female horse, is stronger and
more amenable than the donkey). However, realizing the full potential
of animal power faced formidable technological barriers in the ancient
world.

Donkeys and mules lacked the strength of ponies and horses. The
latter only reached the great centres of civilization from their Central
Asian homeland in the middle of the 2nd millennium BCE. Combined
with another Central Asian import – the composite recurved bow –
they revolutionized warfare. Massed formations of chariots crewed by
warriors equipped with bows and javelins imparted a new mobility and
striking power to the battlefield. But the development of cavalry was
much slower. The earliest representations in art do not appear until
the 1st millennium BCE and then we see riders without the benefit of
saddles, stirrups or spurs. This remained so among the Greeks and the

ABOVE: The war panel of the Standard of Ur
shows horses pulling the chariots that formed an
essential part of the Sumerian war machine.

ABOVE: A section from the Elgin Marbles shows two horsemen. The development of horseback riding was an important military development, but did not emerge until the 1st millennium BCE.

Macedonians. Light cavalry action – shooting arrows or hurling javelins – would have been more difficult without a firm seat. Shock cavalry action – fighting at close-quarters – would have been restricted to swordplay. Precluded would have been the use of the galloping horse to drive home a spearpoint – without saddle or stirrups, the impact would have knocked the rider from his mount.

The Celts may have invented an effective saddle for the mounted warrior – a design that was then inherited by the Romans. We see depictions of it on the tombstones of Roman auxiliary cavalrymen and finds of preserved leather in waterlogged deposits have confirmed the accuracy of these images. The saddle was fitted with four vertical pommels designed to wedge the rider firmly in his seat. Not only would this

ABOVE: The tombstone of Lucius Romanus from the 1st century CE is one of the earliest depictions of a saddle in art.

have afforded him a more secure platform for hurling javelins and wielding a sword; it would have made possible a charge with couched spears.

By this time, stirrups were known, but not yet widely used. They were first developed by Central Asian nomads and only later, in the early 1st millennium CE, adopted by the Chinese and Koreans. They did not reach Europe and the Mediterranean until *c.* 700 CE. Only now did a true heavy cavalry become possible. They can be seen on the *Bayeux Tapestry*, where Norman knights, heavily armoured, mounted on destriers (specially bred war-horses),

LEFT: Stirrups are shown on the *Bayeux Tapestry*. The use of heavy armour and weaponry from horseback was only made possible through the innovations of saddle and stirrups.

firmly seated with saddles and stirrups, charge the Anglo-Saxon shield-wall with couched lances.

One horsey problem remained: lack of a suitable collar for traction. Whereas oxen worked well harnessed to a yoke, horses did not. The yoke and throat-girth left the animal pulling mainly with its shoulders and putting pressure on its windpipe. The solution was to dispense with the yoke, apply a padded breast-collar and attach this to the vehicle with a harness that ran on either side of the animal. In this way, the horse was able to pull with its whole body without constricting its breathing. Again, the earliest artistic evidence for this device comes from China, towards the end of the 1st millennium BCE, whence it spread slowly through Asia, reaching Europe in the 8th century CE, but not coming into general use there until the 12th. Horses work about 50 per cent faster than oxen, but they are more expensive animals and require greater husbandry. Unsurprisingly, therefore, though horse-drawn ploughs are sometimes depicted as early as the 14th century, oxen continued to be used for ploughing throughout the European Middle Ages and across much of Asia up to the present day.

The technical fixes required in harnessing horsepower have their parallel in relation to camels. The 'ship of the desert' was the basis of the Arabian trade in luxury goods. This swelled into an east–west torrent – of gold, silver, precious stones, spices, perfumes, ivory and fine cloth – towards the end of the 1st millennium BCE. But meeting rising demand was impeded by lack of an appropriate saddle. It is obvious where you place the saddle on a horse, mule or donkey: in the curve of the back. It is far from straightforward in the case of a dromedary camel: the hump is in the way. The South Arabian saddle, probably invented around 1200 BCE, was essentially a cushion placed on top of the animal's hump and strapped to the underbelly. This put a strain on the animal and limited its carrying capacity. The solution, when it came, probably around 500 BCE, was very simple.

The North Arabian saddle is essentially a four-sided box placed over the hump, resting on the animal's ribcage, but heavily cushioned to prevent rubbing and sores. The rider sits on a cushioned seat placed on top of the box framework between two high wooden pommels. The cargo is slung evenly on either side,

using the pommels for support, but with the weight transferred to the whole of the animal's upper back by the box framework.

It is difficult to exaggerate the historical significance of the North Arabian saddle. By doubling or more the weight of cargo a camel might bear, it transformed the Arabs into the overland bulk-cargo carriers of the Middle East. It was the equivalent, for ancient desert transportation, of modern containerization. In fact, it is no exaggeration to say, that it so enriched the Arab mercantile elite that they were able to make the transition to urban civilization. The sandstone city of Petra, with its thousand or so rock-cut tombs and its colonnaded street lined with great temples, one of the modern world's most famous archaeological attractions, owes its existence to the North Arabian saddle.

ABOVE: A North Arabian saddle featuring two wooden pommels, allowed for the effective use of camels as mounts.

RIGHT: The ancient city of Petra was the capital of the Nabatean people. The city likely owed its success to the use of camels to transport cargoes vast distances across the desert.

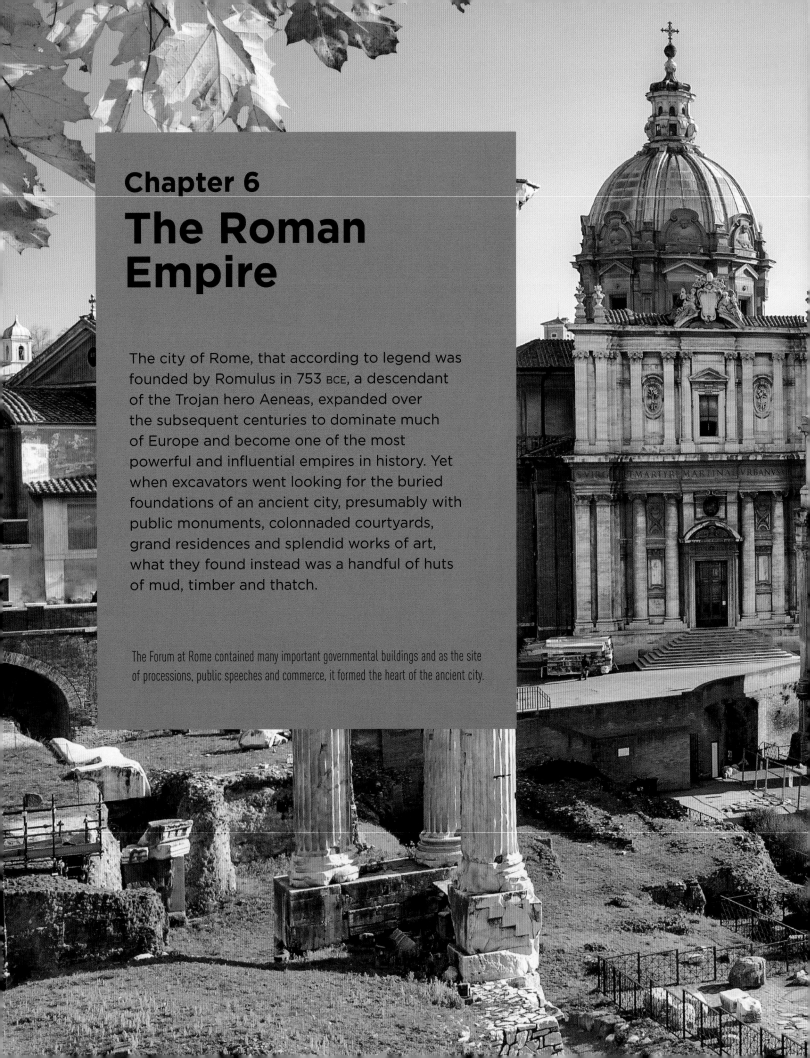

Chapter 6
The Roman Empire

The city of Rome, that according to legend was founded by Romulus in 753 BCE, a descendant of the Trojan hero Aeneas, expanded over the subsequent centuries to dominate much of Europe and become one of the most powerful and influential empires in history. Yet when excavators went looking for the buried foundations of an ancient city, presumably with public monuments, colonnaded courtyards, grand residences and splendid works of art, what they found instead was a handful of huts of mud, timber and thatch.

The Forum at Rome contained many important governmental buildings and as the site of processions, public speeches and commerce, it formed the heart of the ancient city.

Archaeology and Myth

Works of history can turn out to be works of myth. Archaeology, on the other hand, cannot lie: what is there, buried in the ground, is what is there. There was no city on the site of ancient Rome in the 8th century BCE. Three or four hilltop villages were all that existed at that time. One of these – better known to us from excavation than the others – was on the Palatine Hill, the remains of it lying deep beneath the aristocratic mansions of the Late Republic and the imperial palaces of the Early Empire, these dating from some eight centuries later.

The Palatine must always have been a good place for Iron Age farmers and shepherds to settle. The ground rose steeply from the surrounding marsh to a wide plateau, an ideal refuge for men and beasts, where they were protected from both floods and raiders. Plough-land and pasture were in high demand at the time. Territory was often disputed in border clashes, and brigand-chiefs made a living rustling sheep and cattle. The village on the Palatine, girded by cliffs and a palisade, offered relative security and a small Latin-speaking community had long been settled there. The people lived in small rectangular or oval huts, the floors cut into the bedrock, the frameworks formed of timber posts and

ABOVE: A model of the village on the Palatine Hill that would later become Rome, *c.* 750 BCE.

rafters, the walls of wattle-and-daub, the roofs of thatch.

We know the form of these not only from the postholes and slots excavated on the Palatine, but also from the ceramic containers modelled on the houses of the living in which the first villagers had laid to rest the cremated bones of their dead. For, near the bottom of the hill, just clear of the marsh, was an old cemetery, in use since the earliest days of the village in the 10th century BCE, where at first the rite had been cremation, but afterwards, certainly by 750 BCE, the villagers interred the intact bodies of the dead in trenches, along with ceramic jars containing food and drink. The spirits of the ancestors thus hallowed the ground, making good the claims of the living to possess it, guarding the approaches to the village above.

Some of the other hills nearby were also occupied, though we know less about them, for they are covered by modern buildings. These hills next to the Tiber were refuges, places where people gathered for safety in what was, in the Early Iron Age, a marginal, frontier zone – a frontier between nature and agriculture, where much of the land was still a wilderness of swamp and forest; and a frontier between peoples, with Latins to the south, Etruscans to the north, Sabines to the east. Humanity's flotsam and jetsam drifted here – the misfits and outcasts of more ordered societies elsewhere. These were raw new communities, with a rough-and-ready pioneering culture. There is even an echo of this in Livy's *History*. 'In antiquity,' he tells us, 'the founder of a new settlement, in order to increase its population, would as a matter of course embrace a lot of homeless and destitute folk and pretend that they were his native-born fellows. Romulus followed a similar course: to help fill his huge new city … [he threw it open as] a place of asylum for fugitives. Hither fled for refuge all the rag-tag-and-bobtail from the neighbouring peoples, some free, some slave and all of them wanting a fresh start. That mob was the first real addition to the city's strength, the first step to her future greatness.'

But of course, Romulus was a figure of myth and, as we have seen, Rome was nothing more than an Iron Age village in the 8th century BCE. So when was the city founded? To this question, too, archaeology has an answer.

The First City of Rome

The inhabitants of the Early Iron Age village on the Palatine spoke an archaic form of Latin. These were the ancestors of the Romans. But before they could make the transition to urban life, they were, in the late 7th century BCE, overwhelmed by invaders from the north: the Etruscans. A federation of militaristic city-states, the Etruscans had adopted a new way of war, probably copied from the Greeks of southern Italy, based on the hoplite phalanx, a dense bloc of armoured spearmen who fought shoulder-to-shoulder, many ranks deep, behind a wall of overlapping shields and projecting spear-blades. We can see paintings of these hoplites on the walls of tombs in Etruscan necropolises that have been excavated outside their walled hilltop cities and the hoplite 'panoply' of helmet, body-armour, round shield, spear and sword is sometimes found in graves.

Work had begun before the Etruscans took over.

BELOW: The Chigi vase from 650 BCE shows Etruscan hoplites. These soldiers allowed the Etruscans to establish dominance over much of northern Italy.

LEFT: The side wall of the Temple of Jupiter on the Capitoline Hill in Rome. The building was begun by the Etruscans in the 6th century BCE and rebuilt in 83 BCE after a fire destroyed the original.

the Senate House, where the royal council met and the Black Stone, a subterranean sanctuary containing a large black stone inscribed with ritual injunctions. The Palatine began to emerge as Rome's elite residential district, with large patrician houses of standardized design appearing on the lower slopes.

Surpassing all, though, was the Temple of Jupiter, the patron deity of the new city, crowning the Capitoline Hill. The foundations of this vast edifice can be seen today inside the Capitoline Museum. So ambitious was it that it was still unfinished when the last of the Etruscan kings, Tarquinius Superbus, was overthrown in 509 BCE. 'Builders and engineers were brought from all over Etruria,' Livy tells us, 'and the project involved the use not only of public funds but also of a large number of labourers from the poorer classes. The work was hard in itself and came as an addition to their regular military duties, but it was an honourable burden with a solemn and religious significance and they were not, on the whole, unwilling to bear it.'

The Capitoline Temple was about 55m (180ft) wide and 60m (197ft) long, making it one of the largest in the world. It was approached frontally up a steep flight of steps giving access to a high podium. A deep porch of 18 columns arranged in three rows of six covered the front of the podium and a line of columns ran down either side of the building to meet lateral extensions of the rear wall. The shrine itself was a solid-walled structure divided into three long cells, each with a monumental door at the front and a cult image at the back – accommodation for the

Around 650 BCE, the marsh between the hills had been drained and an expanse of beaten earth laid out, creating a place of public gathering at the centre of the growing settlement: the Forum. Another low-lying area close to the river had also been drained, this to serve as a cattle market: the Forum Boarium. Shortly afterwards, the main Forum was repaved in stone and soon, before the end of the 7th century BCE, the earliest stone buildings had been erected nearby. But it was almost certainly the Etruscan conqueror Tarquinius Priscus who formally founded the city and inaugurated a programme of accelerated public works.

During the 6th century, a defensive wall was constructed along the line of the newly established city boundary. It was built from well-cut, carefully laid blocks of *cappellaccio*, a soft volcanic tufa quarried in the Roman countryside and widely used then and later as a building material. The wall enclosed the Palatine, Capitoline and Esquiline Hills and the Forum in between, an area of 285ha. A century of monumental building followed. The city's main sewer became a huge stone-lined culvert, the Great Drain (*Cloaca Maxima*), large enough to have allowed the passage of a wagon-load of hay. In the Forum, new buildings included the Regia, the house of the king,

Capitoline Triad, Jupiter, Juno and Minerva. A gabled, tiled roof extended over both porch and shrine. Exterior architraves, cornices and eaves were decorated with lines of terracottas painted with floral and geometric patterns. Rows of gorgons and other mythic monsters glared down from the guttering. Life-sized gods perched on the roof.

But even in the late 6th century BCE, despite the gargantuan construction project under way on the Capitoline Hill, Rome remained a modest Etruscan-ruled town in control of a territory about 20km wide containing perhaps 35,000 people. There were a hundred or more such places in Iron Age Italy. How come, over the next half millennium, this miniature city-state expanded into the greatest empire in the ancient world? At its peak, centred on the Mediterranean, the Roman Empire would stretch from the Atlantic Ocean to the borders of Persia, from the North Sea to the Sahara Desert. It would control most of this vast territory for 500 years, much of it for 1,500 years.

Rome's historical legacy would be profound and long-lasting. It would be the incubator of three of the world's greatest religions: Judaism, Christianity and Islam. It would give rise to a cultural tradition that would shape Western art and architecture for 2,000 years. Kings and emperors would dress up as Romans, brandish Roman eagles and adopt Roman titles (Caesar/Kaiser/Tsar). Roman columns and arches would be seen everywhere, communicating grandeur and power, from the White House to the Brandenburg Gate. All this and much more would be the imprint of Rome.

How to explain Rome's astonishing success?

BELOW: The ruins of the Palace of Domitian on the Palatine Hill in Rome, built in the late 1st century CE. Little remains of the original settlement in the area and what we see today dates to the high watermark of Roman dominance.

Roman Expansion

The Romans overthrew their Etruscan kings in *c.* 509 BCE. Over the next century and half (the Early Republic), they fought a series of wars against neighbouring Latin states until they had absorbed them all. During this time, they were racked by civil strife (the Struggle of the Orders), essentially a conflict between nobility (patricians) and common citizens (plebeians). This ended in compromise: the nobility admitted plebeians to their ranks and remained politically dominant; the common citizens were enrolled in popular assemblies and had the final say on key decisions.

This distinctive constitutional arrangement suppressed internal class conflict and directed the energies of both nobles and commoners into the profitable business of external warfare.

Between 367 and 133 BCE (the Middle Republic), the Romans waged a series of wars, first against Samnites, Greeks and Celts for control of Italy, then against Carthaginians for control of the Western Mediterranean.

During the 500-year existence of the Roman Republic, Rome was at war every year except two. This was because war enhanced the reputations of the aristocratic politicians who led the legions and enriched the state with booty, slaves, land and tribute; and because the common citizens, who formed the army rank-and-file, were, most of the time, willing enough to fight, since they too shared

BELOW: The ruins of ancient Carthage. When Rome defeated Carthage in the Third Punic War (149–146 BCE), it razed the city. A century later it was rebuilt as a Roman city under Julius Caesar.

in the distribution of largesse. Rome, in short, had evolved into a system of robbery with violence, of predatory military imperialism, a self-feeding process of expansion by which each round of warfare provided the resources for the next.

The rapid growth of empire and the great inflows of wealth consequent upon it, disrupted the existing Roman social order and created new political tensions. Between 133 and 30 BCE (the Late Republic), these tensions exploded repeatedly into civil war, with rival Roman politician-generals leading their armies against each other in struggles for power. Deep currents ran beneath the clashes of armies. The more conservative leaders – known as *optimates* – wanted to uphold the status quo. The more radical – known as *populares* – sought reform in the interests of the *nouveaux riches*, provincial elites ordinary farmers, demobilized soldiers and the city mob. The *populares* wanted to end exclusive aristocratic power and modernize the empire.

The civil wars reached their climax between 49 BCE (when Julius Caesar invaded Italy and thereby declared war on the Senate) and 30 BCE (when Octavian-Augustus, Caesar's chosen successor, defeated Antony and Cleopatra and became master of the Roman world). Rome ceased to be a Republic (ruled by an aristocratic Senate) and became an Empire (ruled by an autocratic Emperor).

During the Late Republic and Early Empire, great wars of conquest continued – in Syria under Pompey the Great, in Gaul under Caesar, and in Spain, the Balkans and Germany under Octavian-Augustus. Then the pace of expansion slowed, before coming to an almost complete halt under the Emperor Hadrian (117–138 CE), whose policy of retrenchment and consolidation on existing frontiers represented the end of some 600 years of Roman military aggression.

The great wars of conquest had subsidized the Roman imperial project. The spoils of war had enriched the Roman ruling class, filled the coffers of the state and provided the wherewithal for a policy of 'bread and circuses' to win the allegiance of key client groups like the citizens of Rome. Some hawkish emperors therefore favoured new wars of conquest,

ABOVE: A statue of Julius Caesar in Rimini, Italy. Caesar's military success led to the growth of what became the Roman Empire.

but there were no more easy pickings. The frontiers had come to rest on regions of mountain, forest and desert. Wars in the wilderness were likely to cost more to wage than they brought back in booty. Rome had found its 'natural frontiers'; it risked perilous over-extension in fruitless counter-insurgency warfare by venturing further. So the Roman Army evolved from an active field army into a frontier garrison army.

This section has relied heavily on historical sources and hardly at all on archaeological evidence. Time to get back to the material evidence. What more can we learn from this about Roman imperial expansion between the 5th century BCE and the 2nd century CE?

Caesar's Army

Let us start with the army itself. Because the Republican Army was not a standing army with permanent barracks, our evidence is much more limited than for the later Imperial Army with its fixed frontiers and stone forts. Most of the evidence we do have is for Late Republican times. Sculptures like those on the Altar of Domitius Ahenobarbus offer depictions of Roman soldiers. A succession of siege camps has been traced at Numantia in Spain. Actual siege lines have been excavated at Alesia in France. Examples of Roman military equipment – helmets, body-armour, weaponry – are relatively numerous. This evidence, combined with that of Greek and Roman historians, allows us to build a picture of the Late Republican Army.

We know that it was very different in character from the Early Republican Army. This had been a city-state militia modelled on the Greek hoplite phalanx – a dense formation not trained for complex manoeuvre or flexible tactics. But the Romans learned from their wars against the Gauls, the Carthaginians and the Celtiberian tribesmen of Spain, and we see them adopting new weapons suited to a looser, faster, more mobile kind of warfare. The Roman helmet was based on helmets worn by the Gauls. The Roman *pilum* (a distinctive armour-piercing javelin) and *gladius* (a short stabbing sword) were copied from the Celtiberians. The Roman *scutum* (a large oval or rectangular shield) was similar to shields carried by both Gauls and Celtiberians. The development of a cavalry arm – usually by employing native auxiliaries familiar with mounted warfare – was probably triggered by encounters with enemy cavalry on the battlefield. Especially important was the adoption of a Gallic style of saddle with four raised pommels designed to wedge the rider in position and enable him to wield weapons forcefully without losing his seat. Other innovations included the recruitment of specialist archers and slingers for long-range shooting and the use of field artillery in the form of torsion-powered engines for propelling high-velocity bolts and stones.

By the time of Julius Caesar, the Roman Army was more or less fully professionalized. Many of Caesar's men served under him for 13 years, first in the Gallic War, then in the Civil War. He is full of praise for his men in his histories of these wars, laying particular emphasis on the role of the centurions, tough veterans raised from the ranks who commanded companies of 60 (later 80) men. Our most vivid archaeological glimpse of this army in action is provided by the 19th century excavations at Alesia sponsored by the French Emperor Napoleon III.

Alesia was the site of the final defeat of Vercingetorix, the leader of the great Gallic revolt of 52 BCE. Caesar provides a detailed description of his siege lines and of the fighting in his *Gallic War*. The

LEFT AND ABOVE: A *scutum* (large shield) and *gladius* (short sword), the essential equipment of the Roman soldier.

accuracy of his description has been substantially confirmed by the excavations. Ancient Alesia was situated on a lozenge-shaped plateau measuring 1,500m (4,900ft) in length, 1,000m (3,280ft) in width and 150m (492ft) in height. Caesar ordered the construction of a complete line of circumvallation surrounding the entire fortress.

This comprised two 5m-wide ditches, the upcast from which was used to form an earth rampart behind. This was crowned with a wooden palisade and wooden towers every 25m (82ft). Immediately in front of the main defences were lines of sharpened

BELOW: This frieze from the Altar of Domitius Ahenobarbus, from the 2nd century BCE, bears images of Late Republican Roman soldiers.

ABOVE: A 19th-century painting of the surrender of Vercingetorix to Julius Caesar at the conclusion of the Siege of Alesia in 52 BCE.

branches forming a hedge of spikes: the ancient equivalent of barbed wire. Beyond was a belt of circular pits covered by brushwood with pointed stakes in the base and then a further belt of small logs hammered into the ground and mounted with projecting iron spikes: the ancient equivalent of minefields. Immediately behind the main line – which extended for 18km (11 miles) in total – were no less than 23 forts. Later, when news reached him that a relief army was on its way, Caesar ordered his men to construct a second line, one of contravallation, that is, facing outwards and this was 23m (75ft) in extent.

The 19th-century excavations revealed only minor variations along the line of the defences and aerial photography has since supplied further confirmation of Caesar's account. So we bear witness here to the exceptional professionalism of Rome's army of citizen legionaries by the 1st century BCE. It had evolved from a small, local, part-time force of urban militiamen into an instrument of world conquest.

BELOW: The excavations at Alesia have confirmed much of Caesar's written account about the course of the siege.

Roman Colonies

The job of the Republican Army was to fight wars and then disband, not to provide a permanent army of occupation. So how did the Romans control conquered territory?

Excavations by American archaeologist Frank Brown at the little Roman settlement of Cosa in south-western Tuscany during the 1950s provide part of the answer. Cosa lies on the coast about 140km (87 miles) north of Rome and was founded in 273 BCE. Today it would seem no more than a village, only 500m (1,640ft) across; but it was built to endure, being perched on a prominent hilltop and girt with some two kilometres of strong defensive walls formed of massive polygonal blocks. The three gateways were heavily defended and the walls were strengthened with no less than 18 projecting towers. For Cosa was a *colonia*, a new town designed to guard conquered territory, its citizen-settlers organized as an urban militia. To support them, 550km^2 (212 square miles) of territory was allocated to the town and this will have been divided up into individual farms.

The town itself was laid out on a symmetrical grid of rectangular blocks. The major public buildings made Cosa a sort of miniature Rome. Two hills encompassed within the town boundary became the site of temples. That on the south was the Temple of Jupiter and this sanctuary also served as a defensible

citadel, an inner keep to which the citizens could retreat if their main walls were breached; water tanks were provided against this eventuality. The forum was laid out in the saddle between the two hills. It was originally a long rectangle measuring 90m (295ft) by 35m (115ft). Facing onto it was a circular *comitium*, where the town council met. The earliest houses were small, austere and uniform; a reflection, no doubt, of the rough equality among the first colonists.

Some 400 towns are known to have had the status of *coloniae*. These include many new foundations like Cosa – Ostia at the mouth of the Tiber is a notable early example – and also existing towns taken over and then resettled by Roman citizens – Pompeii and Paestum, both originally Greek are examples of the latter.

The creation of *coloniae* was connected with another archaeological marker of Roman expansion: centuriation. Flying low over many parts of lowland Italy – and, indeed, many other provinces of the former Roman Empire – it is crystal clear: mile upon mile of rectangular fields which were originally laid out by Roman land-surveyors (*agrimensores*), but have survived to the present day.

The survey grid was usually laid out by extending the north–south *cardo maximus* and the east–west *decumanus maximus* – the two main thoroughfares – of the local town out into the surrounding countryside. A mesh of secondary roads was then added parallel to these main axes, dividing the land into squares measuring 20 by 20 *actus* (a Roman unit equivalent to 35.5m/116ft). Each of these large squares, known as *centuriae* (centuries), was then further subdivided into 100 small squares, known as *heredia* (a Roman unit equivalent to about half a hectare). Finally, each *heredium* was split down the middle, creating two *iugera* – the rectangular fields you can see from the aeroplane. The Latin word *iugum* means 'yoke'. An *iugerum* was a rectangle measuring 71m (233ft) by 35.5m (116ft), which was the amount that a pair of oxen could plough in a day. Why rectangular fields? Because an ox-drawn plough has a wide, slow turning-circle and a rectangular field reduces the number of turns that have to be made. The Roman surveyors had thought of everything!

In the early days, the plots allocated to individual colonists could be very small indeed, barely enough to live on. Later they were much more generous. We often hear of allocations of 50 or more *iugera* (13ha) per settler and that would have made for a community of very prosperous farmers. Moreover, huge amounts of land were implicated. One scholar who made a detailed study of the evidence estimated that in just one decade at the beginning of the 2nd century BCE a million *iugera* (250,000ha) were centuriated and handed out to 100,000 families.

LEFT: The *comitium* (or public meeting place) at Cosa. Similar structures could be found in most of the Roman *coloniae*.

Roman Forts

The Roman Army became a standing army of full-time professional soldiers during the reign of the first emperor Octavian-Augustus (30 BCE–14 CE). Around a quarter of a million strong in all, roughly half was formed by 5,000-strong legions of Roman citizens, while the other half was formed of auxiliaries recruited from the subject peoples of the empire organized in units of 500 or 1,000 men. Legionaries served for 20 years, auxiliaries for 25. All were heavily armoured, superbly equipped, well supplied, thoroughly trained and highly motivated. They represented the finest fighting machine of their age, an instrument of war honed by hundreds of years of experiment and experience in Rome's long ascent to global power.

Because the Imperial Army was largely a garrison army, its former presence marked by numerous frontier works, auxiliary forts and legionary fortresses originally executed in earth and timber, later rebuilt in stone, we have a wealth of archaeological evidence available.

The most impressive set of frontier defences is probably Hadrian's Wall in northern Britain, but comparable remains can be found at many locations on the former frontiers of the empire. Hadrian's Wall ran from sea to sea and comprised a ditch and a stone wall with a signal tower every half of a kilometre (⅓rd mile), a mini fort (for about 30 men) every mile and a large fort (for about 500) men every few kilometres.

Each of the large forts housed an auxiliary unit. It was presumably responsible for manning and patrolling the stretch of wall on either side of the fort where it was

RIGHT: A plan of the Roman fort of Iciniacum that was discovered in 1820 near the municipality of Theilenhofen in Germany. It was built around 100 CE and destroyed c. 260 by the Swabians or Alemanni who were a confederation of Germanic tribes from the Upper Rhine district.

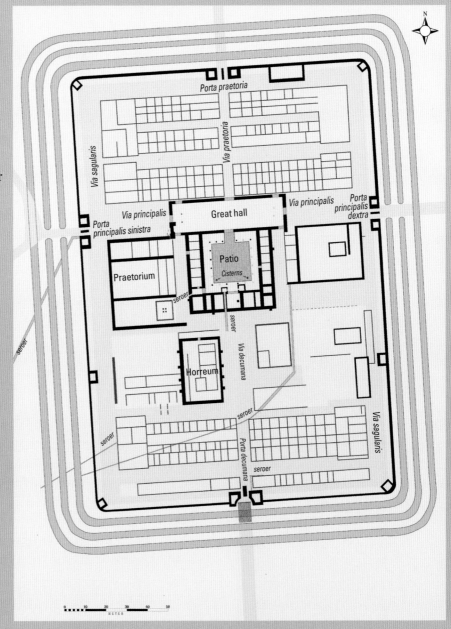

ABOVE: Hadrian's Wall marked the north-west frontier of the Roman Empire.
Along the wall are various ruins of forts and towns.

based. These auxiliary forts had a very similar design:
a 'playing card' shape, a regular grid of streets, a
centrally placed headquarters building (*principia*), a
large commandant's house (*praetorium*), a hospital
(*valetudinarium*), granaries (*horrea*), workshops and
several long rectangular barrack-blocks. Each barrack-
block accommodated a single century (*centuria*) of

80 men. The block was divided into ten *contubernia*, one for each group of eight men, with a much larger apartment at one end for the centurion.

Though accommodation was cramped and basic for ordinary soldiers, the range of amenities available in a Roman fort was impressive and they seem to have got better over time, with the addition of aqueducts, bathhouses and latrines. It was a good life in the army and it was usually possible to rely entirely on voluntary recruitment to maintain numbers.

Many forts endured for centuries and often, too, the very same regiment continued in occupation. This meant that ordinary Roman soldiers – increasingly recruited from the local population – sometimes spent their entire careers serving at a single military post. Such stable garrisons quickly established close relationships with local communities. This is evident in the development of extensive *vici* (attached villages) around Roman forts, where local people chose to build houses and shops, some perhaps the families of soldiers, others artisans and traders supplying the military market.

Extensive excavations at many fort/*vicus* sites have revealed these mixed frontier communities to have been cultural melting-pots. This is especially apparent in the matter of religion, with evidence for the official cults of the army (honouring Jupiter, Mars and the Emperor), the worship of local deities (like the Celtic deity Coventina, who had a sacred well at Carrawburgh on Hadrian's Wall) and exotic 'mystery' religions like that of the Persian saviour-god Mithras (also honoured at Carrawburgh with a temple).

This evidence raises bigger questions about cultural identities. Roman citizenship became ever more widespread, until, early in the 3rd century CE, all free people of the empire were enfranchised. But what did it mean to be Roman when few had been to Rome and most did not speak Latin? How did 'Roman-ness' intersect with other identities – membership of a tribe, citizenship of a local town, adherence to a religious cult? These are live questions in Roman archaeology today.

The archaeology of the Roman Imperial Army reveals not only an instrument of conquest, frontier defence and internal security, but also the epicentre of complex processes of economic development, social interaction and, not least, cultural change.

RIGHT: The Temple of Mithras at Carrawburgh, on Hadrian's Wall in England. The Roman mystery cult of Mithras was born out of older Persian traditions.

Roman Towns

The Roman Republic has been likened to a criminal gang that first robbed its victims and then invited them to join the gang and participate in the next robbery. This is pretty much how it worked. As the Romans expanded their empire, they aimed to win over local communities by offering a large measure of autonomy, respect for native customs and, in the long run at least, a grant of Roman citizenship and full political and juridical rights. This meant local government on the cheap and a steady increase in the manpower pool for recruitment to the legions.

Under the Empire (30 BCE–476 CE), the great bulk of the Army was stationed on or near the frontiers. In the 1st and 2nd centuries CE, behind this defensive shield, during a long *Pax Romana*, elite civilization flourished. Local landowners adopted Roman culture, including the Latin language and built towns and villas, decorated with mosaics and frescoes, in the now-fashionable Roman style. This culture was similar right across the empire, an expression of a common *Romanitas* at the top of society.

The Roman Empire was an urban-based civilization. It was divided into local territorial units (called *civitates* in the Western Empire), each comprising an administrative town and an associated rural *territorium* of estates, farms and villages. The primary official functions of the town were to enforce law and order, maintain state infrastructure and collect the taxes. The towns were the bolts fixing the central state to the local village.

Each town was run by an oligarchy of local landowners and other wealthy men. They formed a town council (*curia*) and from their ranks were elected a small number of magistrates responsible for the day-to-day running of the *civitas*. So long as things went smoothly, these town councillors (*decuriones*) were left pretty much to themselves; there were no centrally appointed officials overseeing their work. Only later, when urban life began to break down in the Late Empire, did the central state start appointing its own district officers.

The origins of these towns were diverse. In many places, especially in the Greek-speaking East, where there was already a strong urban civilization, existing towns were simply taken over; or, more precisely, local urban elites adapted themselves to the realities of Roman rule and otherwise largely carried on as before. Elsewhere, especially in Britain, Gaul, Spain and North Africa, towns were founded *de novo*, though often close to pre-existing native power centres like hillforts.

Whatever its origins, one Roman town ended up looking very much like any other. The municipal councillors invested heavily in urban architecture and the aim everywhere seems to have been to create a kind of miniature Rome, with a complete suite of the public buildings considered essential to *Romanitas*.

The heart of the town was always the *forum* (in Latin) or *agora* (in Greek) – originally an open marketplace, but latterly more multi-functional, with a range of civic and religious ceremonies performed there. Nearby was the basilica, a large rectangular covered hall divided by two internal colonnades into nave and two aisles, used for public meetings and hearing court cases. Also nearby would be the council chamber (*comitium*) and various council offices.

At the centre of the town, too, would be the *capitolium*, an official temple in honour of the Capitoline Triad, Jupiter, Juno and Minerva, the supreme deities of the Roman state. Other temples would be found at various other locations across the town, some to classical deities, some to local ones, some to foreign gods like Mithras, Cybele and Isis. The diversity of cults evident in the archaeology of Roman towns bears testimony to the eclecticism and tolerance of Roman paganism.

Nor would any self-respecting Roman town be complete without at least one public bathhouse – serving as a general leisure-centre – as well as a theatre (for drama, religious ceremonies and public meetings) and an amphitheatre (for gladiatorial combats, beast-baiting and public executions).

Most of these urban amenities were paid for by members of the municipal elite. The leading families competed for the honour of holding high office and for the favour of their fellow citizens by becoming patrons of their towns; numerous inscriptions record

ABOVE: The *capitolium* of Brescia, honouring Jupiter, Juno and Minerva.

their generosity. They gave further expression to their rank and status by building themselves grand town-houses (*domus*) and decorating these with mosaics, frescoes and statuary.

Pompeii and Herculaneum are the prime sites for understanding the Roman *domus*, which typically comprised a more public *atrium* courtyard near the street-front entrance and a more private peristyle courtyard at the rear, where there would be an ornamental garden, sometimes with fountains, a

colonnaded walkway and one or more large dining-rooms (*triclinia*), where the owner would periodically host a Roman-style dinner-party (*cena*).

Both public buildings and private houses were sumptuously decorated with floor mosaics, wall paintings and free-standing statuary. Classical gods and myths were typical subjects of the more elaborate artwork, the best of it executed in superb naturalistic style, the statues cut to show bodies in lively motion, the mosaics and frescoes making full use of perspective and chiaroscuro techniques.

The uniformity of urban planning, public architecture, the design of private houses and the form and content of art across the empire represented a cultural *koine* – a package of forms designed to express a common cultural identity. The Roman provincial town was not simply an administrative centre; it was also an exemplar of *Romanitas*, a model of Roman identity and grand living able to bind together the diverse elites of a very cosmopolitan empire, from the Celtic-speakers of northern Britain to the German-speakers of the Rhineland, the Punic-speakers of Tunisia and the Greek-speakers of Syria.

LEFT: The amphitheatre at Pula, in modern Croatia, could hold 23,000 spectators.

A Note on Roman Coins

The Roman state minted huge numbers of coins. The state had a monopoly on the mining of metals, especially gold and silver, and this was partly because coinage was essential to the operation of the 'tax-pay cycle'. The state levied taxes in the form of coin, and this was used to pay the soldiers and defray other military expenditures. The coins then entered to general circulation when soldiers and military contractors spent their money, oiling the wheels of a whole series of other economic exchanges along the way, and also enabling ordinary people to acquire the coins they needed to pay their taxes in due course.

The Roman economy was never fully monetized, but coins were certainly widely used in everyday life – some tend to be found on even the smallest and most remote of Roman sites. They are, moreover, highly accurate dating tools, for they were routinely stamped with the name and titles of the reigning emperor, and the precise formula for the latter changed each year. So a Roman coin can often be dated to a specific year.

This does not, of course, date the archaeological layer in which the coin was found to the same year, for coins can remain in circulation a long time after minting. What it does do is to show that the layer in question must *post-date* the time of minting. In archaeological terms, the coin provides a *terminus post quem* – a date after which something happened. But combined with other dating evidence from the site, each coin makes its contribution to the chronological jigsaw.

ABOVE: Silver coins found at the site of Augusta Raurica in modern-day Switzerland.

Roman Villas

The Roman elite associated town life with public and private business. One took one's seat in the council, debated the issues of the day, met with one's peers and one's clients, managed one's estates and business affairs. There was even a room in the grand town-house which functioned as an estate office and a place for business meetings: the *tablinum*, usually located opposite the main street-front entrance on the far side of the *atrium*.

The countryside, on the other hand, was associated with 'refined leisure' – with peace and relaxation, reading and writing, entertaining friends and country pursuits like hunting. All men of substance maintained both a town-house and a country villa.

BELOW: The *atrium* of a *domus* from Herculaneum. The *atrium* was an open-air court with a pool at its centre.

The difference was enshrined in language – *domus* for town-house, *villa* for country-house.

The simplest villas comprised a single long rectangular building subdivided into separate rooms accessed via a covered colonnade running down one side. More elaborate villas included a wing at one or both ends and the most elaborate of all involved four ranges of rooms completely enclosing a central courtyard. The richer villas, as well as being highly

ABOVE: The elaborate mosaic in the House of Neptune at Herculaneum shows hunting scenes and has remained particularly well preserved due to the ash that covered the city after the eruption of Mount Vesuvius in 79 CE.

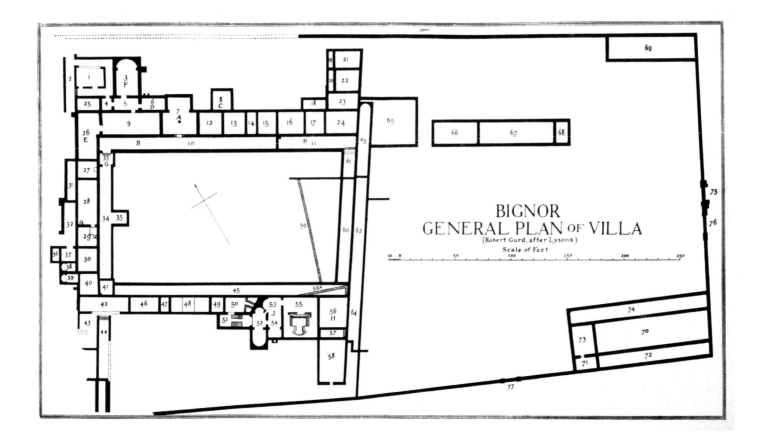

decorated in the usual Roman way, also had their own bath-houses.

Some villas were simply grand country-houses, but most were also estate-centres, with an associated farm complex. The Romans used the terms *villa urbana* and *villa rustica* to distinguish the two parts: the grand country-house for the use of the landowning family and their guests; and the working farm, probably run by an estate manager with a staff of slaves and labourers.

Bignor Villa on the South Downs in England is a fine example. Extensively excavated, we know that it reached its final form early in the 4th century CE, when it became a complete courtyard villa with ranges of rooms on three sides and an enclosing wall and corridor on the fourth, beyond which lay the farmyard with associated farm buildings. It consisted of 65 rooms in all, including both summer and winter dining-rooms and a bathhouse. The winter dining-room and the bathhouse were heated by underfloor

ABOVE: A plan showing the layout of Bignor Villa. It began as a humble farmstead in the late 2nd century CE before expanding to be become an expansive estate two hundred years later.

hypocausts. The best rooms were decorated with some of the finest Roman mosaics to be seen in situ in Britain, including a head of Venus, a head of the Gorgon Medusa, the Four Seasons, the abduction of Ganymede by Jupiter in the guise of an eagle and a scene of fighting gladiators in the arena.

Villa estates tended to operate a mixed-farming regime, with arable, pasture, woodland, wetland orchard and market-garden providing a wide range of produce tending towards self-sufficiency. In addition to a home farm, there might also be tenant farms on which rents were levied.

Beyond the boundaries of the villa estate, there might be land worked independently of the great lords by peasant freeholders – though they would still have obligations of labour service and tribute payment to the central state. Archaeology is increasingly preoccupied with building a more comprehensive picture of the Roman countryside, shifting the focus from villas to villages, roadside settlements, hamlets and individual homesteads. Recent surveys have shown that the Romano-British countryside was much more densely occupied than once assumed, with some sort of settlement every mile or so, at least in the lowland areas. Population estimates have had to be doubled or trebled: we now think there were four million or more people living in Roman Britain, the great majority of them in rural homesteads, hamlets or villages.

The Roman economy was based on agriculture. Slaves, labourers, tenants, freeholders worked the land and some of what they produced was creamed off in the form of rents and taxes to support the great infrastructure of forts, towns and villas that we associate with Roman civilization. But how sustainable was this in the long run? We shall attempt to answer this question in the next chapter.

BELOW: The Medusa mosaic from Bignor Villa. The site contains some of the highest quality mosaic floors of any Roman site in Britain.

Roman Pottery

Though there are some exceptions, virtually all societies since the Agricultural Revolution have made use of pottery. Because ceramic – fired clay – is a very cheap material, ceramic vessels are fragile and often break and because the broken sherds are virtually indestructible, pottery becomes of huge archaeological significance wherever it occurs. The Romans were prolific makers and users of pottery.

A broad distinction is made between coarse ware and fine ware. The former tends to be rougher, undecorated, everyday pottery used as containers, for storage and in food preparation. The latter tends to be more refined, often thinner and more delicate, often more elaborately shaped, often with decoration in the form of mouldings, painted designs and a shiny surface finish achieved through the application of surface slip and careful firing techniques. Most notable among Roman fine wares are the various glossy red-slipped wares, like Italian Arretine Ware, Gaulish Samian Ware and North African Red-Slip Ware. The fine wares were essentially tablewares: they were designed to be seen and admired and to underline the status of the food and drink being served.

Coarse wares, being essentially functional, tended to be more standardized. It is often impossible to guess whether a sherd of Roman grey ware dates from the 1st or the 4th century CE. Fine wares, on the other hand, not only came in a wide range of fabrics and forms, they also tended to change over time, in keeping with cultural fashion. This can make Roman fine ware, especially where there is a large assemblage of sherds to look at, a very accurate dating tool. Many Roman pottery specialists will be confident about assigning an assemblage to, say, a particular quarter century, allowing a sequence of layers on an excavation site to be closely dated.

RIGHT: An example of North African Red-Slip Ware. These forms of pottery could be found across the empire and were designed to be admired.

Pottery has many other uses in archaeology. Perhaps the most important alongside dating is the way it shows connections between different places. Because pottery moves around, we can see the evidence for networks of distribution and exchange; and we can then speculate about the nature of these networks, the underlying mechanisms at work. When, for example, we find large quantities of Black Burnished Ware from southern England up on Hadrian's Wall, we can imagine some sort of military supply chain in operation.

ABOVE: Coarse wares, like this black burnished ware pot, were functional rather than decorative and had standard forms that were maintained for centuries.

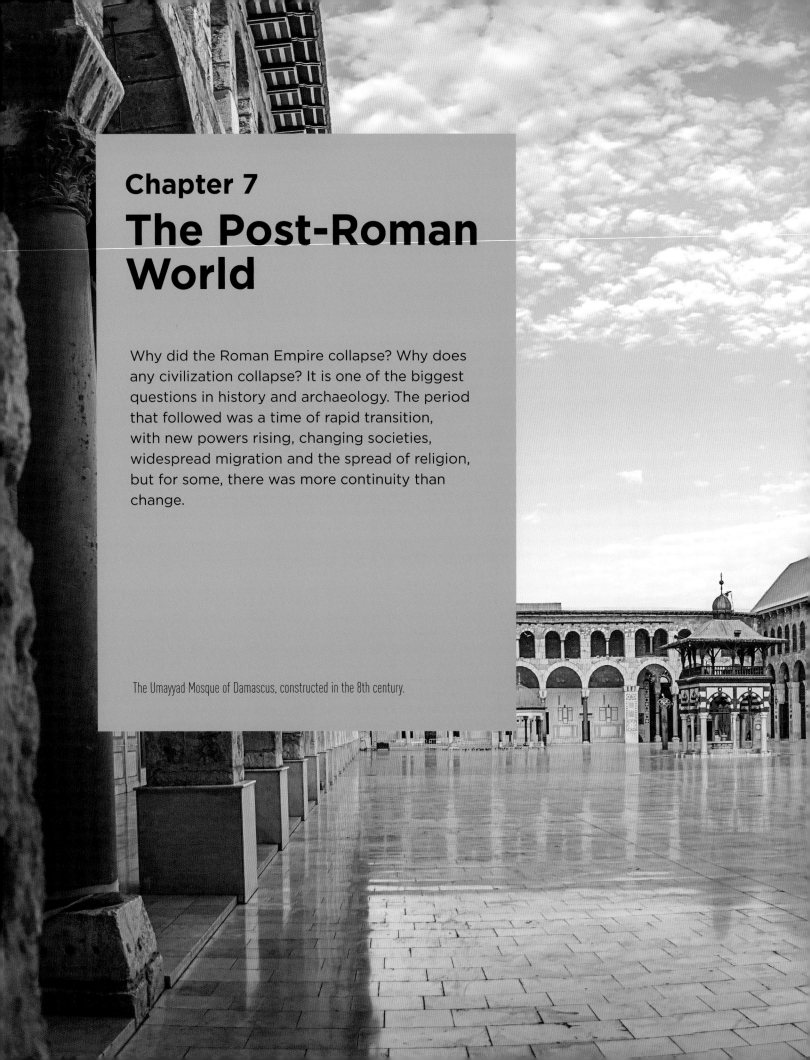

Chapter 7
The Post-Roman World

Why did the Roman Empire collapse? Why does any civilization collapse? It is one of the biggest questions in history and archaeology. The period that followed was a time of rapid transition, with new powers rising, changing societies, widespread migration and the spread of religion, but for some, there was more continuity than change.

The Umayyad Mosque of Damascus, constructed in the 8th century.

The Fall of the Roman Empire

Below the level of the elite, in the ordinary homesteads, hamlets and villages where most people lived, indigenous languages, religions and ways of life continued. Among the provincial peasantry there was great cultural diversity. *Romanitas* may have been the shared cultural identity of town-dwellers and villa-owners across the empire, but it was, at most, the thinnest of veneers in the ancient countryside.

The provincial peasantry had no real stake in the system. They were the beasts of burden on whose backs empire and civilization were built. They performed the labour services and paid the taxes and rents that sustained elite culture. And this burden was slowly increasing in the Late Roman Empire.

The expansion of empire had been subsidized by the great hauls of booty and slaves yielded by wars of conquest. When expansion largely ceased in the early 1st century CE, this subsidy dried up and the empire became reliant on its own resources. We can be certain that expenditure remained

high. We have only to consider the evidence for ongoing investment in the army and frontier defence, not to mention that for the great 2nd century construction boom in town and country, with its public monuments, grand houses and villa estates. The historical sources, moreover, warn of a growing threat from new barbarian states in Central and Eastern Europe; we hear of powerful confederations of Germanic and Gothic tribes pushing against the Rhine and Danube frontiers of the Roman Empire.

A new breed of 'soldier-emperors' – men not tied to palaces but moving around with their armies – emerged in the 3rd century. They siphoned off a growing proportion of the empire's wealth – conscripting labour, raising taxes, requisitioning resources – in an effort to maintain frontier defences. A long-term process of 'decline and fall' can be

RIGHT: The Surgeon's House of Rimini, from the town's high point in the 2nd century.

charted in the archaeology of towns, villas and villages – flourishing in the 2nd century, stagnating in the 3rd, often semi-derelict in the 4th. Shattered by a succession of massive barbarian invasions across the Rhine and the Danube during the 5th century, the Western Roman Empire eventually broke up.

The Eastern Empire, on other hand, richer and with more secure frontiers, survived as the Byzantine Empire for another thousand years, until the fall of Constantinople to the Ottoman Turks in 1453. And in the West, the Christian Church also survived, becoming the principal repository of the old Roman

tradition in the developing medieval world.

The archaeological evidence is clear: after the 2nd century CE, the resources were no longer available, especially in ordinary provincial towns, for heavy expenditures on basilicas, temples, grand houses and fine art. Most 4th century Roman towns looked very different from those of the 2nd century. Many civic buildings became ruinous. Many townhouses were abandoned. Deep deposits of 'dark earth' – a mix of organic debris and assorted other rubbish – accumulated across great swathes of the urban space. Resources were ploughed into building defensive walls and churches. In many cases, the walls enclosed only much reduced circuits, leaving large parts of the former town beyond their protection, so shrunken had the urban population become. We can imagine small numbers of administrators, soldiers and clerics huddled inside these walls, attended by small communities of artisans, traders and labourers.

A snapshot of this Roman rise and fall is illustrated at the seaside town of Rimini in Northern Italy. Archaeologists excavating in the town have traced the town's fall from grace, from a high in the 2nd century, when the town contained rich villas, including a well-equipped Surgeon's House, to its near-abandonment by the 4th century.

A similar malaise eventually overtook the villas. Though many of the grandest courtyard villas appeared only in the 4th century, this proved to be the Indian summer of the villa estates; most were abandoned by their owners in the years around 400 CE. Presumably they were too expensive to maintain as law and order broke down in the surrounding

LEFT: A hunting mosaic from the Villa de Casale, Sicily, from the early 4th century CE, highlights the extraordinary wealth of these villas. Like many villas, it underwent decline and was damaged in the late 5th century, when Vandals attacked.

countryside. Some were then occupied by 'squatters' – to use a term favoured by some archaeologists – with evidence for roofs and walls being propped up, hearths being laid over mosaic floors, animals being stalled in spare rooms, rubbish being dumped in others.

On the frontiers, too, despite the prioritization of military expenditure, many forts were abandoned. The defence of 5,000km (3,100 miles) of frontier was too much for the Late Empire, its resource base shrinking under the weight of military exactions, its enemies becoming ever more powerful and threatening. The Romans were forced to change strategy – from static linear defence to mobile defence in depth, resting their hopes on the ability of fast-moving field armies to deal with both internal disorders and barbarian incursions as and when they arose.

Nonetheless, though the archaeological evidence is clear, there is great debate about its meaning. Was Roman civilization as such really in decline or was it more a matter of continuity and change? The Roman Church was certainly not in decline: its wealth, power

and reach were increasing all the time and it would in due course become one of the main foundation-blocks of the new medieval world. And the Byzantine Empire, of course, would endure for a millennium as a repository and disseminator of Roman culture. A new world was emerging from the womb of the old, but that new world bore a strong and enduring imprint of *Romanitas*.

The Byzantine Empire

Near the eastern border of modern Tunisia lies the ancient Roman city of Ammaedara (known today as Haïdra). It is not on the regular tourist trail, but it should be, as it is one of the most spectacular archaeological sites in a country replete with them; for Tunisia was the richest part of Roman North Africa, which was among the richest regions of the empire. Haïdra's great tumble of ruins, which sprawl across a mile or so of ground beside a wadi, include a *capitolium*, a marketplace, a bathhouse, a theatre,

BELOW: The remains of the Byzantine fortress of Haïdra in Tunisia.

LEFT: A mosaic of the Emperor Justinian in Ravenna. Justinian hoped to restore the Roman Empire to its former glory, but fell short of achieving his aims.

Africa was his first major effort – and among the most successful – but what he found was a world in which Roman urban civilization had shrivelled to mere villages huddled around churches and monasteries. The Byzantine fortress at Haïdra reflected the fragility of the new conquests and also the hollowness of the civilization Justinian aimed to restore, for it occupied only a fraction of the area of the classical city and was built entirely of masonry salvaged from the ruins.

Byzantine remains have this character almost everywhere – in North Africa, Italy, the Balkans, Anatolia and the Levant. Though the Eastern Roman Empire endured for a thousand years after the fall of the Western, it took the form of a conservative military-clerical-bureaucratic complex overlain across a society that was essentially rural and downtrodden. The Byzantine Empire's long struggle to defend its territory – against Goths, Persians, Arabs, Turks and others – drained the lifeblood from local communities.

To pass from a remote border fortress like Haïdra to the very heart of the empire – the imperial capital at Byzantium/Constantinople – is to experience this contrast between centralized wealth and power and provincial impoverishment. Byzantium was originally a Greek city. It was re-founded by the Emperor Constantine the Great in 330 CE as the capital of the Eastern Roman Empire. It became independent of Rome when the empire divided in 395 CE and then the principal repository of *Romanitas* when the Western Empire collapsed in 476 CE. The city expanded in late antiquity and was filled with great monuments – a huge imperial palace overlooking the Bosporus; a hippodrome for

a monumental arch, several Late Roman churches and impressive tomb monuments beyond the former city limits. But for sheer monumentality what impresses the visitor above all are the 10m (33ft) high walls of the Byzantine fortress, the masonry circuit extending 200m (656ft) by 100m (328ft), with heavy reinforcement from projecting towers at the corners and along the sides.

The fortress was built after the Byzantine reconquest of North Africa in 533–534 CE. The Emperor Justinian (527–565 CE) planned to reconquer the whole of the fallen Western Roman Empire. The defeat of the Vandal rulers of North

ABOVE: The Hagia Sophia was perhaps the greatest architectural achievement of the Byzantine Empire and its dome still stands today.

chariot races with seating for 100,000; a patriarchal cathedral which was the largest in the world; a vast underground cistern, its roof supported by a forest of 336 marble columns; a plethora of other churches glittering with wall mosaics; and much more.

Hagia Sophia – the patriarchal cathedral – was a masterpiece of engineering, design and decoration. In the Eastern Christian tradition, it has the form of a Greek cross (in contrast to the Western tradition of a Latin basilica), with a central dome 32m (105ft) in diameter and 56m (184ft) high from floor to crown, resting on a substructure of giant piers and arches.

Though much changed today – the Christian church was converted into an Islamic mosque after the fall of Constantinople to the Turks in 1453 – the whole of the interior was originally decorated with polychrome wall mosaics. Thin tesserae of coloured stone for the figures were combined with tesserae of gold leaf and glass for the backgrounds, the shimmering effect (one has to imagine them illuminated by sunlight and candlelight) giving artistic expression to the Christian

conception of a world suffused with an unseen divine presence.

Byzantium was also a fortress. Located on a peninsula, it was girt with sea walls facing the Sea of Marmara (to the south), the Bosporus (to the east) and the Golden Horn (to the north). But far more spectacular were the land walls, the Walls of Theodosius, the most formidable defensive walls in the world when they were built in the first half of the 5th century CE. Running 6.5km (4 miles) from north to south, they comprised a 20m (66ft) wide by 7m (23ft) deep moat that could be flooded with water, a low wall on the inner side of the ditch to prevent easy egress, an outer wall complete with battlemented walkway and tall projecting towers and then the main defence, the inner wall, 5m (16ft) thick, 12m (39ft) high, with 96 massive projecting towers. The 60m (197ft) distance between the ditch and the inner wall combined with a 30m (98ft) height difference made it exceptionally difficult for attackers to bring effective fire to bear on the main defence, whereas tiered platforms and multiple projecting bastions gave the defenders every opportunity to bring fire down on their enemies – using composite bows, crossbows and catapults.

Almost 2,000 miles from Byzantium, on the most distant fringe of early medieval civilization, lies the legendary site of Tintagel, perched on Cornwall's rugged north coast. Excavations by the Cornwall Archaeological Unit in 2017 turned up fresh evidence for the long reach of Byzantium. The early Cornish kings, it seems, feasted on oysters, roast pork and fine wine, eating and drinking from bowls imported from Byzantium and glass goblets from Spain. Finds included fragments of a fine red-slip ware bowl from Anatolia and amphorae (for transporting wine) from Anatolia or Cyprus.

These discoveries are not exceptional. A number of early medieval sites in western Britain

BELOW: The Walls of Theodosius were almost impenetrable and protected the city of Constantinople from invasion for nearly a millennium before it finally fell to the Ottoman Turks in 1453.

have yielded handfuls of Byzantine sherds that testify to some sort of gift exchange or long-distance trade associating British rulers with the wealth and prestige of the Byzantine Empire. This influence, as we shall see, was destined to endure, acting as a reinforcement for embattled Western Christianity in the face of successive onslaughts by pagan barbarians.

The Germanic World

The village of Feddersen Wierde was founded in the 1st century BCE in the coastal marshes of the Weser estuary in Lower Saxony in Germany. At its peak in the 3rd century CE, it contained more than two dozen longhouses, located on a raised 4m (13ft)-high mound (known as a *terp*) to protect them from flooding and laid out radially like the spokes of a wheel around a central open space. Timber-framed, with wattle-and-daub wall panels and roofs of reeds, the largest were 25m (82ft) long and 5m (16ft) wide. Thanks to waterlogging preserving the lower parts of structural timbers and wall panels, we know that each longhouse was internally subdivided; and thanks to careful recovery and recording of finds from the interiors, we know that one end was used as a cattle byre, the middle section as a working area and the opposite end as living-space, complete with centrally placed hearth. In addition, each longhouse had its own small square granary nearby, with raised floor to protect stored grain from damp and vermin. The population of Feddersen Wierde is estimated to have been about 300 people – a dozen or so per longhouse, so living in extended-family groups. They raised mainly cattle, but sheep/goat, pig, horse and dog remains were also found in the animal-bone assemblages and barley, oats, beans and flax are present among the plant remains. The inhabitants also engaged in craft activity. A workshop area yielded evidence for work in wood, leather, iron and bronze; notable finds were unfinished wood bowls and parts of wheels. One has the impression of a self-sufficient community supplying virtually all its own needs.

One notable longhouse lacked the usual internal partitioning but was divided into three aisles by timber uprights and the assumption is that this was used for meetings and feasts, perhaps under the

ABOVE: This model of Feddersen Wierde shows its characteristic longhouses and the wattle-and-daub architecture that was a common feature of the era.

auspices of a local lord. It was in this area that a litter of Roman imports – coins, bronzes, pottery – was found; these are likely to have been prestige goods and marks of status.

Up to 300ha (740 acres) of the surrounding land may have been used for cultivation and pasture. But in the middle of the 5th century CE, coastal flooding made this land too wet and salty and the village of Feddersen Wierde, no longer economically viable, was abandoned. Where did the people go?

Whole peoples were on the move in the 5th century CE. Welded into powerful tribal confederations, they swarmed across the Rhine and the Danube, wave upon wave, overwhelming the defences of the Western Roman Empire. Their names are preserved in the Late Roman sources: Alamanni, Burgundians, Franks, Ostrogoths, Saxons, Suevi, Vandals, Visigoths and others. They spoke variants of German and had other cultural affinities like shared gods and myths and similar kinship systems, settlement patterns and ways of war. Forced to move by military pressure in Eastern and Central Europe – above all from the Huns – they burst into the Western Roman Empire and then fanned out across the hinterland, eventually coming to rest in North Africa, Spain, France and Italy, where they formed new hybrid states that were part-Roman, part-Germanic; states that would, in many cases, evolve into the states of medieval Europe.

The famous Sutton Hoo boat burial from Suffolk in England, dating from the early 7th century CE, is

RIGHT: The Sutton Hoo helmet.

perhaps the most spectacular illustration of that process of Romano-German cultural hybridization. Anglo-Saxon settlers had established themselves in eastern England during the 5th and 6th centuries CE and by the early 7th century large territories were being melded together to form kingdoms. Sutton Hoo, with its 18 mounds, was the burial place of early English royalty. The greatest of these, Mound 1, was found to have contained a complete Anglo-Saxon ship, 27m (89ft) long and 4.4m (14ft) wide, in the base of which, resting at the centre of the keel, was a burial chamber packed with rich grave-goods. Many of these – the great buckle, the purse lid, the shoulder clasps, the drinking horns – were decorated with Germanic designs of geometric interlace and stylized animal heads, executed in gold, garnets and millefiori glass. Others were Late Roman or Byzantine – the famous helmet was similar to those worn by the Late Roman Army; the Coptic bowl was an import from the Eastern Mediterranean; the 37 gold coins from Frankish mints on the Continent were modelled on Roman prototypes.

RIGHT: A shoulder clasp, purse lid and belt buckle from the Sutton Hoo hoard.

The new rulers of the Western world acknowledged their Germanic roots, but when it came to establishing themselves as kings, they chose to dress up as Romans as the most effective way to substantiate their claims to power. So it would continue for the next millennium and a half.

Carolingian Europe

You can still see Charlemagne's palatine chapel in all is architectural grandeur if you visit Aachen Cathedral in Germany today, for it was incorporated wholesale into the later Gothic church. It comprises a 16-sided polygon measuring 30m (98ft) across, divided into an outer ambulatory and an inner chamber by eight piers supporting round arches. Above runs a gallery, its tall, pillared arches aligned with those beneath and these support a clerestory with a window above each arch and a central dome. Multi-coloured marble veneers give the interior a sumptuous appearance. The dome was originally decorated with frescoes. Charlemagne's throne, on a stepped dais, is still there on the floor of the upper gallery.

The ground plan of the palace of which the chapel was part has been recovered in large part through excavation. It included: an apsed assembly hall in the form of a Roman basilica, with attached porch, treasury and archive; a long connecting gallery with a tribunal midway along it; an atrium, council chamber and secretariat ranged around the chapel; and a large detached bathhouse.

BELOW: The Palatine chapel at Aachen dates back to the reign of Charlemagne. Its aesthetics followed Roman, rather than Germanic, architectural trends.

The chapel was built between 792 and 805 CE, with work on the associated palace continuing for another ten years or more. The whole complex was designed to substantiate Charlemagne's claim to imperial power. The architecture was thoroughly Roman in style, with no trace of the Germanic traditions of the Franks; it was not a cultural blend, but a wholesale adoption of the architectural and artistic tradition of Late Antique Christian Rome. It was an early expression of the style we have come to call 'Romanesque'.

This was quite in keeping with Charlemagne's political ambition. He consciously saw himself as a latter-day emperor, styling himself 'Holy Roman Emperor' and having himself crowned by the Pope at St Peter's in Rome on Christmas Day 800 CE. This was no mere posturing. By the time of his death in 814 CE, his empire extended across the whole of modern-day France, the Low Countries, western Germany, Austria, Croatia and northern Italy; in addition, he had subjugated the Slavic tribes on his eastern border and turned them into tributaries. Charlemagne, in short, the King of the Franks, had made himself master of half of Europe. No wonder he assumed the trappings of a Roman emperor.

The Carolingian Empire became a powerful continuator and transmitter of Roman culture. This included not only architecture and art, but also language, learning, technology and religion. The primary mechanism was the Western Christian Church. Latin became a lingua franca. Monasteries copied ancient manuscripts and filled libraries with Greek and Roman texts. Roman surveying, engineering and industrial technologies were revived. And, of course, the Catholic Church, centred in Rome, became a defining institution of medieval Christendom.

More fragile, however, was Roman-style political centralization. The Carolingian Empire did not long survive Charlemagne's death. Civil war saw it divided into three separate kingdoms by the late 9th century, while new enemies – the Magyars of Hungary, the Arabs (or Saracens) in the Mediterranean and the Vikings on the northern seas – threatened the frontiers. This was to be a recurring pattern in European history: successive hegemons – Charlemagne, Charles V, Philip II, Louis XVI, Napoleon, the Kaiser, Adolf Hitler – would be struck down and the continent would revert to a mosaic of smaller rival states.

Islamic Civilization

A similar fragmentation afflicted the Islamic Empire created by the Arab conquests of the 7th century CE. Similar, too, was the way in which the Arabs appropriated the residual Roman traditions of the vast territories they so quickly overran – in what was one of the most rapid and extensive campaigns of conquest in human history. They took Syria in 636 CE, Iraq in 637 CE, Egypt in 642 CE. They reached Kabul in Afghanistan in 664 CE and the Pyrenees on the borders of the Frankish Empire by 711 CE. At this point, the Islamic Caliphate, with its capital in Damascus, stretched 8,500km (5,300 miles) from the Atlantic Ocean to the Indus Valley; it was far bigger than any of the great empires of antiquity.

When the Arabs emerged from the Arabian Desert in the 630s CE, they were a mix of camel nomads, oasis farmers and small-town merchants and artisans. They carried with them, in addition to a distinctive and highly effective way of war, little more in the way of cultural baggage than their ancient semitic language and their newly minted religion. Everything else – science and medicine, irrigation and the plough, art and architecture, the learning of the ancients – they would assimilate from the more advanced civilizations they conquered; but they would then raise these cultural achievements to a new level, far exceeding that of relatively barbarous medieval Europe.

The unitary caliphate survived for little more than a century. By the late 8th century CE, it was fragmenting into smaller polities. Vast distances and primitive communications made it impossible for caliphs in Baghdad (which succeeded Damascus as the Arab-Islamic capital) to maintain control over their territory; local emirs established independent dynasties – Umayyads in Spain, Idrisids in Morocco, Aghlabids in Tunisia, Fatimids in Egypt, Saffarids in Persia and many more. But these Arab-Islamic dynasties were civilization-builders.

Let us consider the example of Damascus. The ancient city fell to the Arabs in 636 CE and it remained the Arab capital during a century of rule by the Umayyad dynasty of caliphs (661–750 CE). The old city of Damascus dates from as far back as the 2nd millennium BCE. It was successively an Aramaic, Assyrian, Babylonian, Persian, Greek, Roman and Byzantine city before the arrival of the Arabs. The invaders adapted the existing buildings and layout to their own needs. Early Arab-Islamic cities typically featured a citadel with a garrison of soldiers, a palace for the local emir, a great mosque with attached madrasas (schools) and other associated buildings and a grand market or medina. This was exactly the pattern at Damascus. The citadel was built on the site of the former Roman-Byzantine fort in the north-west corner of the city. The Byzantine cathedral – built on the site of a Roman temple to Jupiter – was converted into a great mosque. The main Roman east–west street – a wide, colonnaded *decumanus maximus* – was

converted into a long, covered medina of traditional eastern type. Most of the regular Roman street plan was lost, however, buried beneath a warren of houses, courtyards and winding alleyways, again of traditional eastern type. The new Umayyad buildings used huge quantities of *spolia* – masonry and architectural fragments taken from ruinous or demolished Roman or Byzantine buildings. This, like the conversion of Roman and Byzantine buildings to new purposes, was not just a convenience: it was an appropriation of *Romanitas*, an assertion that the new Arab-Islamic rulers were, by right of conquest and faith, the successors of the pagan and infidel rulers of the past and the inheritors of an ancient urban civilization.

A quite different picture confronts us when we visit Kairouan in Tunisia. When the all-conquering Arab army camped at this barren, dusty, desert-edge spot during its long westward advance, its leader received mystical inspiration to found a city. So Kairouan was a wholly new Islamic city built on virgin ground. It became the capital of the Aghlabid dynasty (800–

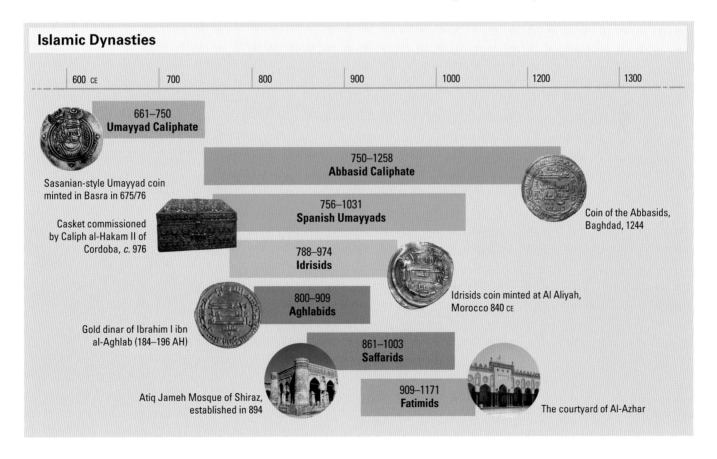

Islamic Dynasties

| 600 CE | 700 | 800 | 900 | 1000 | 1200 | 1300 |

661–750 Umayyad Caliphate

Sasanian-style Umayyad coin minted in Basra in 675/76

Casket commissioned by Caliph al-Hakam II of Cordoba, c. 976

750–1258 Abbasid Caliphate

756–1031 Spanish Umayyads

Coin of the Abbasids, Baghdad, 1244

788–974 Idrisids

Idrisids coin minted at Al Aliyah, Morocco 840 CE

800–909 Aghlabids

Gold dinar of Ibrahim I ibn al-Aghlab (184–196 AH)

861–1003 Saffarids

Atiq Jameh Mosque of Shiraz, established in 894

909–1171 Fatimids

The courtyard of Al-Azhar

LEFT: A gold coin from the reign of the Abbasid Caliph al-Mahdi, 780 CE.

909 CE) when they made themselves independent of Baghdad and they turned it into one of the great cities of early Islam. Its greatest monument was and is the Great Mosque. The slightly trapezoidal courtyard measures 67m (220ft) by 52m (170ft) and is surrounded on all four sides by an arcade of horseshoe arches resting on slender classical columns. The courtyard slopes towards the middle, where a central drain soaks precious rainwater into an underground cistern. The minaret, formed of three tapering square

BELOW: A mosaic from the Umayyad Mosque at Damascus. The mosque was converted from the Byzantine cathedral on the same site.

towers capped by a small dome, measures 11m (36ft) on each side at the base and is almost 32m (105ft) tall; it is the oldest surviving minaret in the world. The prayer hall on the opposite side of the courtyard is a vast interior space almost 71m (233ft) wide by 38m (125ft) deep, the roof supported on a forest of 414

ABOVE: The courtyard and minaret of the Great Mosque of Kairouan. The mosque was first established in 670 CE, but owes its present form to the efforts of the Aghlabid emirs.

classical columns. The *mihrab* (the wall niche indicating the direction of Mecca) is decorated with faience tiles imported from Baghdad. The wooden *minbar* (from which the imam preached) was also ornamented with carvings. Elsewhere, too, marble veneers and wood panels are adorned with Early Islamic motifs – geometric patterns, highly stylized plant forms and Kufic inscriptions with quotations from the Koran.

The columns around the courtyard and in the prayer hall are of marble, porphyry and granite. They are of uneven height, so the bases on which they sit vary in size. They sport a wide variety of capitals – Ionic, Corinthian, Composite – and these are often ill-fitting. The *spolia* used to build the mosque has been closely studied and the conclusion drawn that several distant classical sites across Tunisia were quarried for their fallen masonry. Here again were Arab-Islamic rulers appropriating classical culture – for both functional and symbolic purposes. And just as Roman emperors built infrastructure to supply the cities of the empire with water, so the Aghlabid rulers of 9th century Tunisia built a 36km (22 miles) long aqueduct and a series of pools on the edge of town to supply Kairouan with water, the largest of them 128m (420ft) wide; this urban waterworks included secondary pools and a filtering system designed to remove accumulated sediment. All very Roman.

But the Arabs, for all the enthusiasm with which they embraced and augmented the great achievements of civilization past, were also ruthless warriors. They eventually established themselves across the whole of the southern Mediterranean, even taking the islands of Crete, Sicily, Sardinia and the Balearic Islands and these became pirate bases from which they launched large-scale raids on the coasts of Christian states to the north, seeking portable booty, especially from churches and monasteries and captives who could be sold as slaves.

LEFT: The prayer hall of the Great Mosque is filled with classical columns.

BELOW: The Aghlabad basins in Kairouan could store 68,800m³ (2.4 million ft³) of water.

The Vikings

If the Saracens were the sea-raiders of the south, the Vikings were the sea-raiders of the north. Let us travel to Torksey in Lincolnshire, England, where, thanks to exhaustive fieldwork stretching over three decades, we get an intimate insight into the Viking threat.

'In this year [872 CE],' records the *Anglo-Saxon Chronicle*, 'the army went into Northumbria and it took up winter quarters at Torksey in Lindsey; and then the Mercians made peace with the army.' The assumption had been that the site in question must have lain under or close to the present-day village of Torksey. This began to change when Dave and Pete Stanley happened to be driving past a field a mile or so north of the village where a local farmer was at work on his tractor. They stopped, spoke to the farmer and were granted permission to run their metal-detectors over the freshly ploughed ground. Over the course of several hours they found almost nothing and, with dusk falling, they were set to pack up and go home. Then Pete got a signal and unearthed a bronze coin of Anglo-Saxon date. Over the next 25 years, Dave and Pete returned to the field again and again and recovered an astonishing range of Anglo-Saxon and Viking artefacts.

Dave and Pete reported their growing body of finds to the local museum. The curators brought in specialist academic advice from outside, including coin expert Mark Blackburn and Viking experts Dawn Hadley and Julian Richards. There could hardly be any doubt: the two metal-detectorists had surely located the site of the Viking Great Army's winter encampment.

Systematic coring at Torksey, a prominent bluff standing 5–10m (16–33ft) high, has revealed that it was effectively an island in 872 CE, the River Trent flowing close-by on the west and with wet, marshy ground on all sides. The name gives it away: Torksey means Turc's or Turoc's Island. This made it ideal for a ship-based army that needed a secure base through the winter months. Notable too was its location barely a mile south of a major road-crossing over the river. And it was big. At 55ha (136 acres), it was comparable

RIGHT: Iron ploughshares recovered from the tool hoard at Torksey.

LEFT: A gold Viking ring found at Torksey. Thousands of valuable Viking artefacts were found at the site, indicating that it was one of the encampments of the Great Viking Army.

in extent with the largest known Roman legionary fortresses – on which basis, plausible estimates for the size of the Great Viking Army range from 1,500 to 5,000 men.

Torksey has become what archaeologists call a 'type-site' – one that provides the most comprehensive picture and by which others, less well-defined, may be assessed. Geophysical survey and sample excavations have yielded nothing – no buildings, ditches or pits. But this absence of evidence is itself a form of evidence: an indirect confirmation, surely, that this was a temporary tent-city. On the other hand, the site has produced an enormous collection of Viking artefacts, with more than 1,500 now recorded, including 400 coins (of central significance because they can often be dated to a particular year), along with dress accessories, weights, gaming pieces and hack-metal (items of silver or gold cut into smaller pieces). This gives us a distinctive archaeological 'signature': an assemblage of objects that indicate a Great Army encampment – as opposed to, say, a contemporary Anglo-Saxon village or a later, more permanent Viking settlement.

The earliest Viking raids on England dated back to the late 8th century CE. The army that landed in East Anglia in 865 CE was larger than any seen before. Arriving in 100 longships, it must have comprised several thousand Viking warriors, most of them veterans of many seaborne raids. The attacks had been escalating for the best part of a century, with

sudden descents on the Low Countries, northern France, eastern England and Ireland, hitting coastal communities but also often penetrating deep into the hinterland down estuaries and navigable rivers. The raiders came for silver and slaves and they targeted monasteries especially, for these were known to be rich.

Scandinavia – today's Norway, Sweden and Denmark – was the Viking homeland. But, like pirate crews throughout the ages, they picked up adventurers from elsewhere, so the Norse were probably mixed with Irish, Scots, Frisians, Saxons and others on the rowing benches of the longships. Theirs was a 'heroic' society, where warrior retinues formed around great lords, each a leader, a patron, a 'ring-giver' to his followers. A typical retinue must have been around 30-strong, the capacity of a longship, the men serving as both rowers and fighters. Social power was mediated by flows of prestige goods, accessed by trade or by raid; the greater the booty, the greater the retinue, the greater the lord. So loot was the fuel of a predatory social order in which Viking competed with Viking to build longships and recruit followers.

By the mid 9th century, Viking armies sometimes overwintered where they raided. Their armies were larger now, better equipped, less dependent on hit-and-run, strong enough to defend themselves against local forces even without the benefit of surprise. But what happened in the winter of 865/6 CE was altogether different. Not only was the army unprecedented in size, but this time, though it may not have been clear to anyone at first, including the Vikings themselves, it was destined to stay for good.

During the 9th, 10th and 11th centuries, the Vikings settled in coastal regions and along navigable rivers across a huge swathe of the far north. We find their distinctive archaeological imprint all the way from Greenland and Iceland to the very heart of European Russia. We see them lining the edge of the Baltic, the North Sea and the Atlantic. When they settled, of course, they became farmers and traders, so we may speak of Viking villages and Viking towns. York in northern England is a notable example. Large-scale excavations in the old city over many years, often in waterlogged deposits with exceptional preservation of wood, leather and textiles, have allowed local archaeologists to identify a well-defined 'Anglo-Scandinavian' culture in the 10th and 11th centuries. Following a second wave of incursions, the Vikings even established a short-lived dynasty of kings on the English throne. And across the Channel, in

Normandy, a Viking-ruled duchy would become the base from which another invasion would be launched, in 1066, that would mark one of the great turning-points in the history of the British Isles.

BELOW: The Vale of York Hoard, which dates back to the 10th century, was discovered by metal detectorists in 2007. It consisted of hundreds of silver coins as well as several other Viking artefacts.

Maya and Moche

While Europe struggled to establish new structures in the wake of the fall of the Roman Empire, civilization flourished in the Americas. During this period, the great Maya sites of Mexico's Yucatan peninsula and neighbouring Guatemala, Honduras and Belize were established. These include Tikal, which, at its peak between 200 and 900 CE, had an estimated population of around 50,000. The city was built around a vast ceremonial complex, in this case dominated by five temple pyramids up to 70m (230ft) tall covering the burial places of Maya rulers and linked by giant causeways. Surveys have revealed that the city extended for some 16km² (6 square miles). No less than 3,000 separate structures have been identified.

Mesoamerican specialists distinguish between the Preclassical (*c.* 750 BCE–250 CE), the Classical (*c.* 250–950 CE) and the Post-Classical (*c.* 950–1550 CE) Periods in the exceptionally long-lived Maya civilization. As well as urbanism and monumental architecture, three other notable achievements of the Maya peaked in the Classical Period: art, writing and measurement. Art included relief carving in stone and wood, modelling in stucco, wall painting and ceramic decoration. It is characterized by human figures and heads along with animal totems and vegetal motifs rendered in a distinctive blocky manner, sometimes highly stylized, yet often arranged in scenes that are active, dynamic and visceral. Gods, kings and ceremonials are staple subjects. Many Maya artworks are inscribed with hieroglyphics, using a system of about a thousand glyphs. As well as appearing on sculpture, paintings and pottery, the Mayan script was used to create illustrated books, works of art in themselves, written on bark or leather and sewn together. The symmetrical layout of settlements and the design of temples can leave no doubt about the proficiency of Maya surveyors and architects and we have unequivocal evidence for a numerical system based on units of 20 (including a zero concept) along with astronomical observation and calendrical calculation.

In the same period, a new Moche civilization (1st century CE–750 CE) developed on the Peruvian coast.

LEFT: Mayan hieroglyphics, as seen in the Dresden Codex.

FOLLOWING PAGES: The temple pyramids formed a great ceremonial complex at the centre of the Maya city of Tikal.

By military conquest, they eventually took over much of the highlands. The Moche drew part of their wealth from the sea, but they also built irrigation canals to water the forbidding deserts of northern Peru and turn it into rich agricultural land. Each valley had its ceremonial centre dominated by an enormous temple of mudbrick. The largest, the Pyramid of the Sun, 340m (1,115ft) by 160m (525ft) at the base, 50m (164ft) high, was constructed of an estimated 130 million adobe bricks; though much eroded, it still stands 40m (131ft) tall.

The discovery in 1987 of a series of spectacularly rich tombs at the site of a small pyramid at Sipán has added a new dimension to our understanding of the Moche. The richest of these, that of the Lord of Sipán, is without parallel in American archaeology. The first tomb was found by looters, but was so full of golden artefacts that the robbers fell out over the spoils and one of them informed on the others to the police. The site was sealed off and placed under armed guard. Archaeologists then discovered that the tomb disturbed by the looters was a secondary burial. Inside the pyramid was an intact Moche tomb containing the body of a 40-year-old man who had been laid to rest in a large wooden coffin dressed in the most sumptuous regalia – headdresses, pectorals, jewellery and clothing, most of them made or ornamented with gold, silver, copper and semi-precious stones. The regalia featured symbolic representations of the male sun-god and the female moon-goddess. Six others had been buried with the Lord of Sipán: three young women (wives or concubines?), two males (warriors?) and a child of about ten. The males had amputated feet, perhaps to prevent them deserting their duty as guardians of the tomb. One of them also had a dog. Was he responsible for looking after his lord's favourite pet?

LEFT AND BELOW: Burials from the Lord of Sipán site. The interred were surrounded by elaborate grave goods.

Chapter 8
The Medieval World

Traditionally, archaeologists have focused on elites and either ignored medieval remains entirely or explored only high-status sites. Why research a peasant village when you could study the Hundred Years War or excavate a Cistercian monastery? Yet medieval sites have provided a wealth of data on the lives of ordinary people across the world and the more substantial architecture that has survived – from castles to temples to palaces – shed light on the powers that produced them.

Dingling, the Ming Dynasty tomb of the Emperor Wanli.

European Feudalism: Villages

When historian Maurice Beresford identified the deserted medieval village at Wharram Percy in Yorkshire as a focus of research, in 1948, he was charting a new direction for medieval studies, due to its focus on the lives of ordinary people. But Beresford lacked the skills to excavate properly, so he teamed up with archaeologist John Hurst in 1950. For the next 40 years, Beresford and Hurst led annual summer excavations at the site, slowly building up a complete picture of the layout of the village through centuries of occupation, accumulating an astonishing assemblage of 110,000 artefacts and eventually publishing no less than 13 learned tomes on their findings.

It is hardly an exaggeration to say that the Wharram Percy excavations launched a whole new sub-discipline: the archaeological investigation of the medieval countryside. This was paralleled by a major turn in historical studies from elites to the common people, sometimes called 'history from below'. In fact, the multidisciplinary approach – archaeological fieldwork combined with archival research – has remained very much a feature of medieval village/landscape studies.

The remains of the medieval village at Wharram Percy were evident from the outset in the 'humps and bumps' visible across the site. These were systematically surveyed and then targeted excavation built a detailed picture of what they represented. The

medieval village was laid out on either side of a central north–south road. Ranged along it were almost 40 separate rectangular plots stretching back from the road, most divided into a 'toft' at the front, where there was a house and yard and a 'croft' behind, for use as pasture orchard, cottage garden or whatever. The plots ranged in length from about 50m (164ft) to almost 200m (656ft) and were typically about 10m (33ft) wide. At the south-eastern edge of the village was a stone church (the ruin is still standing), a parsonage, a mill and a millpond. At the opposite north-western edge was the main manorial complex. Beyond lay the open fields, divided into strips, which the villagers worked communally, pooling their resources to provide ploughs and plough-teams (with up to eight oxen per plough).

Traditionally, open fields were worked in rotation, periods of fallow alternating with periods of cultivation, providing time for the fertility of the soil to renew itself, a process assisted by allowing animals to graze and drop manure and by spreading backyard midden waste. These open fields were designed to be ploughed in common. Plough-teams were cumbersome and awkward, with wide turning-circles. Land divided by ditches, banks and hedgerows would have been a great inconvenience. So open fields were ideal and these were divided into strips, with each peasant household allocated a number of strips distributed across the village land. Where the contours have not been erased by modern ploughing, it is often possible to identify the distinctive 'ridge and furrow' of medieval fields – a consequence of the fact that the plough threw the sod first one way, then the other, as it moved up and down the field in opposite directions, creating a hump in the middle with a trough either side.

Sometimes a further distinction can be made between 'infield' and 'outfield', the former closer to the village and more intensively worked, a difference often indicated archaeologically by the density of potsherds, animal bones and shells in the soil.

LEFT: An illustration of the medieval village of Wharram Percy. Through systematic surveys and excavations, archaeologists have been able to reconstruct the life of everyday peasants in this era.

RIGHT: The remains of the church at Wharram Percy.

These artefacts represent midden spreads. Finding them involves systematic fieldwalking across modern ploughland to collect and plot both 'artefacts' (like potsherds) and 'ecofacts' (like animal bones): a key archaeological method in the investigation of medieval landscapes.

Other resources were also important. Many villages were close to rivers and wetlands and most would have had their own pasture and woodland resources, perhaps beyond the limits of the cultivated fields.

Though Wharram Percy was our starting point, we are now making broad generalizations based on the huge number of investigations that have taken place since 1948. But in fact, the broad generalizations are often being challenged, as medievalists, both historians and archaeologists, put more stress on regional variations and the way in which villages and field systems are shaped by diverse ecological and social circumstances. There was, it seems, no 'one size fits all'.

We know from historical sources that the lord of the manor and the priest would have been supported by the labour services and feudal dues paid by the 200 or so villagers of Wharram Percy. (Though we also know that villagers had rights as well as obligations, that these were protected by law and that disputes between lords and peasants were very much a feature of medieval rural life.) We also know that the village was in the possession of the Percies, one of the great baronial families established in the north of England after the Norman Conquest; presumably they maintained a manor house mainly for the use of the bailiff they employed to run this part of their estate, though they presumably made occasional visits. The village and its fields probably constituted a fief – the land granted to a knight in return for military service. The knight and his fief occupied the lowest rung on a feudal hierarchy that extended all the way up to the king. Archaeologically speaking, the higher rungs are represented by two classes of monument: castles and monasteries.

BELOW: A medieval bone and antler comb found at Wharram Percy.

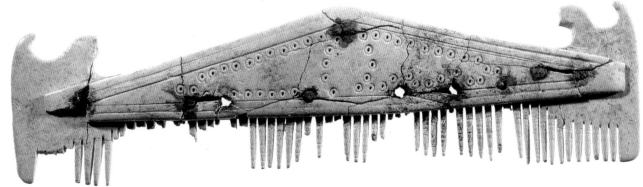

Monasteries

One of the most extraordinary documents to have survived from the early medieval period is a copy dating to around 820 or 830 CE of a complete plan for a monastic complex at St Gall in Switzerland. It depicts the layout of an ideal Benedictine monastery designed to accommodate some 270 people, 110 of them monks, in a life of work, study and prayer. The range of buildings reveals a complete self-contained community. In addition to a great abbey church and its cloister, we have a library and a *scriptorium* (where manuscripts were copied); a monks' dormitory, warming room, refectory, laundry and bathhouse; kitchens, bakehouses and breweries; larders and cellars; a granary and a mill; a large workshop and a house for coopers and wheelwrights; accommodation for sheep and shepherds, goats and goatherds, cows and cowherds, swine and swineherds, and also for hens, geese and their keepers; stabling for brood mares and their foals; a hospice for paupers and pilgrims; lodgings for visitors, graded by social rank; an infirmary with dedicated kitchen and bathhouse; an orchard, vegetable garden and herb garden.

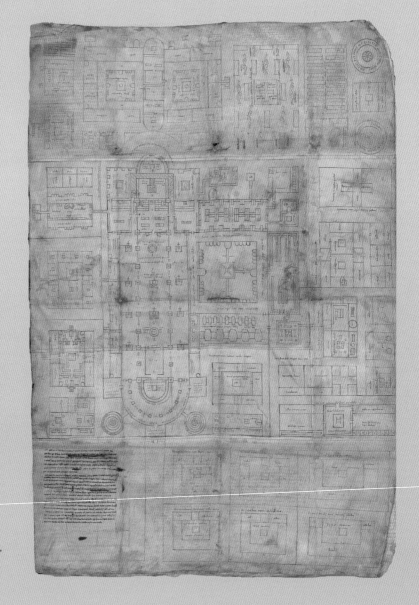

Not the least extraordinary thing about the plan is that it depicts a complex that was never actually built: it expresses an intention and an idealization; it becomes for us a kind of 'virtual' archaeology – the equivalent of an excavation plan, but instantly accessible without all the effort!

When we turn to hard archaeology, we discover a super-abundance of medieval monastic sites. Many survive, never complete but often in part and in particular we are blessed with large numbers of great monastic abbeys and very often with their attached cloisters. Often, too, we have monumental standing ruins, sometimes with the layout of the monastic complex as a whole successfully traced out on the ground, thanks to archive research, field survey and sample excavation. These can be among the most evocative archaeological remains in the modern landscape, perhaps especially Cistercian foundations, an order which favoured remote rural locations.

RIGHT: The Plan of St Gall monastery from the *Codex Sangallensis*, dating to *c.* 820 CE.

ABOVE AND RIGHT: The cloisters of Fontenay
Abbey in France is one of the oldest Cistercian
monasteries in Europe.

Fontenay Abbey in the Côte d'Or in France is an especially fine example. It was founded by St Bernard of Clairvaux in the early 12th century in a remote location but close to a water source. It was constructed in the Romanesque style, but with due attention to the architectural and artistic austerity required of a religious order that was in revolt against the laxity and luxury of the long-established Benedictines. The stark simplicity and functionality of church, cloister, dormitory and refectory were all in keeping with St Bernard's strictures about a life of work, piety and self-sufficiency. But there was monumental grandeur nonetheless. The nave was 66m (217ft) long and 8m (26ft) wide, the transept 19m (62ft) wide, the cloister 36m (118ft) by 38m (125ft). On the other hand, there was no decoration of any kind, for the Cistercians abjured such frivolity, insisting that men in holy orders should not be distracted from prayer, scripture and communion with God. It is possible, then, to interpret the archaeological remains in the light of the monastic rule.

What a contrast with another 12th century foundation: Monreale in Sicily. This was a Benedictine house founded by the Norman king William II. The original church and cloister still stand. Both are a riot of the most elaborate Romanesque, Byzantine and Islamic art it is possible to imagine – a reflection of the extraordinarily cosmopolitan culture of Sicily at the time. The exterior walls are decorated with Islamic-style intersecting arches and rosettes executed in different coloured stonework. The interior is a blaze of gold, like entering a dragon's cave, for it is covered with Byzantine-style wall mosaics, depicting, in sequence, biblical stories, both Old Testament and New and culminating in a vast image of Christ Pantocrater ('the ruler of the world'), who fills the half-dome of the apse at the eastern end, with the heavenly hierarchy ranged in tiers beneath him. The cloister, on the other hand, provides one of the finest displays of Romanesque sculpture to be seen

BELOW: The famous mosaic of Doubting Thomas found inside Monreale.

anywhere, for the capitals of the pairs of columns supporting the delicate horseshoe arches around the ornamental garden are decorated with scenes from the bible, of fighting knights and of mythic monsters. One notable capital shows King William offering a model of the cathedral to the Madonna and Child. Here, then, is another aspect of medieval monasticism: Monreale was a vastly expensive prestige monument designed to symbolize the relationship between secular and divine power in Norman-ruled Sicily.

RIGHT AND BELOW: The Cathedral of Monreale in Sicily and its elaborate interior reflected the prestige and wealth of the rulers who spent lavishly on it.

European Feudalism: Castles

The earliest medieval castles in England were of the 'motte-and-bailey' type. They were thrown up quickly as new Norman lords established themselves on the land they had conquered in 1066. They were designed to overawe the English peasantry and discourage revolt. Vivid depictions of such castles can be seen on the Bayeux Tapestry. A notable archaeological example is Hen Domen in Powys in Wales, for it became the focus of a major research project between the 1960s and 1990s and it remains the most thoroughly excavated timber castle in the British Isles.

A motte-and-bailey castle comprised an earth mound surmounted by a timber keep or inner fortification (the motte), with an attached enclosure containing ancillary buildings surrounded by rampart, ditch and timber palisade (the bailey). The motte at Hen Domen is 8m (26ft) high, very steep-sided and

BELOW: The imposing exterior of Kerak castle in Jordan reflected the insecurity felt by the Crusader states.

the platform at the top is 7m (23ft) across. The bailey below is a rough oval measuring 50m (164ft) by 40m (131ft). The site was surrounded by a double rampart and a 2.7m (9ft)-deep ditch.

The excavations delivered two big surprises: one was just how cluttered with buildings the whole of the interior had been; the other was the rapidity with which old buildings had been knocked down and new ones erected. In the area investigated – about half the extent of the bailey – the excavators found evidence for some 50 major and 20 minor timber buildings constructed at various times over a period of about two centuries. The impression was of bustle and dynamism. Many of these buildings were recognized only in the form of arrangements of postholes, spreads of cobbles and faint impressions where timber beams had once lain. Recovering such ephemeral evidence depended upon meticulous trowelling and recording – a pace of work only possible in research excavations, rarely if ever in the context of development-driven commercial or 'rescue' excavations.

LEFT: The fortress at Kerak offered a commanding view of the surrounding landscape and hoped to give the Crusaders an advantage to compensate for their lack of numbers.

Many motte-and-bailey castles were never rebuilt in stone. Some of those that were turned into huge defensive monuments and, of course, many new stone castles were built later in the Middle Ages. Let us shift our gaze from the Anglo-Welsh border in the 11th century to the Crusader states in the Levant in the 12th century. Here we bear witness to something radically different in both scale and sophistication. Take the example of Kerak in modern Jordan.

The castle sits on a rocky spur with steep cliffs on three sides, reinforced in places by massive *glacis* – sloping walls designed to keep enemy siege engines at a distance, their surfaces ice-smooth to prevent attackers gaining any foothold. Towering above the cliffs and the *glacis* are the main curtain walls, which surround the upper bailey, forming a rough A-shape on the plateau at the top of cliffs, the whole circuit measuring half a kilometre in total. In front of the massive north wall, which fronts the town and affords the only easy approach to the castle is a rock-cut *fosse* or dry moat 30m deep. Projecting towers, casemates and battlements provide numerous positions for the deployment of archers and artillery. Though Kerak was substantially altered by later occupants, the basic 12th-century Crusader design is clear.

This massive fortification was multi-purpose: it was a defensive strongpoint, a military base for the projection of armed might into the surrounding countryside and a combined residence and barracks for the great lord, his retainers and his soldiers. Hastily thrown up, judging by the rough-hewn masonry, it represents a huge investment of labour – no doubt the forced labour of nearby villagers.

One of dozens of Crusader castles in the Levant, Kerak is a measure of the chronic insecurity of the invaders. They had arrived with the First Crusade (1096–1099), but many of their comrades-in-arms had left for home after the fall of Jerusalem, leaving relatively small numbers of Western Christian knights to defend the four newly created Crusader states – from north to south, the County of Edessa, the Principality of Antioch, the County of Tripoli and the Kingdom of Jerusalem. Marooned in a sea of Arabs, Kurds and Turks, the great majority of them Muslims, ruling over potentially rebellious subjects and with exceptionally long land borders to guard, the Crusaders were compelled to compensate for small numbers by ensconcing themselves behind massive defensive walls. It is for this reason that we see some of the most impressive European feudal castles in the distant Levant.

Novgorod

Large-scale excavations at the medieval Russian city of Novgorod have been more or less continuous since the 1950s. The site is situated about 160km (100 miles) south of St Petersburg, but Novgorod long predates the city founded by Peter the Great in the early 18th century: it was, from the 12th to the 15th centuries, the capital of a republican state that stretched from the Gulf of Finland in the west to the Ural Mountains in the west, a distance of 1,500km (932 miles). But the city's former importance is not the only reason for the intensity of archaeological investigation: there is also the site's extraordinary state of preservation.

LEFT: Excavations at Veliky Novgorod have revealed the remains of the powerful republic which preceded the better-known city founded by Peter the Great.

Novgorod sits on a platform of clay beside the River Volkov amid a broad, flat, open plain. The medieval archaeological deposits have remained continuously waterlogged, preventing normal processes of organic decay in contact with the air. This means that wood, leather, food remains and other organic materials have been preserved. This is hugely important at Novgorod, for it was a timber-built city. Houses were constructed of timber beams laid on the ground and then floored with planks. Many examples of these footings have been excavated. Some houses are suspected of having been two, even three storeys high. The streets were also built of timbers. Three or four thin poles would be laid along the length of the street and split logs would be placed width-wise across them. Numerous of these log streets have also been excavated. Because, moreover, timber rots relatively

RIGHT: A birchbark *beresty* from Novgorod from the 12th century.

quickly when it is in contact with both damp and air, Novogorod's medieval houses and streets had to be regularly replaced. Excavators have found layer upon layer of rebuilding represented. In the case of Saints Cosmas and Damian Street, for example, no less than 28 separate levels of paving have been recorded, the earliest laid in 953 CE, the latest in 1462.

The dating of Novgorod is often very precise thanks to tree-ring or dendrochronological dating. This is another reason for the city's exceptional importance among medieval urban sites. The growth rings of tree trunks reflect changing climatic conditions, with wide rings when they are favourable, narrower ones when less so. Archaeological scientists who specialize in dendrochronology have succeeded in building up long sequences by looking at preserved timbers from many different sites. These provide them with what are called 'relative dates': they tell us what happened earlier, what happened later. But dendro dates can then be tied in with known calendar dates, where, for example, the construction date of the roof timbers of an extant building is recorded in historical documents. This provides dendro-chronologists with an anchoring of 'absolute dates', enabling them to assign actual calendar years to all the tree-rings in their sequences. For the northern hemisphere, we now have dendro-chronologies that take us back 14,000 years!

With the successive buildings and streets

securely dendro-dated, it is then possible to date the extraordinary assemblage of about 150,000 artefacts, for careful stratigraphic excavation, layer by layer, allows them all to be assigned to a particular phase in the city's development. Many of the artefacts are themselves organic, so we have objects of everyday life rarely found on other sites, like shoes, combs, bowls, eating utensils, musical instruments, even children's toys. Thanks to the dendro-dating of the layers in which they are found, these can often be assigned a date as close as 15, 20 or 25 years (this being the rough lifespan of earth-fast timber structures).

By far the most important of these wooden objects are the 700 or so *beresty* that have now been excavated. Dating from the 11th to the 15th century, they are birchbark documents. The coarse outer layers of pieces of birchbark were first removed by boiling. Then the soft inner layers were smoothed out and allowed to dry. These could then be inscribed, without the use of ink, simply by impressing the surface using a bone or metal stylus, much as on a wax tablet, but with the advantage that a *beresty* created a permanent record. The language represented – Old Novgorodian or Old East Slavic – would evolve into Old Russian. Specialists can read the texts easily and they provide a fund of information about everyday life, commercial transactions, government business and the laws of the medieval republic.

Along with an abundance of imported artefacts and a range of historical sources, the *beresty* help us to place Novgorod in its regional, indeed inter-continental context. What is clear is that Novgorod was first and foremost a trading city, one connected via the River Volkov, the Gulf of Finland and the Baltic with much of northern Europe and via the Don and the Volga with the Black Sea, the Caspian Sea and the Silk Road. Vessels of Chinese Celadon Ware (a soft, grey-green, glazed pottery) have been found at Novgorod, for example and we know that amber, furs and wax from the Baltic were being traded from the city into the Islamic world. A mid 9th century Viking foundation, Novgorod developed into one of the great mercantile centres of the medieval world; so much so that, despite almost 75 years of excavation, it is still the case that only about 2 per cent of the site has been excavated.

Mound-builders and Pueblo Farmers

Agriculture was also the basis of the Mound-builder culture of the Mid-West and the South-Eastern parts of the United States. Though some mounds may date back as far as 3500 BCE, the majority of the many thousands known are much later. Small conical-shaped mounds were erected over burials by the early Adena culture (1000–300 BCE) and later much larger ones covering elaborate wooden burial chambers. The largest of these, Grave Creek mound on the banks of the Ohio in West Virginia, is more than 18m (59ft) high. The succeeding Hopewell culture (100 BCE–500 CE) continued the tradition. The Great Serpent Mound in Ohio, more than 400m (1312ft) in extent, 6m (20ft) wide, but less than a metre high, represents a giant snake, with the burial located in the beast's mouth. The

Mississippian culture (700–1700 CE) took mound-building to an even more monumental scale, using the mounds as platforms for temples and chiefly residences. The Cahokia complex in Illinois extended across 800ha (1,976 acres), contained 100 earth mounds and featured a log wall around the 200ha (494 acres) inner sanctum. The largest of the Cahokia mounds, Monk's Mound, is a flat-topped platform resting on four terraces more than 33m (108ft) in height. Archaeologists estimate that as many as 30,000 people may have inhabited the immediate area.

Mystery has surrounded the mounds since they first became the subject of serious enquiry in the 19th century. We seem to have a long continuity of tradition crossing over successive cultures, with growing monumentality as power and wealth became more centralized in the hands of paramount chiefs. Grave goods and mortuary figurines further attest the primacy of the individuals buried under the mounds. Snakes, ducks and other animal totems on Hopewell ceramics offer clues about an associated fertility cult. But a host of unresolved questions remain.

Remarkable in a different way were the Pueblo-farmers of the South-West in the early 1st millennium CE. Confronting an environment of exceptional severity, they shifted from dry farming using only natural rainfall to wet farming based on water-capture dams and a system of canals to irrigate fields of maize, beans, squash, tobacco and cotton. So successful was the agricultural regime that large villages of adobe houses were constructed. That at Snaketown in Arizona covered a square kilometre, contained

BELOW: Monk's Mound at the Cahokia site was the centre of a settlement that contained as many as 30,000 inhabitants at its peak in the 12th century.

dozens of houses, numerous refuse mounds and a Mesoamerican-style ball court. Chaco Canyon contained no less than 13 villages built of stone, adobe and timber, the largest, Pueblo Bonito, comprising around 700 separate rooms, some in multi-storey arrangement and 34 subterranean *kivas* (for ceremonies and social gatherings).

A combination of crop failure due to low rainfall and the predations of Apache and Navajo seem to have brought the Pueblo-farmers to crisis soon after 1300, when most of their settlements were abandoned. Theirs had always been a highly marginal and precarious existence, their striking cultural achievements a measure of their struggle to survive in such a hostile arid environment.

RIGHT: A tablet from Cahokia depicting a birdman tablet. Anthropomorphic animal figures are commonly found on artefacts from the Mississippian culture.

BELOW: Pueblo Bonito in Chaco Canyon was constructed between 850 and 1150 CE. At the time, it was surrounded by forest, but the trees were cleared to support the construction of the settlement, leading to environmental crisis in the following years.

Toltecs, Aztecs, Chimú and Incas

Waves of invaders from the north entered the geopolitical space left by Maya decline at the end of the Classical Period (see page 195). The Toltecs established themselves in central Mexico from *c.* 950 to 1170 and, after a further period of fragmentation and warfare, the Aztecs made their capital at Tenochtitlán on the northern shore of Lake Texcoco in 1345. Between 1428 and 1519, the Aztecs built an extensive empire based on a centralized autocracy served by a warrior and high-priestly ruling class and a large professional army. There appears to have been no attempt to assimilate subject-peoples or develop productive technique. Tribute – gold, cotton, turquoise, feathers, incense and vast quantities of food – were sent to Tenochtitlán, the largest city in the pre-Columbian Americas. Much of this was then consumed in grotesque rituals in which individuals were sacrificed at the Great Temple, their hearts torn out as offerings to the gods, their bodies then tipped down the steps.

Until relatively recently, much of what we knew about this formidable Aztec city came from documentary evidence: the temple, like most of the rest of the city, was destroyed by the Spanish invaders. But excavations over the past four decades have fleshed out the story. We now know that the Templo Mayor or Great Temple, was one of 45 monumental public buildings built in a walled ceremonial precinct – 500m (1,640ft) to a side – in the centre of Tenochtitlán. Of all the structures, The Great Temple was the focal point of Aztec religious life, its architecture mirroring the Aztec

LEFT: A 15th-century Aztec model of a temple. Human sacrifice was a regular occurence at such places.

RIGHT: This Toltec relief shows an eagle eating a cactus fruit. The eagle had an important role in both Toltec and Aztec mythology.

LEFT: The remains of the Templo Mayor in Mexico City. It was rebuilt seven times, with the prior structures nesting within the new construction each time. Construction of the first temple began in 1325, while its final incarnation was only completed shortly before the arrival of the Spanish Conquistadors in 1519.

vision of the cosmos. Built in the form of a pyramid, reaching 200m (656ft) in its seventh and final version, its four tapering tiers represented four heavenly levels. At the summit was the supreme level, with two shrines to the Aztec god of war and to the god of rain and agriculture. The Great Temple was nothing short of the symbolic centre of the universe and the place where the supreme earthly ruler interceded with the gods and most particularly with the gods of war and food. But of course, it was not the gods nor the elite, but the everyday people who really facilitated the food supply.

The exceptional agricultural wealth that was the basis of Mesoamerican civilization – based on raised fields, irrigation systems and the cultivation of maize, beans and squash ('the three sisters') – had been achieved using Stone Age technology. The lack of metals and a way of war based upon them, was to prove a crippling disadvantage in the imminent encounter with European colonialism – a disadvantage compounded by the fact that the region's wealth had been appropriated by a highly exploitative and brutal class of alien rulers, such that the common people either welcomed the defeat of their masters or even participated actively in the struggle to bring them down in the early 16th century.

In South America, the Moche succumbed to the Chimú around 750 CE. The Chimú were colonialists who established a communications network that enabled them to control an empire that extended some 1600km (1,000 miles) along the Peruvian coast. The capital at Chan Chan eventually sprawled across 15km^2 (6 square miles). It centred on ten royal compounds, built over a period of 250 years, each containing a sealed mausoleum beneath a pyramid, reached via a single gateway, a vast entrance courtyard and a complex of residential and storage buildings.

These successive Peruvian civilizations provided the platform on which the greatest of them all was erected: that of the Inca. It had its origins in the Cuzco area of the Andes in the 12th century. It eventually developed into a formidable military autocracy. The Sapa Inca was an absolute ruler who combined the roles of warlord and high priest with the power to decide all political, military and religious matters. Beneath him was an aristocracy formed in large part of his relatives. Beneath them was a layer of state officials, local administrators and military commanders. Between 1438 and 1533, the Inca incorporated a large part of western South America into their empire, which eventually stretched along 3500km (2,175 miles) of coastland and extended inland for around 300km (186 miles). To bind this vast territory together, the Inca built a 40,000km (24,850 miles)-long network of roads and rest-houses, reserved for official use. Teams of runners could relay messages as rapidly as 250km (155 miles) a day. The roads were built by forced labour, including tunnels dug through rock, causeways laid across marshes and bridges of stone, wood and rope across chasms. The major causeways, up to 16m (52ft) wide, were designed for the movement of armies.

Forced labour was also employed in the construction of irrigation systems, agricultural terraces and, of course, Inca cities and monuments. Around two-thirds of total agricultural produce was taken in taxes. At the heart of the empire lay a series of major Inca sites built from vast blocks of irregular masonry fitted together with astonishing precision – notably, the administrative capital at Cuzco, the massive fortress at Sacsayhuamán immediately north of it and the ceremonial centre at Machu Picchu that lies

LEFT: Detail of a pelican glyph from Chan Chan.

perched on a ridge of rock 600m (1,969ft) high, its flanks lined with tiers of narrow agricultural terraces.

Peruvian civilization, like Mesoamerican civilization, was based on sophisticated agricultural technique, but one limited by tools of stone, wood

BELOW: The adobe walls of Chan Chan, the capital of the Chimú. It was the largest city of pre-Columbian South America, containing approximately 40,000 inhabitants.

ABOVE: The fortress of Sacsayhuamán, on the outskirts of the Inca capital of Cuzco. The huge stones that make up the walls are not connected by mortar, but instead have been precisely cut so that they fit together.

RIGHT: Atahualpa, the last Inca Emperor or 'Sapa'. The Sapa Inca ruled with absolute power and was at the head of a complex administrative apparatus that stretched across the length of the empire.

and bone. Gold, silver and copper were worked in abundance, but they were used for ornament, ritual and artistic representation, valued, along with turquoise and other semi-precious stones, for the sun-redolent symbolism inherent in their shininess. Given primitive technique, brutal exploitation was necessary to extract the surpluses of labour and produce necessary to create the stone cities, mudbrick pyramids and rich burials on which archaeological attention tends to focus. The Inca ruling class, like the Aztec, made few friends in its century of imperial hegemony.

OPPOSITE: The site of Machu Picchu was occupied c. 1420–1532 and was likely used as both a ceremonial centre and a royal estate.

Wind Power

Medieval Chinese pottery brought up in the nets of Korean fishermen in 1975 first alerted archaeologists to the presence on the seabed of what came to be called 'the Sinan shipwreck'. It proved to be a 200-ton keeled sailing ship of the 14th century and during nine seasons of underwater exploration half the wooden hull was recovered together with more than 20,000 pieces of pottery, 28 tons of coins, more than 1,000 lengths of red sandalwood, in excess of 1300 everyday objects and much more; so much, in fact, that the remains of the ship and its cargo are the main focus of a new purpose-built museum.

The ship – 32m (105ft) in length, 10m (33ft) in the beam, 3.5m (11.5ft) deep amidships – was divided into seven or eight compartments by internal bulwarks. Only the lower hold survived to be salvaged, the upper decks lost to the ocean, presumably with large quantities of lighter objects which simply floated away. Nonetheless, the Sinan ship bears testimony to the dynamism of the trade in Chinese celadons and porcelains, two ceramic wares in high demand in communities around the Yellow Sea. The wreck confirms the evidence that strong maritime trade connected China, Korea and Japan in the medieval period.

Ocean-going sailing ships date back to the 3rd millennium BCE in the Far East. Chinese ships equipped with fore-and-aft rig may have been trading as far west as

India, Arabia and East Africa before the end of the 1st millennium BCE, as they most certainly were doing by the time of the Tang Dynasty (618–907 CE), for porcelain of this date has been recovered from Kenyan villages. Fore-and-aft rig – where the sails are aligned with the keel – make it possible to sail into the wind. Square-rigged vessels – where sails are aligned beam-to-beam – can also be designed to do this, but the evidence is that for thousands of years this crucial technical advance was not achieved.

Sailing ships plied the waters of the Eastern Mediterranean throughout the Bronze Age and quite possibly long before, but these vessels usually carried a single mast and sail and were entirely dependent on a following wind. Greek and Roman ships were much the same, both cargo-carriers and warships, as were the longships of Anglo-Saxons and Vikings centuries later. The famous Oseberg ship, excavated from a burial mound in the early 20th century and now displayed in Norway's Viking Ship Museum, confirms it. Dating from the early 9th century CE, the ship is 22m (72ft) long and 5m (16ft) broad and is clinker-built of oak planks (meaning that the planks of the hull overlap). There is a centrally placed mast which

RIGHT: The Oseberg ship combined oars and sails for its power and would likely have been used for both transport and military purposes.

is estimated to have been 10m (33ft) tall and to have carried a sail of *c.* 90m² (970ft²), allowing a maximum speed of 10 knots. But only in the event of a following wind. That is why the ship was also provided with 15 pairs of oar-holes, allowing 30 men to row the ship. The Oseberg ship is very similar to the ships with which William the Conqueror invaded England more than two centuries later, as depicted on the *Bayeux Tapestry*.

The *knarr* ship was a variant of the longship specifically designed for carrying cargo. Relatively wider in the beam, it was capable of carrying about 25 tons. It was superseded by the cog in European waters during the Middle Ages. Cogs were generally much bigger, often capable of carrying up to 200 tons and very occasionally as much as 1,000 tons. The best-known example is the Bremen cog, a 14th-century vessel dredged from the River Weser in the early 1960s and now displayed in the German Maritime Museum. Some 24m (79ft) long, 8m (26ft) in the beam and 4m (13ft) high amidships, its carrying capacity is estimated to have been between 90 and 130 tons. But it was a square-rigged vessel with single mast and sail incapable of sailing into the wind: an enduring technical problem that left capital invested in shipping and cargo idle in port when the wind was unfavourable.

The cog was eventually replaced by the carrack, developed during the 14th and 15th centuries, especially by the Portuguese, who were in the forefront of oceanic exploration and long-distance maritime trade in the Late Middle Ages. The carrack was a square-rigged sailing ship, but carrying three or four masts and multiple sails, designed for tacking into a headwind. The *São Gabriel*, a three-masted Portuguese carrack, for

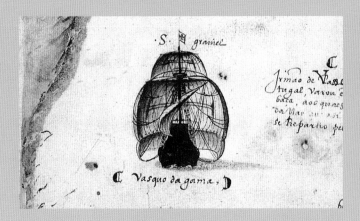

ABOVE: The *São Gabriel*, Vasco da Gama's flagship, was a carrack, designed for long-distance trade and exploration.

example, carried six sails: bowsprit, foresail, mainsail, mizzensail and two topsails. This was the flagship of Vasco da Gama when he sailed from Europe to India around the Cape of Good Hope in 1497. Carracks making the India or China run during the 16th century often had a capacity of 1,000 tons.

The voyages of discovery, the explosion in long-distance maritime trade, what has been described as 'the first globalization', were dependent on a critical technological breakthrough: the mastery of wind power at sea.

RIGHT: The Bremen cog. Vessels like these were most common in northwestern Europe, where they replaced the *knarr* as the preferred ship of traders due to their high cargo capacity.

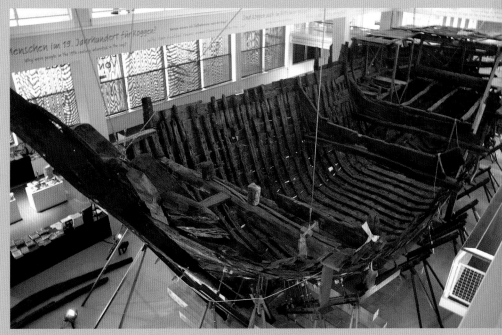

Angkor Wat

It was once described as 'an architectural achievement which perhaps has not and never will have an equal in the world'. The French traveller Henri Mouhot, writing in his Le Tour du Monde (1863), was referring to Angkor Wat, the former capital of the medieval Khmer Empire. The ruins, built beside the Great Lake of north-western Cambodia, extend for 25km (15 miles) east–west and 10km (6 miles) north–south. They are dominated by a temple complex of 163ha (403 acres), the largest in the world by land area. The main temple comprises four corner towers and a central tower that rises 65m (213ft) above ground level. The towers surmount a rectangular ground-floor gallery and this in turn is surrounded by two further galleries arranged concentrically around the first. The four sides of the outer gallery measure 3.6km (2.2 miles) in total length and surrounding this is a rectangular moat no less than 5km (3 miles) in total length. The monumental road to the site runs for well over a kilometre. The design combines two architectural concepts, the tower temple and the gallery temple, to create what is, without doubt, the supreme monument of the medieval civilization in South-East Asia.

Angkor Wat (meaning 'City of Temples') was constructed in the early 12th century by order of Khmer King Suryavarman II (1113–1150). Originally built in honour of the Hindu god Vishnu, it was later adapted for Buddhist worship and in fact the blending of Hinduism and Buddhism (both imported from India) was a feature of medieval religious practice across much of South-East Asia. This is reflected in the $1,200m^2$ ($12,917ft^2$) of bas-relief stone carvings that decorate so much of the temple, arranged in a story-telling sequence (once described as 'the greatest known linear arrangement of stone carving'). They

BELOW: The main temple of Angkor Wat. Built in the early 12th century, Angkor Wat served as the Khmer Empire's state temple.

ABOVE: Angkor Wat bas reliefs, featuring the Battle of Devas and Asuras.

depict numerous Hindu myths, Hindu concepts of heaven and hell, Hindu-Buddhist spirits (*asparas*) and deities (*devata*) and of course Buddha; there is also a procession of the founder-benefactor, King Suryavarman.

The cost was astronomical. Inscriptions record that the temple took 35 years to build, required 5 million tons of sandstone hauled from a holy mountain 50km (31 miles) away and involved the work of 300,000 labourers and 6,000 elephants. Where did the resources come from to make this colossal investment possible?

Angkor Wat is located at the edge of a vast alluvial floodplain. During the dry season the Great Lake drained into the Mekong River, but during the wet season the flow was reversed as water backed up, raised the level of the lake and flooded much of the plain to the north. Each flood deposited a rich sediment, renewing the fertility of the soil, while an elaborate system of ditches, canals and reservoirs, built and maintained by the Khmer kings, created a vast wet prairie ideal for rice cultivation. So abundant was the harvest that the region became home to a million people and provided the resources for world-beating waste expenditure on prestige monuments.

All told, the Khmer Empire constructed around 900 temples in its heyday between the 9th and 13th centuries, while other South-East Asia states – from Thailand and Vietnam to Malaya, Sumatra and Java – also invested heavily in monumental religious architecture and art. This was 'the Age of Kingdoms' – with frequent wars, shifting borders and faltering dynasties – and temple-building was not just a matter of piety, but part of the competitive power-play of the epoch. It was the spread of rice cultivation which made possible the huge expansion of population and resources represented by complexes like Angkor Wat, but also important, especially in Malaya, Sumatra and Java, was maritime trade. This was expanding rapidly in this period, especially that through the Straits of Malacca linking the South China Sea and the Indian Ocean; and many of the great cities of the South-East Asian islands and peninsulas were mercantile emporia.

The classical age of South-East Asian civilization ended in the 15th century. As ever, debate rages around the reasons. What is certain is that there is nothing to rival the great monuments of the 9th to 14th centuries and the relative decadence and backwardness of the region thereafter left it wide open to penetration and occupation by European colonialists – the Dutch, the French and the British.

Ming China

It is to China's Ming emperors what the Valley of the Kings is to Egypt's New Kingdom pharaohs. The 13 imperial tombs lie in a valley 45km north of the imperial capital at Beijing. The only one so far excavated is that known as Dingling, which is the Tomb of the Emperor Wanli (1573–1620), the 13th ruler of the Ming Dynasty. It was discovered accidentally when archaeologists encountered loose brickwork giving access to a tunnel filled with earth. At the end of the tunnel was a small inscribed stela giving directions to the burial chamber. The massive marble doors had locked themselves when closed for the last time and it was necessary to use a strip of flexible metal to reach in and dislodge the marble columns behind. Once beyond this, the excavators

discovered a monumental complex comprising outer hall, central hall, two side chambers and at the far end the burial chamber itself. As well as the body of the emperor, the tomb contained the bodies of his two

BELOW AND RIGHT: The treasures of Dingling tomb: the Empress Crown and jewellery in the shape of the Chinese character 心 (xīn), which means heart.

empresses and a stunning collection of undisturbed grave-goods. Some 3,000 artefacts were recovered – gold and silver objects, imperial regalia, brocade fabrics, the personal effects of emperor and empresses. Most spectacular is the Dragon and Phoenix Crown of Empress Xiaoduan. Featuring nine dragons and nine phoenixes, it is inlaid with precious gemstones and is considered to be the most valuable artefact of its kind in the world. What treasures await discovery in the other dozen imperial tombs in the valley?

Earlier Ming tombs have been excavated elsewhere. That of Prince Zhu Tan contained clothing, lacquer-work furniture, silk scroll paintings, a collection of printed books and a miniature ceremonial parade of 400 small, finely carved wooden figurines representing the princely retinue. Another such princely tomb, that of Prince Zhu Yuelian, also contained a model retinue, this formed of 500 glazed ceramic figurines ranged around a ceramic model of the royal carriage.

Spectacular in a quite different way was the Ming capital at Beijing. During the 15th and 16th centuries, this was the most heavily populated city in the world. By the mid 14th century, the city had been reduced to about 100,000 people. A century later, it was ten times that, as the Ming emperors invested vast resources in creating a prestigious imperial capital – at a time when the population of London was 20,000, Paris 200,000 and Constantinople 400,000. They employed 100,000 skilled artisans and a million slaves and conscripts to build the central palace complex, the Forbidden City, which contained the imperial audience chambers and residences. Around this core were the offices of the eunuch bureaucracy, the offices of the imperial, civil and military hierarchy, along with treasuries, storehouses, granaries, arsenals, parks and gardens. The whole of this inner city, 6.5km (4 miles) east–west, 5.5km (3.4 miles) north–south, was walled. So, too, was a new outer city to the south, measuring 8km (5 miles) east–west, 3km (1.8 miles) north–south, where huge enclosures housed the Temple of Heaven complex.

No less impressive was the Grand Canal dug to link the Ming capital with the port of

LEFT: Ceramic figurines from the tomb of Zhu Yuelian. These models inform us about the fashions and customs of Ming dynasty officials.

Shandong on the Chinese coast, some 350km (217 miles) distant. An estimated 165,000 labourers were employed on this project and when it was completed, it made possible grain deliveries of 200,000 tons per annum, more than enough to feed the vast city that Beijing had become. For, in addition to the swollen imperial court and bureaucracy, hundreds of thousands of traders, artisans and labourers were resident in the city, making a living by supplying goods and services to the state, but also dependent on state-managed flows of food and raw materials.

The Ming Dynasty (1368–1644) had emerged from the chaotic decline of the preceding Mongol or Yuan Dynasty (1271–1364), consumed by internal rebellion and disintegrating central power. The Ming established an effective autocratic state, with tight control by a bureaucratic-military complex centred on Beijing, but extending downwards through provinces, prefectures, sub-prefectures and counties, each with their responsible officials and local administrations of clerks and garrisons of soldiers. The countryside was dominated by a parasitic class of landlords. The peasants were ground down by rents, taxes and labour services. The towns flourished, with vibrant trading and craft-work, but they lacked the independence and freedom of medieval towns in Europe. Imperial China was a thoroughly top-down society. Though the Ming Dynasty sponsored economic development – for this was the foundation of imperial power – with large-scale canal building and encouragement of the silk, cotton and ceramic industries, Chinese civil society remained tightly controlled and in harness to the state and the bureaucracy. Population increased from less than 60 million in 1350 to almost 200 million by 1550, but the essential structures of Chinese society remained frozen. This would continue to be the case under the succeeding Manchu Dynasty (1644–1912); and this enduring conservatism would leave China, despite its vast manpower and wealth, too weak to resist the predations of modern imperial powers during the 19th and early 20th centuries.

LEFT: The Forbidden City, constructed between 1406 and 1420, was the royal centre of Beijing and the home of both the Ming and Qing Emperors.

Samurai Japan

In contrast to medieval China, where the central state was predominant, medieval Japan bears comparison with medieval Europe, where the central state was weak in relation to a class of feudal warriors with local landholdings. In fact, in the case of Japan, centralized authority broke down in 1185 and was not properly restored until the time of the Tokugawa Shogunate (1603–1868). During the century and a half from 1467 to 1603, civil war was almost continuous as rival regional magnates (*daimyo*) struggled for power and huge resources were ploughed into armies and fortifications.

The rise of Japanese feudalism is represented archaeologically by the appearance of *yakata* type manor-houses from the 12th century onwards. These bear a remarkable similarity to European manor-houses of the same period. Some had the form of a motte-and-bailey castle, with a mound surmounted by a timber fort and one or more enclosed courts below. Others were simple rectangular enclosures, perhaps surrounded by a moat and a timber palisade. The manor-house at Yajima-Yakata was of this form, the moated enclosure measuring 150m (492ft) east–west by more than 200m (656ft) north–south. Inside the compound were various buildings, the largest measuring 8m (26ft) in length, a mix of residential accommodation, storehouses and service areas. The *samurai* warrior who held the manor – the equivalent of a European knight – was supported by an estate worked by tied peasants.

We are exceptionally well-informed about *samurai* armour, weapons and fighting techniques, thanks to an abundance of contemporary artworks and many fine museum collections. Japanese warriors developed a form of 'lamellar' armour early on. This made use of

RIGHT: Samurai armour from the 16th or 17th century. The central lamellar cuirass was made up of overlapping scales.

small pieces of metal or leather that were sewn into strips and coated with lacquer as waterproofing. The strips were then laced together horizontally to form separate pieces of armour for chest and back, neck and shoulders, arms, thighs and legs. The armour was completed by a metal helmet, often with ferocious face-mask and elaborate decoration. The warrior might also have an identifying banner attached to his back. A full set of *samurai* armour might weigh around 30kg (66lbs) – similar to the weight of equipment carried by a British Tommy of the First World War.

The principal weapons of the *samurai* were swords, various pole weapons and longbows. The swords in particular were works of consummate craftsmanship and were highly prized objects: forged over weeks, exceptionally hard and sharp, they were supreme symbols of warrior status. Peasant-soldiers fought alongside the *samurai*, seemingly in increasing numbers in the late medieval period, when they were equipped to fight either as arquebusiers or spearmen. *Samurai* battles often had a somewhat ritualistic character: first an exchange of firearms at perhaps 50m (164ft) range; then an advance of massed spearmen;

finally an attack by the *samurai* elite, on foot or mounted depending on circumstances. Military manuals prescribed a range of elaborate tactical manoeuvres with names to match – birds in flight, arrowhead, keyhole, crane's wing, yoke, fish scales, half moon, tiger's head, long snake, lying dragon. It is questionable how useful these attempts to reduce warfare to formulas were.

The Tokugawa shoguns who brought the *samurai* civil wars to an end were like the absolute monarchs of Renaissance Europe. They crushed the regional warlords, restored peace and allowed agriculture and trade to recover. Farmers, artisans and merchants prospered, the economy became increasingly monetized, towns grew in size and prosperity. But the shoguns feared innovation, worrying that it would destabilize their power and attempted to shut Japan off from the outside world. The country became a closed society under a political dictatorship suspicious of new ideas and resistant to change. The shock of modernity would be correspondingly acute when it came.

BELOW: A *wakizishi*, a short sword used by *samurai*.

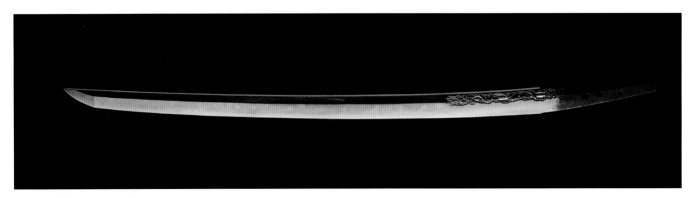

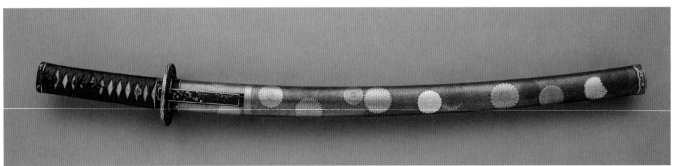

Pacific Societies

The Maori *pa* (hillfort) at Mount Wellington, built on the site of a volcanic crater, provides evidence of an advanced social system which developed on the islands of New Zealand. Half a kilometre wide and defended by ditch, rampart, palisade and raised fighting platforms, it enclosed terraces for houses and gardens and many pits for storing sweet potatoes. It combined the functions of chiefly residence, ritual centre and fortification.

The temperate climate of New Zealand provided a greater abundance of food resources, allowing the accumulation of substantial social surpluses and the emergence of chieftainships in the Classic Maori period (1350–1800 CE). The *pa* seem to have become more numerous and well-defended over time as tribal warfare intensified and the Maori would eventually put up a formidable military resistance to European colonization during the 19th century.

The Polynesians of the South-Western Pacific islands also developed a rich culture based on the consumption of fish, shellfish, pigs, poultry, dogs along with such plant staples as banana, taro, yam, breadfruit and sweet potato. Here, too, the evidence of sacred sites, ritual objects and figurative art,

ABOVE: The Maori *pa* at Mount Wellington. The site consists of extensive earthworks and perhaps as many as 2000 people lived at the site.

supplemented by anthropological studies, leaves no doubt about the complexity and variety of Polynesian culture. But one site stands out among all others, for it is unique, monumental, and one of world archaeology's greatest and most mysterious wonders: Easter Island.

What are we to make of this extraordinary place? A remote and tiny outcrop of volcanic rock a mere 170km² (66 square miles) in size, it is renowned for its hundreds of giant stone *moai*, which were quarried,

LEFT AND FOLLOWING PAGES: The front and back of an Easter Island *moai*. These stone statues weighed hundreds of tons and in total more than 900 *moai* were produced by the people of Easter Island.

carved, transported and erected on stone platforms across the island. Ranging in height from 2m (6.5ft) to 10m (33ft), some weighing as much as 80 tons, sometimes arranged in rows of up to 15, they were all of similar type: giant heads with sloping forehead, large angular nose and projecting chin, with bodies cut off at the abdomen and arms held tightly at the sides and crossed at the front. Some 400 still stand in the quarry at various stages of completion. One of these, known as 'El Gigante', weighs 270 tons and would have stood more than 20m (66ft) tall had it ever been erected.

Recent research has focused on the intricate carvings decorating the backs of many *moai* and of associations with the bird-man cult on the island. This was an elaborate fertility rite that involved a race to swim the narrow strait between Rapa Nui (the main island) and Motu Nui (a small offshore island) and return with the first sooty tern's egg of the season – a race laden with hazard, for many contestants drowned, were eaten by sharks or fell from the cliffs. The relationship between the *moai* and the bird-man cult is just one of the many mysteries which shroud the archaeology of Easter Island. A bizarre twist may be that the *moai* religion, with its enormous investment in waste expenditure on a tiny island, may have exhausted the available resource base and condemned the whole society to collapse – fate perhaps implicit in the quarry-full of unfinished statues.

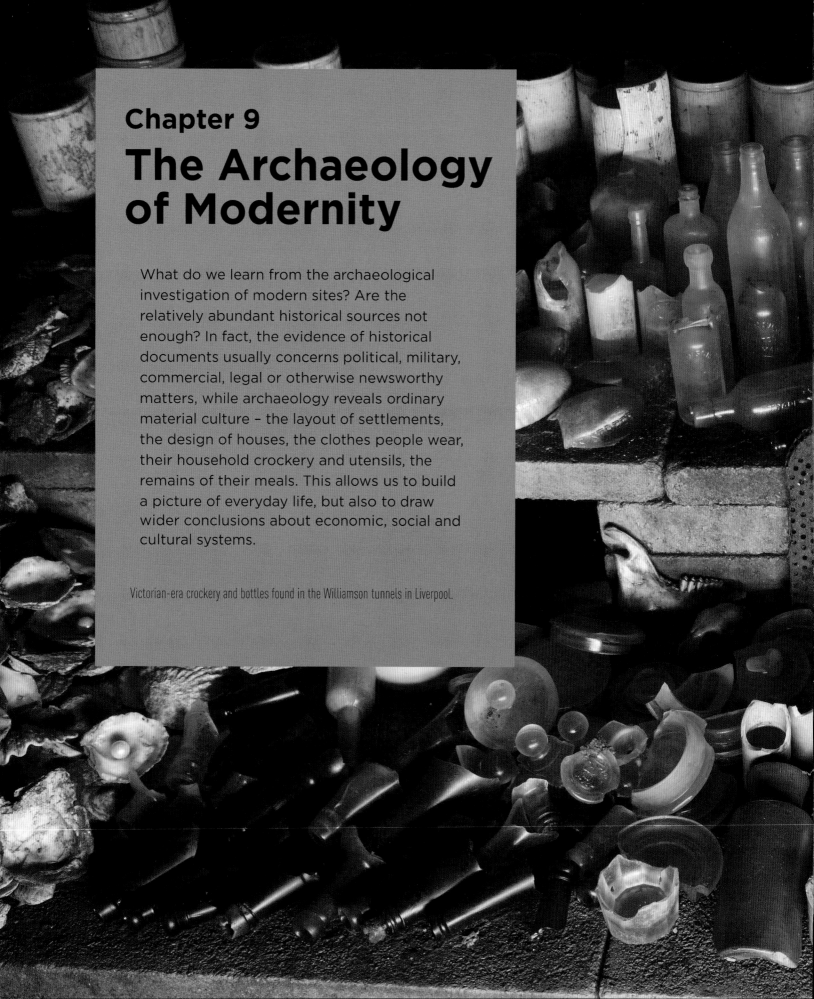

Chapter 9
The Archaeology of Modernity

What do we learn from the archaeological investigation of modern sites? Are the relatively abundant historical sources not enough? In fact, the evidence of historical documents usually concerns political, military, commercial, legal or otherwise newsworthy matters, while archaeology reveals ordinary material culture – the layout of settlements, the design of houses, the clothes people wear, their household crockery and utensils, the remains of their meals. This allows us to build a picture of everyday life, but also to draw wider conclusions about economic, social and cultural systems.

Victorian-era crockery and bottles found in the Williamson tunnels in Liverpool.

Settlers, Slaves and Ships

In 1994, archaeologist Bill Kelso was invited to set
up a project to investigate the remains of Jamestown,
Virginia, the first permanent English settlement in
America. The settlers – 104 men and boys – had
landed in May 1607 with a royal charter empowering
them to 'make habitation, plantation and … deduce
a colony of sundry of our people'. The investigations
originally planned to last only ten years, have been
so rewarding that they have continued ever since and
visitors to the site can see ongoing excavations in
progress.

Part of the original 1607 fort, a church constructed
in 1608, a storehouse ordinary houses, temporary
shelters and wells have been revealed, along with
human remains, some with grisly stories to tell, like
the young man who died from a musket shot which
shattered the bones in his lower leg and a teenage girl
who appears to have been cannibalized.

The archaeology is thus giving visceral support to
historical accounts, for cannibalism is indeed recorded

ABOVE: An archaeologist at work at Jamestown. The excavations of the
settlement have brought to life the story of the first English settlers in the
Americas.

during the 'Starving Time' in the grim winter of
1609/10.

The site has yielded an astonishing two million
artefacts, many in quite exceptional states of
preservation – everything from routine bulk finds
like potsherds, tobacco pipes, beads, knives and
cheap knick-knacks to wooden dolls, hornwork
books, children's shoes and combat armour. Many
of the finds were imports to be traded for food
with Native American tribes. Others were made
locally, with evidence for the presence of bricklayers,
coopers, fishermen, glassmakers, goldsmiths, masons,
perfumers, pipe-makers and tailors among the settlers.

The Jamestown project is providing an
archaeological foundation-block for the whole
subsequent history of European colonization in the
Americas, a unique and intimate insight into the

lives of the earliest pioneers. Other fieldworkers are exploring the dark history of New World slavery. One recent discovery, at Newtowne Neck State Park in Maryland, on the known site of a Jesuit plantation, is an exceptionally well-preserved slaves' quarters. Excavators uncovered the remains of slave cabins associated with ceramic cups and broken tobacco pipes a short distance from the 18th-century brick-built manor house, still standing, that was once occupied by the Jesuit missionaries. Again, as with Jamestown and other colonial sites, there is a tie-in with historical documentation, in this case a record of the sale of 272 slaves from the area in 1838, including some from the Newtowne Neck plantation, who were loaded onto three ships bound for Louisiana, among them dozens of children, some as young as two months. The complicity of the Catholic Church in the slave trade is apparent.

Shipwrecks also offer close-up views of European colonization. That of the Dutch East Indiaman *Amsterdam* was exposed at low tide on the beach at Hastings on England's South Coast in 1969. She was recorded as lost on her maiden voyage on 26 January 1749, bound from the Netherlands for Batavia in Java, laden with cloth, wine and silver. The story is that the crew of 300 was racked with disease, the ship lost its rudder in severe gales and the sailors mutinied and forced the captain to run her aground. She then sank in 8m (26ft) of soft sand and silt before her cargo could be salvaged. Archaeological investigations in the 1980s made a huge haul of 18th-century artefacts, but the wreck remains in situ and can still be seen on the beach at low tide (where it is under legal protection). A full-size replica of the *Amsterdam* is on display at The Hague.

BELOW: Pottery sherds from Jamestown come from a variety of places, including England, France and Germany.

Tudor London

It did not look much: about 3m (10ft) of battered brick walling, a chalk and stone pad and a robbed-out foundation trench – the sort of scruffy bits and pieces that one routinely finds on an urban excavation. The relentless churn of redevelopment, the constant levelling of buildings, the digging of foundations, the sinking of pits and wells, the laying of pipes tends to leave an immensely complex

LEFT: Several artefacts have been found at Newtowne Neck.

BELOW: The wreck of the *Amsterdam* at low tide at St Leonard's on Sea, England.

three-dimensional jigsaw of partial remains of many different periods that archaeologists must then make sense of. Excavation and recording have to be meticulous and detailed if the 'stratigraphic narrative' – the story of sequential development implicit in the remains – is to be revealed. Compounding the challenge is the fact that virtually all urban archaeology is development-driven and therefore restricted to the excavation only of those remains scheduled for destruction – known as 'preservation by record'. This means archaeologists cannot chose where to dig: they are restricted to snapshots of the buried remains determined by construction plans.

But there was something special about the brickwork revealed in 2008 on a redevelopment site in Shoreditch: the wall was not straight but turned a corner, as if part of an octagonal building. Moreover, this excavated fragment of wall matched the results of a geophysical survey done in 1999. Though not confirmed by excavation, the survey appeared to have picked up a curving 'anomaly' about three metres inside the 2008 wall and conforming with it. And these two structural fragments – the inner wall

implied by geophysical survey and the putative outer wall revealed at the bottom of the excavation trench – provided a perfect fit with the speculations of an antiquarian scholar called W W Braine, who, in 1917, using a combination of old maps and property deeds, had proposed a precise location for 'The Theatre' – the playhouse where some of the earliest of Shakespeare's plays had been first performed.

The locations of later Shakespearean theatres – The Rose and The Globe – were already known. Rescue excavations on the site of The Rose in 1989 had, in fact, triggered a major public row, with archaeologists, actors and the general public organized into a 'Save the Rose Theatre' campaign to prevent the destruction of the remains. The decision was made to suspend the new building over the top, leaving the archaeological remains preserved beneath. Equally high profile was actor and director Sam Wanamaker's decision to build a full-size replica of The Globe very close to the known site of the original and run it as a modern Shakespearean theatre. The shape, age and location of the remains found in 2008 make it almost certain that they belong to Shakespeare's first theatre. Further

LEFT: The excavations of 'The Theatre' in Shoreditch, London, the playhouse where Shakespeare's plays were first performed, in 2009.

LEFT: Excavations of the Rose Theatre in 1989. The redevelopment of the area threatened the destruction of the remains of the original theatre, leading to a campaign to preserve the original and intense archaeological excavation of the site.

work on the South Bank since has also revealed remains of The Curtain and The Hope, allowing us to map out and reconstruct London as Shakespeare would have known it, based on archaeological evidence, supplemented by contemporary maps and documents.

Shakespearean theatres were about 30m (98ft) in diameter and polygonal in design. They comprised three galleries, one above the other, placed between the high outer and inner walls of the structure, roughly 3m (10ft) apart; here the more affluent spectators would sit. The galleries surrounded an open yard where the 'groundlings' stood to watch, with the projecting stage to one side and the tiring-house comprising dressing-room, prop-room and musicians' gallery behind. Perhaps the most fascinating contemporary reference to the form of the theatre is that of Shakespeare himself. 'But pardon, gentles all,' announces the opening chorus of *Henry V*, 'the flat upraised spirits that hath dared to this unworthy scaffold to bring forth so great an object. Can this cockpit hold the vasty fields of

France? Or may we cram within this wooden O the very casques that did affright the air at Agincourt?' A war of nations was to become a drama performed by a handful of players in a 'little place … within the girdle of these walls'.

Again, we might pose the question: what has archaeology added to what is already known? But this may not be the right question. Perhaps what matters here is what might be called 'power of place'. We seek contact with the material remains of the past not simply in pursuit of knowledge, but also in pursuit of less easily defined emotional and aesthetic experience. That is why we conserve heritage sites even after thorough investigation has mined them of information. We still crave direct physical contact with the place, the structure, the object; we still want to 'touch the past'. That a modern developer might have destroyed the remains of The Rose – where Shakespeare's first play, *Henry VI, Part 1*, premiered in 1592 – was perceived to be cultural vandalism, a violation of a shared heritage embodied in material remains.

Victorian York

In 1901, Seebohm Rowntree, a philanthropic-minded chocolate manufacturer, wrote one of the classics of early sociology. His work inspired decades of social reform to eradicate poverty and construct a welfare state. There was a time when archaeologists would have bulldozed away the remains of the 19th-century industrial suburbs investigated by Rowntree to get at the medieval and ancient remains beneath. Not any more: not, at least, so far as the most responsible urban authorities are concerned. When a part of the Hungate area of historic York the size of four football pitches came up for redevelopment early this century, the plan was to excavate the entire urban sequence from top to bottom. The excavators aimed to test and refine Rowntree's testimony.

The original study, during which investigators had visited every working-class home in the city, making records on 11,560 families and 46,754 individuals, had been fine-grained. Rowntree had distinguished between different grades of housing, amenities and well-being. He distinguished, for example, between

relatively well-constructed artisan houses on the one hand and jerry-built terraces with brick floors on bare earth, thin partition walls, poor ventilation, rising damp and risk of winter flooding on the other. Archaeological investigation confirmed this. A sizeable late 19th-century house in Palmer Lane had fine quarry-tiled floors. By contrast, five houses fronting onto Lower Dundas Street had at some point been divided into ten back-to-backs, each house then comprising a tiny one-up/one-down hovel. The former backyard area now contained five front doors and became Dundas Court. A five-cubicle toilet over a cess-pit was rebuilt as a communal toilet block shared by round 50 people, half of whom would have had to walk round the block to use it; this facility remained in use until the 1930s. The two-up/two-downs in Haver Street were so small that the houses were barely the width of two outstretched arms. Either

BELOW: Excavations underway in the Hungate area prior to housing construction in the area. The whole area was examined and an array of artefacts shedding light on everyday Victorian life uncovered.

side, separating people from their neighbours were partition walls formed of a single course of bricks. Underfoot was a layer of dirty bricks laid on bare earth. A major home improvement at some point was a layer of concrete over the top.

A large assemblage of finds added to the picture of 19th-century working-class life in 'the workshop of the world'. Archaeologists found kilos of glass bottles, stoneware porter bottles, ale bottles, and flasks and flagons once used to store and serve all manner of alcoholic drinks. The main collection came from the site of the former Bricklayers' Arms on the corner of Palmer Lane, known to have been in existence from at least 1838 to 1937. As with all 'historical archaeology' – the term we use when the period under investigation is one for which good written records exist – the value of the material evidence is greatly enhanced by tie-ups with contemporary references. We learn from a report of the Chief Constable in 1902, for example, that the Bricklayers' Arms was a 'fairly good house' with club room, smoke room, dram shop, kitchen and cellar; between 1871 and 1915, it was renowned for linnet-singing competitions!

The slums of 19th-century York seem as alien as the medieval world. For archaeologists involved in excavating such sites, the experience can be viscerally real. To uncover the squalor of the communal latrines, the heaps of animal bones buried in backyards and iconic objects like one of Dr Giles Robert's ointment jars, a cure-all quack remedy for 'piles, cuts, burns, leg ulcers and gout', is to come into close contact with the common people of the industrial revolution. This is 'archaeology from below' to stand alongside 'history from below', where the focus shifts from powerful elites, architectural monuments and grand living to the ordinary working population on whom past civilizations depended.

Conflict Landscapes

World War I has been the main focus of the new sub-discipline of modern conflict archaeology. This is different from battlefield archaeology, battlefield salvage and, indeed, simple battlefield looting. Battlefield archaeologists are primarily concerned with testing and refining written accounts, usually through extensive metal-detector survey to locate and plot the distribution of metallic artefacts. Claims to have thereby revised the historical record can be overblown, but there have certainly been some notable success stories, notably in the case of Doug Scott's seminal investigation of the Little Bighorn battlefield, the site of Custer's last stand in 1876, where the team demonstrated that the Sioux had been much better armed than previously assumed and that they had engaged in sustained long-distance sniping. So forensic was the investigation that it included tracking the positions and movements of individual combatants across the battlefield.

Modern conflict archaeology, on the other hand, addresses the huge escalation in scale and violence represented by industrialized warfare. The mobilization of armies of millions, their supply by total-war economies and the transformation of entire landscapes by trench-digging, concrete emplacements, underground tunnelling, shell-fire, along with the

ABOVE: Archaeological objects found during excavation of a Turkish Army camp at Wadi Rum: Ottoman spoons, star-and-crescent Ottoman Army button, padlock and curiously a prehistoric stone tool.

construction of rear-area infrastructures of depots, barracks, hospitals, railways, ports and much more, has created a vast wealth of archaeological remains to be investigated. The challenge is to devise appropriate research frameworks, field methods and sampling strategies for getting to grips with this abundance of material remains. One aspect of this is a strong commitment to a multi-disciplinary approach, one involving archaeology, anthropology and history in combination.

The Great Arab Revolt Project offers a good case-study. Working in the deserts of southern Jordan over nine annual seasons between 2006 and 2014,

LEFT: Excavation of the Ottoman trenches at 'Tel Shahm Fort South'.

the aim was to recover evidence for the campaigns for Lawrence of Arabia during World War I. This involved operating at several different registers. The conflict was essentially a struggle between camel-mounted Arab guerrillas and British special forces on one side and Ottoman garrisons defending a railway line on the other. This meant that the war ranged over huge areas of open desert with no clearly defined front-lines. So the team carried out a systematic survey down the entire length of a 120km (75 mile) stretch of the former Hijaz Railway, locating and recording all visible military sites. They then focused down on selected areas and carried out more detailed survey work, looking at the relationships between military sites within a defined locality. They also selected certain sites for systematic clearance, artefact recovery and recording. In this way, moving from macro to micro, they aimed to build a picture of the war as a whole. The overall distribution of fortified stations, hilltop redoubts, entrenched camps and blockhouses told its own story about the Ottoman counter-insurgency strategy. The excavation of individual trenches and tent-rings, on the other hand, with finds of cutlery, crockery, glassware, buttons, combs, matchboxes, cigarette papers, playing cards and so on, told another story about the experience of individual Ottoman soldiers.

An unusual aspect of the project was the opportunity afforded to 'excavate a legend' and test the reliability of a world-famous war memoir. The trustworthiness of T E Lawrence's *Seven Pillars of Wisdom* has been in question since its formal publication in 1935. The more extreme detractors have accused Lawrence of being a serial liar and self-promoting charlatan. The archaeological evidence has proved otherwise. The match between places and events recorded in *Seven Pillars* and the remains of military posts located on the ground proved to be exceptionally close. A notable example was Tooth Hill Camp, an overnight campsite mentioned in a couple of brief references. Using a combination of air-reconnaissance sketch maps and unpublished archive photos, the archaeological team identified the location and carried out a thorough archaeological investigation, excavating two campfires and recovering numerous artefacts – ration tins, gin bottles, rum jars, vehicle parts, spent cartridges, even part of the trigger mechanism of a mountain-gun. It was astonishing archaeological confirmation of the reliability of the historical testimony.

RIGHT: A poster for the 1923 film *The Ten Commandments*.

The Archaeology of the Contemporary Past

Modern conflict archaeology is the most developed form of what is sometimes called 'the archaeology of the contemporary past'. There is even an academic journal dedicated to this new sub-discipline. Active research results remain limited, but the intention is clear: to recognize that archaeology means the study of the past – the whole of it – through the lens provided by material remains. That being so, there is no inherent reason why a 21st-century landfill site should be any less worthy of archaeological

LEFT: The imposing Gates of Rameses, as seen in the original film of *The Ten Commandments*. To prevent competition, DeMille dismantled and buried the entire set for the movie once filming was complete.

BELOW: The archaeologist John Parker reveals part of the plaster-of-Paris statue of the pharaoh from the set of DeMille's movie.

investigation than, say, a Sumerian tomb, a Roman bathhouse or a Cistercian monastery. It may even be the case that we do not yet know what our research questions should be. As Einstein quipped, 'If we knew what we were doing, it wouldn't be called research.' It may be that the investigation of modern material remains will give answers to questions we would never have thought to ask.

How about the archaeology of cinema? We have a wealth of material remains to explore – cinemas, studios, film sets, locations, souvenirs and so much more. Very little has been done so far, but a start has been made. Take the example of Cecil B DeMille's 1923 silent classic *The Ten Commandments*. Building the set for the City of Rameses, DeMille employed 1,500 construction workers for a month and used 150km (93 miles) of timber, 30 tons of plaster, 11,000kg (24,250lbs) of nails and 120km (75 miles) of reinforcing cable. The towering city walls were ten storeys high. The monumental entranceway was flanked by four colossal statues of the pharaoh weighing 39 tons a piece and the avenue of approach was lined with 21 concrete sphinxes of four tons each. What happened to this Hollywood version of Ancient Egypt built in sand dunes near Guadalupe in California?

After filming, DeMille, worried that rival filmmakers would reuse the set to make movies on the cheap ordered the whole thing to be broken up and buried. The city walls were bulldozed into a 100m (328ft)-trench and covered over. In

1985, these remains became the focus of a University of California at Santa Barbara research project. Geophysical survey – by magnetometry and ground-penetrating radar – was used to plot the buried remains. Then a series of digs using trowels, brushes and blowers to clear the loose sand has recovered a sample of the actual material – ranging from huge fragments of plaster reliefs and architecture to mock Roman coins and glass bottles, including, in breach of Prohibition Era law, cough mixture bottles that contained up to 12 per cent alcohol!

These remains represent a kind of 'virtual' Ancient Egypt at two removes. They reveal how 1920s filmmakers and presumably the audiences for whom they catered, imagined Ancient Egypt. But they were temporary structures only, made of flimsy materials, not an artwork in their own right, for the intention was to capture them on celluloid; it was the movie image that mattered, after which the set was disposable.

Other archaeologists have been exploring film locations where elements of the original sets survive in situ. Surveys of sets used in the making of David Lean's epics *Lawrence of Arabia* (1962) and *Ryan's Daughter* (1970), for example, have also thrown light on the artistic imagination at work. A desert 'oasis' constructed in a canyon in Almeria in Spain turns out to bear no relation to any real oasis: with its pool of clear water and floppy date palms, it is a comic-book construct. The schoolhouse built on the Dingle Peninsula of Ireland's Atlantic coast seems to embody the rich symbolism of *Ryan's Daughter*, with its tragic love-triangle and its conflict between conventional morality and wild passion.

As with modern conflict archaeology, the emphasis is on a multi-disciplinary approach, where archaeological fieldwork intersects with the evidence of the films themselves, with film history and more broadly with cultural studies and art appreciation. The potential of the archaeology of the contemporary past to enrich knowledge and understanding of our own world is apparent.

RIGHT: Dunmore Head, one of the locations for the 1970 film *Ryan's Daughter*.

Conclusion

The Meaning of Archaeology

When we consider the whole compass of archaeological knowledge, from the earliest hominins to modern warfare, what are the stand-out conclusions?

First – and in direct contradiction with much contemporary political ideology – human-beings do not prosper through competition and rivalry. On the contrary, all the evidence is that humans are defined as a species by the fact that they form cooperative social groups and engage in collective creative labour. They share ideas, work together, and thereby enhance their capacity to solve problems and provide for their needs. We see this represented again and again in the archaeological record – from the hand-axe to the computer – where good ideas are quick to spread and everyone benefits. There is no evidence that secrecy, hoarding and property rights have ever been anything other than barriers to human social development.

Second – not always in the short run, but certainly in the long run – human-beings make progress. Experience and experiment, ingenuity and invention, working out new ways of doing things means a growth of knowledge and technique which is essentially cumulative. Even when civilizations and empires collapse, the advances that really matter – the wheel, the plough, the watermill, the steam-engine – are retained, passed on to succeeding generations and provide a raised platform for fresh endeavour. In short, we get better and better at providing for ourselves.

Third, the pace of change – and advance of progress – has the potential at least to accelerate over time. There are many barriers and there can be long periods of stagnation, even regression, but in the long term our growing corpus of scientific and technical know-how shortens the time between one jump and the next. Take communications. The earliest forms of written script date from around 3200 BCE. But for almost 5,000 years after this, all writing had to be done by hand, making all kinds of written communication slow and expensive. The printing press was an invention of the early 15th century. But the next major advance – continuous rotary printing instead of one-at-a-time flatbed printing – followed in the mid 19th century. And since the 1960s, we have seen a whole series of new forms of printing – dot-matrix, laser, inkjet, 3D – in rapid succession.

Finally, however, we must acknowledge there have also been formidable barriers to progress. We have alluded to these in several places in the text. We have seen how in some cases powerful and wealthy elites divert resources into various forms of waste expenditure. There have been periods and places of cultural dynamism, where the creative potential of humanity was unleashed, as well as long periods of stagnation. Broadly, the pattern seems to be that the greater the resources and freedom from restriction enjoyed by the working population, the more chance there is that progressive social evolution will resume and accelerate.

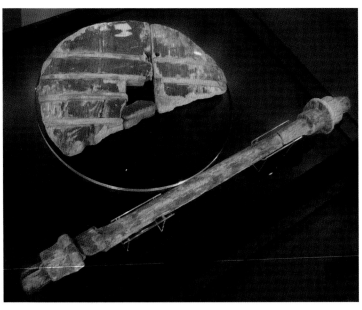

ABOVE: The Ljubljana Marshes Wheel, the oldest wooden wheel discovered.

LEFT: A replica of a 15th-century wooden printing press stands alongside 19th-century cast iron printing presses. The pace of change in communications technologies has continued to accelerate and has advanced especially quickly since the mid-20th century.

The Archaeology of the Future

People sometimes debate what sorts of things the archaeologists of the future might investigate. Perhaps the famous Tucson Garbage Project set up by William Rathje in Arizona in 1973 provides a partial answer. Rathje decided to investigate the contemporary waste deposits created by the citizens of the modern city. Interesting discoveries followed: what people said they did and what they actually did (on the evidence of their garbage cans) did not always tally; people tend to buy more than they need (and therefore waste more) during economic recessions; things people expect to degrade easily may not do so (like newsprint, which can remain readable in a landfill site after half a century!).

But the assumption that we will be exploring material remains at all a century from now, let alone a millennium from now, may be unduly optimistic. For, after seven million years of hominin evolution, 300,000 years in the cultural development of our own species, 5,000 years in the advance of complex society and 250 years since the industrial revolution, we have arrived at a compound crisis that seems to threaten the survival of any kind of human civilization.

The crisis is unfolding in four dimensions: ecological, military, social and ideological. Global warming is driving us towards catastrophic climate change and an accelerating breakdown in the Earth's ecosystems. Nuclear arsenals, rising arms expenditure and an increasingly tense geopolitical situation risks triggering warfare so destructive that it kills us all. Rampant corporate power is siphoning wealth to the top, condemning billions of lives to unremitting toil, poverty and deprivation and giving rise to global social inequalities beside which the excesses of Roman emperors and Renaissance princes pale into insignificance. And, in the face of this potentially terminal crisis, rational and planned responses seem to be precluded by a global pandemic of nationalism, racism, fascism and narcissistic individualism.

Archaeology has rich lessons to teach: about our creativity, our ascent through history, our ability to make life better, healthier, more prosperous, more rewarding for all, but also other lessons about the destructive role that can be played by exploitative, oppressive and violent social orders – lessons that have never been more urgent.

Recommended Further Reading

'*Dead archaeology is the driest dust that blows.*' That was Mortimer Wheeler, one of the 20th century's greatest archaeologists, writing in 1954. Unfortunately, all too few of his colleagues have heeded his warning in the decades since. Archaeology books can be terribly dull.

Matters are not helped by widespread academic prejudice against 'popularization'. The view seems to be that if it is accessible and fun, it cannot be rigorous and reliable. One even gets the sense that the assumption in some quarters is that the more impenetrable the text the more worthy it must be. In my experience, more often than not, when writing is impenetrable, it is because there is nothing to penetrate. If ideas are clear and coherent, they can be expressed in plain English. And we should avoid overloading text with masses of raw data. The general reader really does not need to be told about the contents of every Bronze Age founder's hoard discovered in Scotland. One or two good examples should suffice to make the point. We do not want to wade through mud before reaching our destination.

This little diatribe explains my recommendations for further reading. I have not listed all the latest academic tomes. I have listed only books that I consider both sound and 'a good read'. This includes a fair number of older works where some factual information may have been superseded by later discoveries; but they make it onto the list either because they offer good simple story-telling (e.g. the Leonard Cottrell books), or because the interpretations they contain are clear and compelling (e.g. the Gordon Childe books). Of particular value are big, bold, overview books that synthesize a mass of data to offer an engaging grand narrative; whether we agree or not, these provide the essential maps of the past without which we are liable to get lost in the woods. I have also included some introductions to archaeological techniques which I happen to rate highly and some accounts of actual archaeological projects which include good explanations of techniques along the way. Many of the books listed, I should say, are those that have inspired me.

I must confess that my selection is skewed towards British, European and Mediterranean archaeology. This reflects my own expertise and experience. I can only hope that the selection is sufficiently representative of approaches to archaeological interpretation to be of generic relevance. I have no doubt there are good reads to be had on the archaeology of parts of the world less familiar to me, but I have not yet stumbled upon them.

In each case, I have usually given the original publication date of the first edition. In virtually all cases, readers will find there are later reprintings and sometimes new editions. They will also find second-hand copies readily available online.

Paul Bahn, 1989, *Bluff Your Way in Archaeology*, Horsham, Ravette.

Paul Bahn, 1996, *Archaeology: a very short introduction*, Oxford, Oxford UP.

Paul Bahn, 2014, *The Archaeology of Hollywood: traces of the Golden Age*, Lanham, Rowman & Littlefield.

Philip Barker, 1977, *Techniques of Archaeological Excavation*, London, Batsford.

George Bass, 1966, *Archaeology under Water*, London, Thames & Hudson.

Guy de la Bédoyère, 2020, *Gladius: living, fighting and dying in the Roman Army*, London, Little, Brown.

J D Bernal, 1954, *Science in History*, Vol 1, *The Emergence of Science* and Vol 2, *The Scientific and Industrial Revolutions*, London, Faber & Faber.

Iain Browning, 1973, *Petra*, London, Chatto & Windus.

Iain Browning, 1982, *Jerash and the Decapolis*, London, Chatto & Windus.

Martin Carver, 1998, *Sutton Hoo: burial ground of kings?* London, British Museum.

Vere Gordon Childe, 1936, *Man Makes Himself*, London, Watts.

Vere Gordon Childe, 1942, *What Happened in History*,

Harmondsworth, Penguin.

Vere Gordon Childe, 1944, *Progress and Archaeology*, London, Watts.

Vere Gordon Childe, 1951, *Social Evolution*, London, Watts.

Vere Gordon Childe, 1956, *Piecing Together the Past*, London, Routledge.

Vere Gordon Childe, 1956, *A Short Introduction to Archaeology*, London, Frederick Muller.

Peter Connolly, 1979, *Pompeii*, Oxford, Oxford UP.

Peter Connolly, 1986, *The Legend of Odysseus*, Oxford, Oxford UP.

Peter Connolly, 1988, *Tiberius Claudius Maximus: the legionary*, Oxford, Oxford UP.

Peter Connolly, 1988, *Tiberius Claudius Maximus: the cavalryman*, Oxford, Oxford UP.

Peter Connolly, 1991, *The Roman Fort*, Oxford, Oxford UP.

Peter Connolly and Hazel Dodge, 1998, *The Ancient City: life in Classical Athens and Rome*, Oxford, Oxford UP.

Leonard Cottrell, 1953, *The Bull of Minos*, London, Evans Bros.

Leonard Cottrell, 1963, *The Lion Gate*, London, Evans Bros.

Leonard Cottrell, 1965, *The Land of Shinar*, London, Souvenir.

Leonard Cottrell, 1966, *The Penguin Book of Lost Worlds*, Harmondsworth, Penguin.

Glyn Daniel, 1981, *A Short History of Archaeology*, London, Thames & Hudson.

Joseph Jay Deiss, 1989, *Herculaneum: Italy's buried treasure*, Malibu, John Paul Getty Museum.

Jared Diamond, 1997, *Guns, Germs and Steel: the fates of human societies*, New York, W W Norton.

Brian Fagan, 1991, *Kingdoms of Gold, Kingdoms of Jade: the Americas before Columbus*, London, Thames & Hudson.

Brian Fagan, 2001, *Egypt of the Pharaohs*, Washington, National Geographic.

Brian Fagan, 2008, *The Great Warming*, London, Bloomsbury.

Brian Fagan and Nadia Durrani, 2021, *Climate Chaos: Lessons of Survival from our Ancestors*, New York, Hachette.

Neil Faulkner, 2012, *A Visitor's Guide to the Ancient Olympics*, London, Yale UP.

Neil Faulkner, 2018, *A Radical History of the World*, London, Pluto.

Michael Grant, 1971, *Cities of Vesuvius: Pompeii and Herculaneum*, London, Weidenfeld & Nicolson.

Philip Grierson, 1975, *Numismatics*, Oxford, Oxford University Press.

Dawn M Hadley and Julian D Richards, 2021, *The Viking Great Army and the Making of England*, London, Thames & Hudson.

Ian Hodder, 1982, *The Present Past: an introduction to anthropology for archaeologists*, London, Batsford.

W G Hoskins, 1973, *English Landscapes: how to read the man-made scenery of England*, London, BBC.

Louise Humphrey and Chris Stringer, 2018, *Our Human Story*, London, Natural History Museum.

Martin Jones, 2001, *The Molecule Hunt*, London, Allen Lane.

Martin Jones, 2007, *Feast: why humans share food*, Oxford, Oxford UP.

Marcel Mauss, 1954, *The Gift: forms and functions of exchange in archaic societies*, London, Cohen & West.

Michael Pitts and Mark Roberts, 1997, *Fairweather Eden: life in Britain half a million years ago as revealed by the excavations at Boxgrove*, London, Century.

Adrian Praetzellis, 2000, *Death by Theory: a tale of mystery and archaeological theory*, Walnut Creek, Altamira.

Francis Pryor, 2003, *Britain BCE: life in Britain and Ireland before the Romans*, London, Harper Perennial.

Michael Pye, 2014, *The Edge of the World: how the North Sea made us who we are*, London, Viking.

Philip Rahtz, 1985, *Invitation to Archaeology*, Oxford, Blackwell.

Philip Rahtz, 2001, *Living Archaeology*, Stroud, Tempus.

Alice Roberts, 2009, *The Incredible Human Journey: the story of how we colonized the planet*, London, Bloomsbury.

Nicholas J Saunders, 2010, *Killing Time: archaeology and the First World War*, Stroud, History Press.

Mortimer Wheeler, 1954, *Archaeology from the Earth*, Oxford, Oxford University Press.

Mortimer Wheeler, 1955, *Still Digging: adventures in archaeology*, London, Michael Joseph.

Mortimer Wheeler, 1964, *Roman Art and Architecture*, London, Thames & Hudson.

Mortimer Wheeler, 1966, *Civilizations of the Indus Valley and Beyond*, London, Thames & Hudson.

Mortimer Wheeler, 1968, *Flames over Persepolis*, New York, Reynay.

Michael Wood, 1985, *In Search of the Trojan War*, London, BBC.

Rebecca Wragg Sykes, 2020, *Kindred: Neanderthal life, love, death and art*, London, Bloomsbury.

Index

A

Aachen cathedral 185–6
Achaemenid Empire 104–7
Acheulian tools 22, 23, 29
Acropolis 125–9
Aeneas 144
African Iron Age 94–8
Agathocles 130
agricultural revolution 42, 44–7, 50, 54–5
Ajanta 116–17
Akrotiri 73
Ai-Khanoum 130
Alesia 152–5
Alexander the Great 107, 108, 130
Amsterdam 235, 236
Ancient Society (Morgan) 52
Angkor Wat 222–3
Anglo-Saxon Chronicle 192
animal usage 138–43
Arikamedu 112–13
Ashoka 108, 112, 114, 115
Assyrian Empire 99–103
Athens 124–9
Aurignacian blades 35, 38
Australian Aborigines 50–2
Australopithecus afarensis 22, 23, 38
Aztecs 215–16

B

Bachofen, Johann Jakob 53
Bantu Empire 97
Baü 60, 61
Beijing 225–6
Beresford, Maurice 202
Bernard of Clairvaux, St 206
Bignor Villa 170, 171
Blackburn, Mark 192

Boxgrove 29
Braine, W. W. 237
Bremen cog 221
Bronze Age
    bronzeworkers 59
    Chavín de Huantar 70–1
    Eastern Mediterranean 72–85
    Hittite Empire 80–3
    Indus Valley 64–5, 86–7
    New Kingdom Egypt 72–3
    Old Kingdom Egypt 63–4
    Olmecs 66–9
    Shang Dynasty 88–9
    social class in 58
    Sumer 60–2
bronzeworkers 59
Brown, Frank 156
Byzantine Empire 178–82
Byzantium 179–82

C

Caesar, Julius 151, 152, 154
Cahokia complex 213
Capitoline temple 148–9
Carolingian Empire 185–6
Carter, Howard 72
Carthage 150
castles 208–9
Celts 134–7, 139
Chan Chan 216, 217
Charlemagne 185, 186
Chauvet Cave 39, 40
Chavín de Huantar 70–1
Chimú 216
China
    animals in 140, 141
    Iron Age 88–9, 118–23

Medieval 224–7
ship-building in 220
Christie, Agatha 100
cinema archaeology 243–5
Classical Greece 124–9
Clovis culture 35
coinage 166–7
conflict archaeology 240–2
Constantinople 179–81
Cosa 156–7
Crickley Hill 46
Cro-Magnon fossils 35
culture history 110–11
Cuneiform script 82–3
Cuzco 216, 217, 218–19

D
Damascus 187
Darius I 107
DeMille, Cecile B. 243–4
dendrochronology 210–11
Dingling tomb 224–5
Dionysus theatre 126–7
Dmanisi fossils 26
Dunning 54

E
earth-mother cult 53–4
Easter Island 229–31
Egypt, Ancient 63–4, 72–3, 83, 138
El-Beidha 44–5
Etruscans 147–9

F
Feddersen Wierde 182
Fertile Crescent 42, 44–5
First World War 240–2
Fontenay Abbey 205, 206
Forum (Rome) 144–5, 148
future archaeology 247

G
Gallic War (Caesar) 152
Germanic peoples 182–5
Gimbutas, Marija 53, 54, 55
Giza 63
Gough's Cave 38–9
Grave Creek 212
Great Arab Revolt Project 241–2
Great Drain 148
Great Serpent Mound 212
Great Wall of China 122–3
Great Zimbabwe 97
Greece, Ancient 124–9, 130–1
Gudea 60

H
Hadley, Dawn 192
Hadrian's Wall 158–61
Hagia Sophia 180–1
Haïdra 178–9
Hallstatt culture 135
Hambledon Hill 48
Harappa 64, 86
Hattusha 80–2
Hellenistic Greece 130–1
Hen Domen castle 208
Herculaneum 163, 165, 168, 169
Hittite Empire 80–3, 84, 94, 98
hominins
Australopithecus afarensis 22, 23, 38
early tool–making 22–3
Homo antecessor 28–9
Homo erectus 25, 28–9, 31, 38
Homo floresiensis 31
Homo habilis 25
Homo heidelbergensis 29, 31
Homo sapiens 31
human evolutionary tree 18–19
Lucy 21
Neanderthals 29–31

Paranthropus 22, 24

Sahelanthropus tchadensis 20, 21

taphonomic processes 26–7

Homo antecessor 28–9

Homo erectus 25, 28–9, 31, 38

Homo floresiensis 31

Homo habilis 25

Homo heidelbergensis 29, 31

Homo sapiens 31, 32–41

human evolutionary tree 18–19

I

Inca Empire 216–19

India

Bronze Age 64–5, 86–7

Iron Age 108–17

Indus Valley 64–5, 86–7

Iron Age

Achaemenid Empire 104–7

in Africa 94–8

Assyrian Empire 99–103

Celts 134–7, 130

in China 88–9, 118–23

Classical Greece 124–9

in India 108–17

ironworking 92–5

and Rome 146–7

Sythians 132–4

ironworking 92–5

Islamic civilization 186–92

J

Jamestown 234, 235

Japan 227–8

Johnson, Donald 21

Justinian, Emperor 179

K

Kadesh, Battle of 83

Kairouan 187–91

Kelson, Bill 234

Kerak castle 208, 209

Kurgans 132–3

L

La Almoloya 58

La Tène culture 135, 136

Language of the Goddess, The (Gimbutas) 53

Lawrence, T. E. 241, 242

Lawrence of Arabia 244

Layard, Austen Henry 100, 102

Leakey, Louis and Mary 25

Lean, David 244

Linear B script 75, 79

Linearbandkeramik culture 53, 110

Livy 148

Lomekwi tools 22

London 236–8

Lucy 21

M

Machu Picchu 217, 219

Maiden castle 134–5

Malinowski, Bronisław 52–3

Mallowan, Max 100, 103

Manchu Dynasty 226

Maori 229

Maurya, Chandragupta 108

Mauryan Empire 108, 116

matriarchal societies 52–4

Maya 195, 196–7, 215

Medieval world

Angkor Wat 222–3

in China 224–7

European castles 208–9

European villages 202–3

in Japan 227–8

in Pacific societies 229–31

pre–Columbian America 212–19

monasteries 204–7

Novgorod 210–12
Medinet Habu 84
Ming Dynasty 224–7
Minoan Crete 73, 74–5, 79
Moche civilization 195, 199, 216
modern world
    cinema archaeology 243–5
    colonization 234–5
    conflict archaeology 240–2
    Tudor London 236–8
    Victorian York 239–40
Mohenjo-daro 64, 65, 86–7
monasteries 204–7
Monk's Mound 212–13
Monreale cathedral 206–7
Morgan, Lewis Henry 52
Mother Rights (Bachofen) 53
Mouhot, Henri 222
Mound-builder culture 212–13
Mycenaeans 75, 78–9, 84, 85

N
Neanderthals 29–31
New Kingdom Egypt 72–3, 83
Newtowne Neck State Park 235, 236
Nimrud 99, 100
Northern Black Polished Ware culture 110
Novgorod 210–12

O
Old Kingdom Egypt 63–4
Olmecs 66–9
Olduvai Gorge 22, 25
Omo remains 32
Oseberg ship 220–1

P
Pacific societies 229–31
Painted Grey Ware culture 110–11
Paranthropus 22, 24

Pataliputra 109
patriarchal societies 54–5
Persepolis 104–7
Peter the Great 210
Petra 44–5, 142–3
Pompeii 163, 165
pottery 172–3
printing 245, 246
Priscus, Tarquinius 148
Pueblo farmers 213–14

Q
Qafzeh cave 34
Qin Shihuangdi 118–19, 123

R
Ramsauer, Georg 137
Rameses III 84
Richards, Julian 192
Rising Star cave system 26–7
Rome/Roman Empire
    army in 139–40, 152–5,
      158–61
    coinage 166–7
    colonies 156–7
    expansion of Empire 150–1
    fall of 176–8
    forts 158–61, 178–9
    origins of 146–7
    pottery 172–3
    rise of city 147–9
    towns in 162–5, 177
    villas 168–71, 177–8
Romulus 144
Rowntree, Seebohm 239
Ryan's Daughter 244

S
Sacsayhuamán 217
saddles 139–42

Sahelanthropus tchadensis 20, 21
St Gall monastery 204
samurai 227–8
San Lorenzo 69
Sanchi 115
São Gabriel 221
Schletz 46
Schliemann, Heinrich 75
Scott, Doug 240
Sea Peoples 84, 85
Seven Pillars of Wisdom (Lawrence) 242
Shabik'eschee 66
Shang Dynasty 88–9
ship-building 220–1
Sipán pyramid 199
Skhul cave 34
Snettisham Hoard 134
social anthropology 52–4
Standard of Ur 61–2, 138
Stanley, Dave and Pete 192
Star Carr 41
Sumer 60–2
Superbus, Tarquinius 148
Suryavarman II, King 222
Sutton Hoo 182–4
Sythians 132–4

T
Talheim 48–9
taphonomic processes 26–7
technological progress 246–7
Temple of Jupiter 148
Ten Commandments, The 243–4
Tenochtitlán 215–16
Teotihuacán 69
Terracotta Army 118–21
theatres 237–8
Tikal 195, 196–7
Tintagel 181–2
Tokugawa Shogunate 227

Toltecs 215
tool–making
      Bronze Age 59
hominid 22–3
Upper Palaeolithic 35, 38–9, 41
Tooth Hill Camp 242
Torksey 192–3
Trobriand Islanders 52–3
Troy 73–4, 76–7
Tutankhamun 72

U
Upper Palaeolithic 35, 38–41

V
Vale of York Hoard 194
Venus of Willendorf 39
Vikings 192–4, 220–1
villas 168–71, 177–8

W
Wanli, Emperor 224
White Sands National Park 34, 35
William II, King 206, 207

Y
Yajima-Yakata 227
Yang Zhifa 118
York 239–40

Z
Zhou Dynasty 88, 89, 119
Zhu Tan, Prince 225

Picture credits

t = top, b = bottom, l = left, r = right

Alamy: 11 (Landmark Media), 58 (Lanmas), 59 (PA Images), 71 (Jesse Kraft), 137 (The History Collection), 142 (Heritage Image Partnership Ltd), 153tl (Artokoloro), 170 (Pawel Kowalczyk), 178 (Ivan Vdovin), 183 (World History Archive), 199 (Reuters), 202 (Heritage Image Partnership Ltd), 216 (Roy Johnson), 218b (World History Archive), 221t (Granger), 232 (S. Forster), 235 (M. Timothy O'Keefe), 238 (Chris Davies), 239 (Purple Marbles York 1)

Auckland War Memorial Museum: 229t

British Museum: 193

Diomedia: 54 (Werner Forman Archive), 101 (DeAgostini/M. Seemuller)

Ephorate of Antiquities of Athens: 124 (American School of Classical Archaeology of Athens)

Flickr: 225 (Gary Todd)

Getty Images: 13 (DEA/Archivio. J. Lange), 21 (Bloomberg), 42 (DEA/G. Dagli Orti), 66 (Werner Foreman), 65 (DEA/A. Dagli Orti), 67 (DEA/Archivio. J. Lange), 103 (Bettmann), 146 (DEA Picture Library), 176b (Mondadori Portfolio), 237 (Peter Macdiarmid)

Historic England: 203b

Lovell Johns: 85, 95

Metropolitan Museum of Art, New York: 13 (Gift of John D. Rockefeller Jr., 1932), 14 (Rogers Fund, 1939), 15 (Bequest of Arthur M. Bullowa, 1993), 23 (Purchase, Arthur Ochs Sulzberger 2018), 88 (Gift of Paul E. Manheim, 1967), 92 (Gift of John D. Rockefeller Jr., 1932), 93 (Rogers Fund, 1903), 99 (Rogers Fund, 1960), 133 (Gift of Ernest Erickson Foundation, 1988), 188t (Rogers Fund, 1939), 215t (Bequest of Arthur M. Bullowa, 1993)

N. J. Saunders: 240, 241

Science Photo Library: 16 (Mauricio Anton), 18 (Volker Steger), 27 (Daniel Born/Greatstock)

Shutterstock: 8, 10 19 (x12), 15, 32, 36, 38, 51, 76, 78, 82t, 90, 120, 144, 150, 151, 155, 164, 174, 180, 196, 203t, 210, 214b, 219b, 226, 229b, 231, 234

Shutterstock Editorial: 243b (Reed Saxon/AP)

United States Geological Service: 34b

Wikimedia Commons: 12 (x2), 13 (x3), 14 (x2), 15 (x3), 19 (x4), 20, 22, 24, 25, 28, 29, 30, 34t, 35, 37, 39, 40, 41, 44, 45, 46, 49, 52, 53t, 53b, 55, 56, 60, 61t, 61b, 62t, 62b, 63, 64, 68, 70, 72, 73, 74, 75, 81, 82b, 83, 84, 86, 89, 94, 96, 99, 102t, 102b, 105, 106, 108, 109t, 109b, 110, 111, 113, 114, 115, 117, 118, 119, 122, 125, 126, 127, 128, 130, 131t, 131b, 132, 134, 135, 136, 138, 139, 140, 141, 143, 147, 148, 149, 152, 153tr, 154, 156, 158, 159, 161, 163, 167, 168, 169, 171, 172, 173, 176t, 177, 179, 181, 182, 184 (x3), 185, 187 (x7), 188b, 189, 190, 191, 192, 194, 195, 198, 200, 204, 205t, 205b, 206, 207t, 207b, 208, 209, 211t, 212, 214t, 215b, 217t, 217b, 218t, 220, 221b, 222, 223, 224t, 224b, 227, 228, 236t, 236b, 242, 243t, 244, 246, 247